W0246916

PENGUIN BOOKS
THE INDIAN PANTRY

Vir Sanghvi is probably the best-known Indian journalist of his generation. He became editor of *Bombay* magazine at twenty-two, making him the youngest editor in the history of Indian journalism. He went on to edit *Imprint*, and *Sunday*, which was then India's largest-selling weekly news magazine. From 1999 to 2004, he was the editor of *Hindustan Times* before being promoted to editorial director, a post he held till 2007, after which he continued at the paper as a columnist. His television career has included several award-winning shows on the Star TV network, NDTV, Discovery and other channels. His weekly political show *Virtuosity* on CNN-News18 is one of the channel's top-rated programmes.

He has a parallel career as India's leading food and travel writer. His many books include the bestselling *Mandate: Will of the People*, *Men of Steel*, *Rude Food* (which won the Cointreau Award for Best Food Literature Book in the world) and *Madhavrao Scindia: A Life*.

The
INDIAN
Pantry

The Very Best of Rude Food

Vir Sanghvi

PENGUIN BOOKS

An imprint of Penguin Random House

PENGUIN BOOKS

USA | Canada | UK | Ireland | Australia
New Zealand | India | South Africa | China | Singapore

Penguin Books is part of the Penguin Random House group of companies
whose addresses can be found at global.penguinrandomhouse.com

Published by Penguin Random House India Pvt. Ltd
4th Floor, Capital Tower 1, MG Road,
Gurugram 122 002, Haryana, India

First published in Penguin Books by Penguin Random House India 2019

10 9 8 7 6 5 4 3 2

ISBN 9780143440178

Typeset in Adobe Caslon Pro by Manipal Digital Systems, Manipal

Printed at Manipal Technologies Limited, India

www.penguin.co.in

For the same two people as the first Rude Food collection:
the Significant Other who is now the Significant Wife
and the Petit Fromage who is now a Grand Fromage himself.

Contents

≈

Staples

Sweet

Introduction

≈

This book has been a long time coming. But then that has been true of pretty much everything about my career as an accidental food writer.

It all started way back in 1979 when I was editor of *Bombay*, a city magazine that was inspired by the *New York* magazine template. We needed brief reviews of restaurants and so I wrote them. Then, in 1981, I graduated to full-length restaurant reviews for *Sunday Observer*, a pioneering publication in Bombay (now Mumbai), which was really a magazine disguised as a newspaper.

And yet, by the time I shifted to Calcutta (now Kolkata) in 1986 to edit *Sunday*, there was no more talk of food writing. *Sunday* was a hard-core political weekly and though my brief was to expand its scope (think of *Newsweek* on the cheapest newsprint available), we decided that there was very little interest in food. So, though I did write the odd food piece, my fledgling career as a food writer in Bombay ended once I had left that city.

When I started doing television in 1994, at first on Doordarshan and, after 1996, on the new satellite channels owned by Star TV, there was never even any question of food shows. In that era, food on TV consisted only of chefs who leered at housewives from the screen while demonstrating how to make paneer butter masala.

And so, from 1986 to 2001, I forgot I had ever written about food. I did discussion and interview shows on TV, anchored election coverage, wrote political stories for *Sunday* and then, for *Hindustan Times* where I became editor in 1999.

It was while at *HT* that my food-writing career resumed. We were revamping the paper's Sunday supplement and I argued that the twenty-first century would see the rise of food and eating out in India.

This was a daring view at the time, but I was the editor, so nobody argued too hard when I said we had to include a food column in the revamped supplement. But this wasn't easy to do. Hard as it is to believe in this food-mad era, there were no bloggers of any consequence, virtually no food journos, and Instagram did not exist.

As we couldn't find anyone to do the column, I did it myself and discovered, to my relief, that I had been right. There was a huge market for food writing as India was finally discovering food and the restaurant scene was exploding.

The success of 'Rude Food', as we called the column, had two consequences. Within a couple of years, Penguin Books came to me and asked if they could publish a collection of the columns. I said yes, the book was published and, fifteen years later, people still come up to me and ask if I can sign their copies. (Sign their copies? I am so flattered that anyone is still reading the book that I just want to hug the people who ask me to sign their copies!)

The second was that Aditya Tripathi, who was then with the Discovery Channel, came to see me. Discovery ran a second channel called Discovery Travel and Living and Aditya wondered if they could turn 'Rude Food' into a show.

I was sceptical. I can't cook so I could hardly put on chef's whites, make eyes at housewives from the TV screen and say things like: '*Yeh garam garam pakode koi bhi banaa sakta hai . . .*'

The only kind of show I was willing to do was one where I could travel around India dealing with the subjects my columns had dealt with. Who invented tandoori chicken? How did the masala dosa make its way north? Why is milk so important to Indians? And so on.

To my surprise, Aditya said yes, Discovery would do such a show. He hired his old schoolfellow Robin Roy to produce and direct, and we travelled across the country shooting the show that became the TV version of 'Rude Food': *A Matter of Taste*.

The book and the show pushed me finally into the food space, an odd place for the editor of a national newspaper to be in. But it is another measure of how quickly India was changing that no one thought that was odd either.

Since then, 'Rude Food', the column has continued to run in *Brunch*, the Sunday magazine of *HT*. As *Brunch* is the largest-circulated magazine in India (by virtue of going out free with *Hindustan Times* every Sunday— in addition, of course, to its own high quality), 'Rude Food' has had a disproportionate impact both on the food scene in general and on my career in particular. It may now be the thing that I am most frequently associated with. And though these days anyone with a smartphone is a food critic, the sheer ubiquity of *Brunch* means that 'Rude Food' reaches many more people than any other food column.

My adventures with food TV were less successful in the years that followed. Aditya moved on, and though Discovery commissioned another set of episodes from Robin and me, they wanted them to be more Asian in character and (inevitably) more glamorous.

So our second season was called *Vir Sanghvi's Asian Diary* and was even better received than *A Matter of Taste*. Because it was shown in nearly every East Asian country, I had the brief thrill of being an all-Asia food celebrity for a year, being welcomed at hotels and restaurants in Singapore and Hong Kong by managers and chefs who had seen the show.

Then, Discovery Travel lost interest in the genre, switched to more fun-filled programming, rejected anything that seemed even vaguely cerebral and the prospect of doing an intelligent food show for them died a sudden death.

I have done lifestyle TV since then, mostly for NDTV Good Times, and have been part of some hit shows. (*Custom Made for Vir Sanghvi* is my most-remembered show.) But I have never found anyone else willing to spend the kind of money on high-quality food programming that Discovery did in those early years. And so, it has been back to political television once again.

As for books, we started talking about a second 'Rude Food' collection within a year of the success of the first one. At first, I was ambivalent because I thought it was too soon. 'Give it another couple of years,' I said, 'for the columns to accumulate. Then we can pick the best ones.'

But there were frequent personnel changes at Penguin, so all the people I began conversations with kept departing, leaving the discussions hanging. Other publishers offered to publish a collection. I said no, arguing that as the first *Rude Food* had been published by Penguin it would make the most sense to have the same house do the second volume, which would be called 'More Rude Food'.

And so it went on for several years till one evening Meru Gokhale and Tarini Uppal of Penguin Random House India took me to a cafe in Sunder Nagar and made me sign a paper giving them the rights to a second book on the spot. Meru can be very persuasive, and Tarini volunteered to go to the *HT* office and spend hours going through back issues to choose the pieces they would use.

We disagreed on a few things. They didn't want to call it 'More Rude Food'. They preferred the name 'The Indian Pantry'. At first, I was incredulous! What was this—a cookbook? What was I—a pantryman? Why not just give it a simple title that explained things clearly?

They reckoned that a neutral title would increase its appeal. Perhaps they were right. Or perhaps publishers don't like putting out collections of columns that have already been published elsewhere. Maybe it seems better to give the book a fresh, new title.

I have no idea. But I trust them.

Many thanks to Tarini who spent months going through my old columns to choose the ones she wanted for this collection and whose book this really is—even more than it is mine. Thanks are also due to the people who put the original columns together: to Poonam Saxena who launched and edited *Brunch* far longer than it is polite for us to remember; to my friend Jamal Sheikh, who took over from her; to all the copy editors who made the pages, from the wonderful Samreen Tungekar to the incomparable Rachel Lopez, the best and most imaginative editor any writer can ask for.

As for the book itself, what can I say?

This is a collection of articles written over a decade, so it is hard to find a single theme, and I am not going to pretend that we went through hundreds of pieces in search of an overarching theme to give this collection a deep internal logic.

Nevertheless, some changes in the Indian food scene are self-evident.

Tarini, who chose the pieces, wanted to document how the Indian idea of food had changed. She knew that many of my *Brunch* pieces were about restaurants, hotels, travel and the like. She was determined to exclude anything that did not conform to her idea of the Indian pantry.

So despite the subtitle (which I insisted on) about the best of 'Rude Food', this is not a collection that seeks to identify the best columns I wrote over the last decade.

Instead, this is a book that focuses on Indians in the kitchen. It looks at the ingredients that have become available to us, and traces the history of many that we often take for granted.

It also looks at some of the dishes that we regard as essential components of Indian cuisine and considers their origins and the way in which they have spread all over India—and in many cases, all over the world.

When Tarini sent me the final list of articles, I looked at many of them with mild astonishment. I am still staggered by the way in which so many of the ingredients I wrote about all those years ago no longer seem exotic or novel.

Much of this has to do with how much India has changed in the two decades since the first 'Rude Food' collection was published. In that era, we still lived in siege economy. Yes, liberalization had begun in 1991, and we should no longer have regarded an open economy as a novelty. But the truth is that in 2003–04, we still regarded foreign foods with awe and wonder.

All that has changed, of course. Not only are we completely integrated into the global economy but there is also very little food that we read about these days that seems strange to us. This was driven home to me a couple of years ago when I hosted four events featuring Gary Mehigan. Gary is a judge on *MasterChef Australia*, an Antipodean version of a global TV franchise.

Gary's food was international and he was (and remains) a star among TV viewers. But what surprised me was the way in which audiences in all four cities were knowledgeable, and blasé even, about the food he talked about. Gary raved about a dish he had eaten in San Francisco that made imaginative use of sea urchin. As the anchor, I prepared to explain to the diners what a sea urchin was. But there was no need. They knew exactly what he was talking about.

As examples piled up, I came to some broad conclusions. The first was that when it came to knowing about dishes, Indian foodies were increasingly on par with the rest of the world.

Since the 1980s, urban Indians have had a general idea of what a pizza is. But now we can tell the difference between a thin crust and a deep-pan pizza. Foodies will know that pepperoni means different things in America and Italy, and they will be able to discuss the differences between the flavours of black and green olives.

So, are we eating better than we used to?

The general view is that we are not. That old family recipes have been forgotten and that regional food has lost its relevance.

This is not a view I subscribe to.

I believe that when it comes to food, Indians have never had it so good.

Partly, it is that we know more about global cuisine than even before because of satellite TV (where *MasterChef Australia* is one of the most popular shows) and the Internet. Partly, it is because the global fast-food chains have targeted India. And mostly it is because our chefs now benchmark themselves against global standards.

Once upon a time, Indian chefs had no idea what was going on in the world. Now, the world's best chefs cook in India. Gaggan Anand, Asia's best chef for the last four years, is an Indian who cooks in India every year. Massimo Bottura, the world's number one chef, cooked in Mumbai this year. Daniel Humm, who was the world's greatest chef last year, also cooked in Delhi and Mumbai a few months ago.

For home cooks, the wider integration of India into the global food scene has been accompanied by an enormous increase in the kinds of ingredients available. Only a decade ago, I wrote a column about olive oil, explaining what it was. Now my columns focus on how to find the best extra virgin olive oil. Some years ago, I wrote about balsamic vinegar. Now I have to explain to my readers what the difference between the balsamic vinegar they get in the shops and real balsamic vinegar is.

When I first started writing about risotto, I advised readers to hold out for genuine Italian rice. Now I have to distinguish between Arborio and Carnaroli rice and their suitability for risotto.

Even within India, levels of knowledge have increased. When I first began writing about *bhut jolokia*, the super-hot north-eastern chilli, I had to explain what it was. Now I handle the issue of why the bhut jolokia is no longer the world's hottest chilli—or is it?

Most foodies now know the basics. The job of the food writer today is to go beyond simple explanations and deal with details and nuances.

At a personal level, I am thrilled. I started writing about food when it was still a minority interest, something nobody would agree to write about. Now, it is finally at the centre of the mainstream.

But something more significant is going on. As the Indian middle class discovers the world it finds that it has money to spend, that new prosperity is finding its first expression in its food choices.

So the food boom is not just a boom for hacks like me. It is a symptom of a nation that is now confidently exploring the world, if not with its mind, certainly with its stomach!

Vegetables

The Troublesome Tomato

≈

You can't get good tomatoes in India.

Among the many food items that I bring back from abroad in my luggage are tomatoes. This nearly always provokes derision among my friends. 'Caviar, we understand. Even truffles. Or maybe unusual spices and herbs from foreign countries,' they sneer. 'But what kind of idiot brings back tomatoes?'

And yes, I have to concede that it seems a little silly, especially as the tomatoes I buy are not some rare, little-found variety but are just normal vine-ripened tomatoes bought at some good supermarket like England's Waitrose chain.

So, why do I struggle to keep my tomatoes fresh on the long journey? Why do I take care to see that they are not squished under the weight of the other stuff in my suitcase? Why do I bear the snide remarks of my friends? Well, the answer is the simplest one of all: because you can't get good tomatoes in India.

Now that I've your attention with that seemingly ridiculous assertion, let me try to give you a little historical background.

3

As far as we know, the tomato was brought back from the New World (i.e., South America) by Christopher Columbus. Many of the fruits and vegetables that came from the New World (even the potato) were so rare and expensive that Europeans credited them with aphrodisiac powers. (Anything expensive is immediately regarded as an aphrodisiac by stupid people—to this day!) Some people argued that they were the forbidden fruit from the Garden of Eden and said that they were the fruit (a tomato is a fruit, by the way, not a vegetable, in strict botanical terms) served up by the serpent. The Italian name for tomatoes, *pomodoro*, translates literally as the 'golden apple' so the confusion may have been widespread throughout Europe in those days. (Apparently the Hungarians called it the *Paradice Appfel* or the 'apple of paradise'.)

But why blame the poor tomato for the apple's misdemeanours? Well, I guess it was because the apple looks like a well-behaved, celibate fruit. But the tomato, on the other hand, is a slutty, scarlet fruit, squishy in all the right places, oozing delicious juice, one taste of which is enough to cause an explosion in the mouth.

Whatever the reason, Europeans took to potatoes and other New World produce before they got around to tomatoes. For a century and a half after Columbus brought back the tomato, it remained a little-eaten fruit that was hardly ever mentioned in polite company.

Only much later did Europeans realize that it had potential in the food department (even if it was a flop in the sex department) and start eating it. But even then, they treated it as a fruit rather than a vegetable. (In botanical terms, this is fair and proper, of course.)

Think about it. Vegetables are cooked and eaten at meals. Fruits are eaten raw, treated as desserts or are puréed to add flavour to other dishes. The tomato's treatment in the West was very fruit-like. Nobody cooked it. When they did eat it, it was raw. And the Italians, who first took to it, used it as a purée for pasta and pizza. (If you look at it that way, a pizza is to a tomato what apple pie is to an apple.) When the tomato finally reached North America (i.e., the US) via Europe, it was subject to similar shock-horror responses till enterprising American companies popularized tomato ketchup. But even then, you will note, it was treated less as a vegetable and more as a condiment or a flavouring agent.

Which brings us to the Indian experience. The Portuguese brought tomatoes to India but the Brits, their heads turned by all the European misconceptions, resisted them till they reluctantly agreed to let them be used for soup (which I guess did not count as actually eating the vegetable in their minds).

Nobody can say, with any degree of certainty, when tomatoes were introduced into the Indian diet but we do know two things. The first is that the tomatoes that the Portuguese brought to India were not round. They were long and shaped vaguely like baingans. And two, they were sour, much sourer than today's tomatoes.

So, influenced perhaps by British attitudes to the tomato, Indian cooks started using it like a fresh spice. We used it primarily as a souring agent and then, as the tomatoes grown all over India became less sour, we used them to add colour and taste to our food. In nearly every dish where tomatoes have been used in early-Indian cooking, their prime purpose has been to add a sour taste (think of Punjabi black dal or of Bengali cuisine where tomatoes were first widely used) and only now do we find any other use for them in the kitchen.

But this is where our paths separated. The West soon realized that the raw tomato had potential. It became a popular salad vegetable and hundreds of breeds were cultivated, some for the purpose of sauce, some for salad, some for sun-drying (in Italy, especially). So, the tomato, unlike the potato and many other New World vegetables, soon had two roles. It was used as a flavouring agent (in sauce, in ketchup, etc.) and it was eaten raw.

In India, however, the tomato remained a condiment. It is true that we Indians treat our vegetables with scant respect, cooking them till all the original flavour disappears and subjecting them to spice assaults, but the tomato has not even been granted the status of a proper vegetable. How many tomato subzis have you come across? We rarely regard the tomato as being worth very much on its own.

When we use tomatoes, it is either as part of the cooking process or as a chutney or some other condiment. Every Indian kitchen will have tomatoes but few of us will pay them much attention. Even when we do sometimes place sliced raw tomatoes on the table, we include potent onion (which kills any delicate tomato flavours) and cucumber (for the bite). Really tasty tomatoes are rarely a priority in Indian homes.

If you don't believe me, conduct an experiment. Go to your local subziwallah and buy some tomatoes. Cut them into slices, sprinkle some good salt (sea salt is best) over them and drizzle a little olive oil over the slices. I am willing to guarantee that the dish will taste like tomato-flavoured cardboard.

If you love tomatoes, as I do, it is almost impossible to get flavourful fresh tomatoes in India. Oh yes, they are fine for cooking (if they lack flavour, you just increase the quantities) but that's about it. The sweet-sour flavour tango which is the true test of a good tomato is rarely found in Indian tomatoes.

Slowly but surely, Indian chefs are coming round to this view. We laughed at Hemant Oberoi when he imported cherry tomatoes for his salad nearly two decades ago, but he was right. Many expatriate chefs will now import their salad tomatoes (it is a nuisance but it is not that expensive) from Europe and some chefs have sourced flavourful tomatoes from small artisanal growers, but these are not available to the general public.

I used to complain about the Indian potato—too much sugar for frying—but fortunately, companies such as McCain have set up farms that produce excellent potatoes (which is the reason why McCain's fries, tikkis and hash browns are such a hit in the home cook market).

But the tomato remains an exception. I am told that one reason is that the two main sources of demand are not quality-conscious. You don't need great tomatoes for an Indian curry, and food companies who use tomatoes (for baked beans and the like) buy tomato paste from industrial manufacturers. The restaurant and hotel sector only needs good tomatoes for salad. (Pizzas, etc., are made with paste usually.) So it is not comparable with the demand for French fries, which was so massive that it became worthwhile for McCain to set up its own potato farm in Gujarat.

A small market does nevertheless need somebody to meet its requirements. Take organic eggs. Most Indian eggs are industrial and disgusting and sadly even our chefs do not know better. But a producer like Keggs Eggs has flourished by supplying those who can tell the difference between a free-range egg with its golden yolk and firm white, and a nasty industrial egg with its pale yolk and watery white.

My guess is that if some enterprising farmer began selling artisanal tomatoes (the sort of thing they do in California), he would find buyers even if his prices were slightly higher. (Nobody minds paying more for

Keggs.) I know such producers do exist. But if they would only identify themselves and market their tomatoes properly, we would finally get decent tomatoes in India.

And my bags would not have to be full of little tomatoes still on their vines!

The King of Vegetables

≈

There is no other vegetable that can be eaten in any shape, or at any consistency than the potato.

If the vegetable kingdom were actually a kingdom, which vegetable do you suppose would be the king? If you answered 'artichoke' or 'asparagus' or any other exotic vegetable, I would have to disagree with you.

I think the answer is clear. The potato is the king of vegetables.

This is a case I am prepared to fight to the end. And my reasons for backing the humble tuber's nomination are easy to set out.

First of all, there is the potato's versatility. How many vegetables can you think of that can be eaten in any shape or at any consistency? You can boil or bake a potato whole and enjoy its flavour. You can cut it into little pieces and make a subzi with it. You can slice it thinly and get delicious potato crisps from it. Or you can abandon the shape entirely and pulverize the potato to nothingness. Even then, as mashed potato, it makes for a classic dish.

You can also cook the potato any way you like. You can boil it, roast it, bake it, fry it or cook it in a subzi, and it will still taste as good.

I am hard-pressed to think of a single vegetable that can be cooked in so many different ways and still give up none of its delicious characteristics.

Apart from versatility, there is also the remarkable speed of the potato's rise. As is well known, the potato was virtually unknown in most of the world till the Spanish brought it from South America. Though it reached England in the sixteenth century, it took another two centuries to become widely available throughout Europe.

Once that happened, there was no stopping the potato. For instance, the French Revolution was accompanied by another revolution—the introduction of the potato into French cuisine—that was almost as far-reaching in its consequences. Paris went so berserk over potato dishes that the royal Tuileries Garden was transformed into a potato field in the centre of Paris. In Ireland, the potato became such a staple that when a fungus wiped out the crop in the 1840s, the population starved and millions died (or went off to America).

To have some sense of how quickly the potato has spread throughout the world, consider the rise of the potato in India. It was brought here by the British (though some claims have been advanced for the Dutch) and you would have thought that Indians might have regarded it as an alien vegetable. Instead, we took to the potato with a rare enthusiasm and within a century of its widespread cultivation, it had become an integral part of the Indian diet.

The next time you sit down to a plate of puri aloo or eat an aloo paratha or bite into an aloo samosa, consider what would have happened if the British had not taken it upon themselves to cultivate the potato in India. Perhaps these dishes would have evolved anyhow as the potato made its way to our country through trade but I doubt very much if potatoes would have become as central to our cuisine as they are today. Even the south, which prides itself on its vegetable tradition, has come to terms with the fact that the single most popular south Indian dish in the world—the masala dosa—is made with potatoes.

Another reason I advance for the potato's claim to be the king of vegetables is its international popularity. No other vegetable crops up in so many different cuisines. Forget about the cuisines of South America where the potato was first grown, but consider the cuisines of Europe.

The Italians will use the potato for gnocchi. A Spanish omelette is essentially an omelette with potatoes. The British national dish of fish and chips requires potatoes. The Germans subsist on meat and potatoes. The Swiss national dish is potato rösti.

In the United States, the French fry is so ubiquitous that it may well be the national dish of America. In Mediterranean cuisines, fried potatoes are a popular starter (as they are in many Arab countries). And of course, South Asia loves its potatoes.

I used to be told by the potato's detractors that my claims for its supremacy would forever be punctured by the failure of East Asia to embrace the potato. How can it be the king of vegetables, the sceptics would ask, if a billion Chinese refuse to eat it?

In the last decade, I have found the answer. Go to any Far Eastern city of your choosing and check out what the locals are doing for fast food. Almost without exception, they are queuing up at Burger King or McDonalds or KFC for an order of French fries. It may not be a part of the local cuisine, but the potato now rules all over East Asia as well.

Then, there is the unique ability of the potato to work equally well as a haute cuisine dish or as a poor man's subsistence food. It does not cost much to make a simple aloo ki subzi, and indeed in many societies (most notably, Ireland and England in the nineteenth century) the poor have survived on a diet of potatoes. Even today, the potato is an integral part of cheap office lunches either as a French fry or as the filling in a masala dosa.

But the potato can also be a rich man's food. One of the best ways to enjoy good caviar is to hollow out a boiled potato, squeeze in a dollop of sour cream and then ladle on the beluga. Similarly, potatoes and truffles have a sacred connection. Grate white truffles over potatoes (ideally, buttery mashed potatoes) and the two flavours will combine in a joyous union.

The French have always recognized the potato's ability to be a part of haute cuisine, which is why so many of their recipes combine potatoes with butter and cream. The great French chef Joël Robuchon (generally considered one of the world's two greatest chefs—the other is Alain Ducasse) created a mashed potato that is now so famous and influential that it is rare to find a chef at a good restaurant anywhere in the world who does not borrow some element of Robuchon's recipe.

The secret of Robuchon's mashed potatoes is dairy. Basically, he adds a lot of butter and hot milk (some chefs use cream) to mashed potatoes and keeps sieving the potatoes repeatedly till he gets a perfect silky texture. Because he uses strongly flavoured potatoes, the dairy products do not detract from the basic potato taste but actually enhance it. I've read interviews where Robuchon claims that guests at his restaurants often ask for a portion of mashed potatoes instead of dessert. (God knows, they are richer than most desserts.)

It is somehow typical of the potato that even a great chef like Robuchon who has created a gourmet classic like his buttery mashed potato should concede that the greater challenge is to make an excellent French fry. Most of us are used to the fast-food French fry (and very good it is too, these days, thanks to the companies that supply the fries to fast-food chains) but the Robuchon French fry is in a league of its own. The secret lies in frying the potatoes twice. The first frying cooks the potato while the second frying gives it the texture: crisp on the outside and soft inside.

Of late, I find myself eating more and more potatoes. Partly, this is because of the vast variety of frozen potato dishes that are now available in the Indian market, thanks to such companies as Lamb Weston and McCain. It takes only a few minutes to cook a Lamb Weston hash brown in the oven, and because no frying is involved, the dish is healthier than it tastes. Similarly, a McCain aloo tikki can be pan-fried in a minimum of oil and still taste delicious.

If the potato has a problem, it comes from the health fanatics who keep telling us that the potato is the unhealthiest vegetable of all. This is nonsense. Potatoes contain important minerals and nutrients and are actually good for you. The problem is not with the potato itself. It is with the deep-frying techniques that are used in many potato dishes.

Fortunately, the new generation of potato products more or less eliminates the need for deep-frying. And yes, even when potatoes are fried, they still contain less calories than many oily Indian snacks (the pakora, in particular, is a serial offender).

So, here's my recommendation. Forget about the health fanatics. Eat your potatoes in moderation. Take a crisp French fry and dunk it in ketchup. Bite into a Kettle chip and feel its texture crumble on your tongue. Dip your puri into an aloo subzi. Munch away at the boiled potatoes that are an integral part of bhel puri. And as a special treat, smear a little home-made achar on an aloo paratha and feel the tastes of the Indian street fill your mouth.

When you eat a potato, you never dine alone. You eat with the king of vegetables.

Two
Peas in a Pod

≈

Fresh is nearly always better than frozen, but in the case of peas, be prepared to make an exception.

It's hard for you and me to understand quite how glamorous the fresh pea has become in the West. Yes, I do mean the matar, the vegetable we put into pulaos or cook with aloo or paneer. We may have grown up seeing piles of pea pods heaped on the kitchen table before they were shelled and the peas extracted for the cooking of the evening meal. But there's a whole generation in the West that has never seen a pea pod and regards the fresh pea as a strange and exotic vegetable.

In his book, *The Man Who Ate the World*, the British food writer Jay Rayner recounts going to dinner at the Michelin three-star Guy Savoy restaurant in the centre of Paris. The waiter came over to discuss the order and pushed the pea dish. Rayner wanted to know what was done with the peas. It turned out that they were not accompaniments to some meat but were the main ingredients of the dish. In fact, the peas were deemed important enough to get an accompaniment of their own: a poached egg.

The peas were completely fresh, probably picked off the branch early that morning. Besides, as Rayner recalls, the waiter was proud of the extra effort that the kitchen had put into the dish.

'Every pea in this pea salad is sliced in half,' Hubert [the waiter] said in a conspiratorial whisper. 'Every pea.' Pause. 'In half . . . and do you know why they slice every pea in half?' He dropped his voice to even more breathy whisper. 'Double the pleasure,' he hissed.

When the dish did arrive, it consisted of a light pea purée topped with the pea halves. In the centre was a coarser pea purée, topped with a poached egg. In 2007, this dish cost 47 euros, and I am sure it costs a lot more now. It is, as Rayner notes, an awful lot of money for a handful of peas and an egg.

So, why do great chefs make such a tamasha about peas? Much of it has to do with the flavour of the ingredient. When we use peas in Indian cooking we are—let's be honest now—not as concerned with the taste of each pea as we are with the texture of the vegetable. We put peas into keema matar or matar pulao because we like the reassuring plop that each pea makes in our mouths as we squish down on it. It is not as though we don't like the taste of peas. It is just that we don't focus too much on it.

In European cooking, on the other hand, peas are valued for their taste largely because chefs don't use the kinds of masalas that our cooks have access to. The French began the craze for petit pois. These are small peas that manage to actually taste of the garden and have a wonderful sweet centre. I used to think that these were a different variety of pea. In fact, they are pretty much the same as normal everyday peas. The French just pick them early, before they've had a chance to mature fully and retain a sweet freshness.

It is that sweet freshness that brings us to the problem of fresh peas. At the centre of each individual pea is quite a lot of sugar. We know that once vegetables are picked their ingredients tend to become unstable. (The classic example is the potato, which tastes very different when it is new from the kind that has been kept in storage for a while.) But pea sugars are more unstable than most other vegetable ingredients. Within hours of the pod being picked off the branch, the sugars begin to deteriorate. Usually, they turn into starches, which completely alter the taste of the pea.

It therefore becomes an incredibly expensive business to serve a pea before its natural sugars have transformed. Such French chefs as Guy

Savoy and Pierre Gagnaire pay vegetable growers to pick their peas in the morning and then rush them to their restaurants either by car or by high-speed train. At Gagnaire's restaurant in London, French peas, which have travelled through the Channel tunnel that very day, are served only in the evening of the day that they have been picked. Any uneaten peas cannot be served the next day because they will have lost their sweetness.

There is, of course, an easy way around this. If you freeze peas soon after they have been picked, they retain their sugariness. When you defrost them, they will taste exactly as they tasted when the freezing process began.

Consequently, the majority of peas consumed in the Western world are frozen after being shelled. That's why a whole generation of Americans and Europeans has never seen a pea pod. They think of peas as something that comes out of a packet.

My policy on vegetables is that fresh is nearly always better than frozen. But in the case of the pea, I am prepared to make an exception. Of course you should eat fresh peas, if like Guy Savoy you can cook them on the day they were picked. But given that most of us do not have that privilege, frozen peas actually—bizarrely enough—taste fresher than genuinely fresh peas.

Does this make a difference in other cuisines? I reckon it makes very little difference in Indian food what kind of peas you use. The taste is not that important; so if you are happy shelling your peas and buying them from the local subziwallah, good luck to you. If, on the other hand, you find it easier to pick up a packet of frozen peas, I doubt it will make much difference to the flavours of your cooking.

The unusual thing about peas, of course, is that they are an international vegetable. (You can be pedantic and claim that scientifically speaking they are actually a fruit, but that seems like a pointless discussion in our context.) Archaeologists have found peas in Indus Valley Civilization sites and they seem to have existed in other ancient civilizations dating back to 3000 BC. Even China, where the pea is called *hu tou* (which means foreign legume), has known the vegetable since the seventh century AD, which might explain why it turns up in so many Chinese dishes (including most famously, egg fried rice) and is sprouted so that chefs can cook with pea shoots.

As you may have guessed, I am something of a pea fanatic myself. I have experimented with the peas that you get in Delhi markets and unfortunately, many of them taste only slightly of pea, perhaps because they were picked too long ago. Some Indian frozen peas are better, but the problem is that they sell them by weight, which means that they wait till the peas are large before plucking them and freezing them. This means that all traces of the sweetness that should be at the heart of the pea have often vanished when the freezing process begins. If you are prepared to spend a little bit more, you can buy imported frozen peas at many supermarkets. These are a little more expensive (but much cheaper than meat or fish) and allow for more versatility in your cooking.

Because I like the taste of peas, I have invented a warm salad that is not only easy to make but also captures the taste of fresh peas.

First, chop lots of onions and garlic. Then take a good spicy salami or a chorizo (buy a chunk not slices) and cut it into pieces the size of the garlic and onions. Next, put a pot of water on the boil and defrost some bacon.

The actual cooking process is simplicity itself. While the water is boiling, sauté the salami in a little olive oil. When it begins to release its fat, throw in the onions and garlic and sweat them. As soon as the water boils, empty the contents of a packet of frozen peas into it. In a few minutes, the peas will begin to rise to the surface, meaning that they are cooked. As each layer of peas rises to the top of the water, start to remove it to make room for the next layer. When you have removed all the peas, add them to the onion, garlic and salami. Toss them all together over low heat for a minute or so to allow the flavours to mingle.

What you do next is up to you and depends largely on the quality of your ingredients. The salad should have a slightly spicy, garlicky taste, which should contrast with the sweetness of the peas. If you find that this has not happened, it is easy enough to correct. You can stir in a little garlic purée or add a few drops of Tabasco. If the peas have contributed too little to the taste, a few drops of balsamic vinegar, like Balsamico, should add the necessary sweetness. The chef's trick would be to now add a little butter to coat the peas but I find that this is unnecessary.

The salad is ready. I like to add a little fresh parsley once the dish is in the bowl but parsley is not always available. My current penchant is to cook a little bacon till it is very crisp and then add a few pieces to the salad for texture and extra pigginess.

It's a dish that you can eat on its own, that requires relatively few ingredients. And it is delicious. Try it and see.

THE INDIAN PANTRY

Corn Star

≈

Though the freshly made masala bhutta is an entirely Indian invention, the bhutta is actually an American vegetable discovered by Christopher Columbus.

Ever since I was a small boy, I have been fascinated by corn. I imagine that my interest was first aroused by the bhutta that I ate every evening. In Bombay, in the 1960s, there was a bhutta seller at every street corner. His corn was fresh and it was cheap.

I still remember staring avidly at the smouldering coals as the bhuttawallah roasted his wares. When the kernels had changed colour and before they could turn black and burnt, he would take the bhutta off the coals and ask how spicy I wanted it.

My answer was always the same: as spicy as possible. And so, the bhuttawallah would take a wedge of lemon, dunk it into a mass of chilli powder and other spices that he kept by the side of the coals and then smear my bhutta with a delicious chilli-lime mixture. Because a single application was never enough for me, he would repeat the process twice or thrice till I was satisfied.

I was told that the bhuttas came from rural Maharashtra though the men who roasted the corn seemed to come from all over India. They purchased their bhuttas from wholesale vegetable markets and set up their little stalls at every street corner and on the seaside at Marine Drive, Bandra Bandstand and Cuffe Parade—in the days when there was still sea in that area.

Of course, we didn't use the term *bhutta* then. That was a north Indian usage that I discovered later when I went to school in Rajasthan. The bhuttawallahs knew who their customers were and so they preferred the Gujarati term, *makai*. (Strange how closely the Gujarati and Punjabi words for bhutta parallel each other!)

I suppose I should have made the connection, but it took me a long time to work out that my other childhood favourite—masala popcorn—had exactly the same roots. But because popcorn looked so different from a bhutta and perhaps because I was not a very bright child, I never realized that popcorn consisted of bhutta kernels that had been popped by the application of heat so that the starch content caused them to swell up.

What did puzzle me, however, was the cornflake. If the English word for bhutta was corn, surely the cornflake should be made of crushed makai? Except that the painting on the box showed fields full of what looked remarkably like wheat. There was not a bhutta in sight.

Perhaps this was American corn, I decided. Indian corn was bhutta. I was somewhat encouraged when I read in American storybooks about Indian corn, favoured in the Wild West. I never figured out how the bhutta had reached Buffalo Bill and the Lone Ranger, but here it was in black and white: the term Indian corn.

My confusion was compounded when my parents took me to a restaurant in London on my ninth birthday. They suggested that I order Chicken Maryland, a dish that was novel to me but which I now place as Kentucky Fried Chicken with a slice of canned pineapple. Chicken Maryland came without any potatoes. Instead, it was served with what the menu called corn on the cob. This turned out to be a white man's version of the bhutta. It looked paler and fatter than our home-grown variety, and rather than use chilli and lemon, the restaurant poured melted butter all over it.

My sole concern at that age was that we are in a fancy restaurant. How in God's name do I eat this firangi bhutta with a knife and fork? I was told that it was okay to use my fingers, which meant that the moment of panic passed. But the dish did nothing to clarify my confusion. If the bhutta came from Maharashtra, how did its gora brother land up in some place called Maryland? It took me many years to resolve all the mysteries of the bhutta. And the solutions turned my childhood illusions upside down.

First of all, the bhutta is not native to Maharashtra. It is an American vegetable and was discovered by Christopher Columbus. Secondly, the American corn that so sustained Buffalo Bill did not come from Mumbai. It was the same bhutta that we ate but it was called Indian corn after American Indians (i.e., Native Americans), not after the bhuttawallahs on Marine Drive. Thirdly, the term corn doesn't actually mean anything. In Europe, it is used as a generic for any kind of cereal grain, one reason why there appear to be so many different kinds of corn. Fourthly, the bhutta is part of the maize family. Some of us may remember maize from our school geography lessons when we discussed the kharif crop and such grains as ragi and jowar. But even maize is a vast category. Bhutta represents just one small part of it.

Maize is actually a kind of grass and it dates back 70,000 years, making it one of the oldest cereals known to man. All maize does not consist of bhutta. Some of it has much smaller seed heads (cobs) and other kinds (squaw corn) have cobs that are even bigger. All maize is believed to have originated in America and did not reach Europe till 1492. Within years, the colonialists had taken it to Africa and to Asia where it quickly became a part of the diet.

The British brought maize to India because it had the advantage of growing quickly. But it wasn't till about 300 years ago that its cultivation caught on in this country. As far as I can tell, the masala bhutta is entirely an Indian invention. It is possible that the Aztecs ate something like it, but the version that is sold by our seasides is our own creation (though it may put it in perspective to realize that the chilli powder that is an essential ingredient of masala bhutta also came from America and was introduced to the subcontinent by the colonialists). Similarly, proponents of the ancient history of Punjabi cuisine should note that makki di roti is, by definition, a relatively recent invention.

More extraordinary still is the journey of maize into South-east Asia. All of us are familiar with baby corn, an important vegetable in Thai and Chinese cooking. This is no more than a kind of maize, a bonsai bhutta if you like, that has been bred from the original strain that Columbus discovered. If you actually taste baby corn on its own (without soya sauce) you'll find that it doesn't really remind you of bhutta. And wherever they've tried to introduce corn on the cob in South-east Asia, the experiment has failed. The only kind of maize that

East Asians will eat is baby corn, and that's probably because it doesn't taste like maize.

However, their cuisine is largely dependent on the use of cornflour (also called cornstarch in North America) as a thickener. You cannot extract cornflour from baby corn. It comes from the bottom of the kernels of fully grown bhutta. So, most of East Asia imports its cornflour from Western countries and from India. That should tell you something about Chinese food as well—if they put cornflour in everything now, what did they do in the days before Columbus discovered America?

I was in Mumbai some time ago and as I walked past the bhelpuriwallahs and the bhutta sellers by the seaside at Bandra Bandstand, I thought back to my childhood makai. In some strange way, it was reassuring to think that in this era of fast-food hamburgers, pre-packaged biscuits and polythene-wrapped potato crisps, there was still one dish that did not depend on large corporations or on the food industry.

Bhutta is no good unless it's fresh. It reaches us soon after it is harvested. It is made in front of you on hot coals by a man who has done this for years and whose palms bear the burns that come from moving the coals around. Each bhutta is individually seasoned to your liking. And every penny you pay for it goes to the man who made it and not to some faceless corporation that employs him.

And yet, maize is not Indian at all. It is an American vegetable brought to our shores by the British.

If that isn't globalization, what is?

Bringing Home the Brinjal

≈

The glorious history of the humble brinjal.

Brinjal is an original Indian vegetable. Around three evenings a week—and often more—we make a baingan bharta for dinner in my home. It is not that difficult a dish to master, baingan is relatively easy to find in the market, and it may well be my favourite (or at least one of them) of all market subzis.

When foreign guests try the bharta, they usually love it. Not only is it relatively mild in its spicing—you can actually taste the flavour of the original vegetable, which is not always true of other Indian-style subzis—but it is also a flavour that many foreigners recognize immediately. Their reference point, though, is not some restaurant version of the dish—baingan bharta is not a popular dish at most Indian restaurants abroad—but the baingan dishes of Middle Eastern cuisine. (Pedants may want me to point out that the baingan is a berry, in scientific terms, and not, technically speaking, a vegetable. But we shall ignore them!)

Sometimes guests will tell me that it reminds them of the Turkish Imam Bayildi. This baingan dish is probably more famous than it deserves to be because of its unusual name that translates loosely as 'the Imam fainted'. There are many stories about how the name originated. One version has it that an Imam swooned with joy because the dish was so wonderful. Another has it that one day, when his wife ran out of olive oil, she could not make it. On hearing that the dish would not be served, the Imam was so angry that he fainted. A third, more cynical version, is that the poor man fainted when he heard how much olive oil was used in the preparation of the dish.

Personally, I have never found more than a very tenuous parallel between our baingan bharta and Imam Bayildi. But I do see the point. The food of the Middle East, and the Mediterranean region as a whole, uses lots of baingan. Melanzane Parmigiana, one of the world's most famous Italian dishes, for instance, is based on baingan.

Over the years, bitter experience has made me cautious about claiming anything as our own. Many of the vegetables, pulses and flavours that we consider central to Indian cuisine turn out to have come from the Americas and were introduced to India by European colonialists: chilli, potato, rajma, etc.

So it is with dishes. They are not always of indigenous origin. Our pulao comes from the Turkish pilaf; the samosa is a variation of the Middle Eastern sambusak. The jalebi came to India from West Asia. Tea was planted in Darjeeling by the British who brought the plants from China. Coffee came from the Arabs. And so on.

So I have never made any great claims about baingan. And Western authors have told us that even the word *baingan* comes from the Persian *bádinján*. The other 'English' name we use for the vegetable, brinjal, is said to come from the Portuguese *berinjela*.

And indeed, fancy people in the West don't use any of these names. In America, they call it eggplant. In England, they call it aubergine. The Italians call it *melanzana* (which is why their famous dish is called Melanzane Parmigiana.)

No doubt, I thought, it would turn out that the Turks or the Europeans sent us baingan. Or perhaps it came to India with European imperialists.

But, I am happy to say, I was completely wrong. The baingan is ours. We gave it to the rest of the world. The Turks, the Italians and everybody else, took it from us. They may give it fancy names. But it is an ancient Indian vegetable. It appears in all our ancient texts—even our epics—and we have had the first-ever name for it: the Sanskrit vātiṃgaṇa from which the Hindi baingan came.

As for the Arabic name of which so much is made, well, it looks like bādinjān is derived from the Sanskrit vātiṃgaṇa.

What's more, I don't think we took any of our recipes from Arabs or other foreigners either. The food historian, Colleen Taylor Sen, has tracked down a baingan recipe from the first-known Indian cookbook, the *Pakashastra*. Because this is a work of 760 verses, passed down orally, it is difficult to date accurately. But most estimates place it in the same period as the Mahabharata.

One baingan recipe, discovered by Sen, requires you to take cubes of baingan and mix them with ground coriander, cumin, black pepper, imli, mango powder and dahi. When the baingan pieces are fully coated with the paste, they are fried in ghee. Then, they are wrapped in palm leaves along with aromatic flowers and camphor and sautéed in hot ghee. Eventually they are removed from the leaves and served on their own.

Not only is this recipe, with its double frying, quite complicated but it also sounds a lot like the Indian cooking of today. So, thousands of years ago, long before Jesus Christ was born, India already had a sophisticated cuisine in which the baingan played a key role.

By the medieval period, the famous baingan dishes of modern Indian cooking—including the baingan bharta—had already been created and documented.

So how did the Middle East get into the baingan act? Well, before we worry about that, consider the role of the baingan in the Far East. The Thais have several different kinds of baingan, including the little pea aubergine that they put into curries. The Chinese also use baingan in their cooking. And so do the Japanese.

Where did they get their baingans?

From us, probably!

Most theories suggest that the baingan plant travelled from India to South-east Asia, and then China, during the prehistoric or ancient periods. By the time the rest of the world discovered the baingan, we, in South and East Asia, already knew it well.

So when did the Arabs/Turks get hold of it?

Long after the Far East. That's for sure.

It is hard to say exactly when because, contrary to popular belief, India and the Middle East were trading partners much before the birth of Islam. The Indus Valley Civilization was a trading partner of

Mesopotamia (roughly equivalent to today's Iraq) and the commercial links continued to flourish through the centuries.

Moreover, while there are extensive records of how the Arabs took the baingan to Europe, there seem to be relatively few records of how it got to the Middle East from India in the first place. What seems likely, judging by the baingan's appearances in Arab culinary texts, is that it did not actually become common or popular till about the eighth century AD or several centuries after the first Indian recipes for early begun bhaja had already been recorded in Indian texts.

The Arabs had opened trade routes (and military supply lines—they first invaded Spain as early as the eighth century AD) with Europe and these were probably used to export the baingan. The Italians saw their first baingans in the thirteenth century. The variety the Arabs sold them was white in colour and looked like eggs on stems. This version reached England in the 1600s, was called eggplant, and described thus: 'the bigness of swan's egg, of a white colour and sometimes yellow and often brown'. The characteristic purple colour we associate with the baingan came much later as new varieties were farmed.

Opinions will vary but I believe that people who live in cold countries do not understand the flavour of the baingan or know how to cook it. Arabs, Turks and Persians have warm weather cuisines so they have created great baingan dishes. And the only Europeans who make good use of it are those in warmer Mediterranean Europe where ratatouille and Melanzane Parmigiana were created.

But none of those dishes—neither Turkish nor southern European— seem to me to even come close to the glories that the baingan has been raised to in our cuisine. No matter which part of India you go to, there is a great baingan dish: the begun bhaja of Bengal, the bharta of north India, the simple ringan nu shaak of Gujarat or the many wonderful baingan preparations of Andhra, such as vankaya peanut kura.

So whenever a foreign guest tells me he likes the bharta at my house and asks if it is Middle Eastern in origin, I have my answer ready.

'No,' I say. 'It is an original Indian vegetable. We cultivated it. And we gave it to the world.'

And then I smile. It's nice to be proud of the lesser-known glories of Indian vegetarian cuisine.

Fungus Phobia

≈

Move over briny, canned mushrooms; it's time to try these fresh varieties.

Mushrooms have been part of the South Asian diet for centuries. So why don't they play a larger role in the Indian gastronomical lexicon?

In the most commonly accepted version of the legend, the Buddha died after eating an offering of rotten meat. This story never fails to shock Hindus because we believe—at some deep and subliminal level—that all holy men of the East were vegetarians. In fact, Buddhists are not necessarily vegetarians—until he was forced to alter his diet for medical reasons, the Dalai Lama counted beef amongst his favourite foods.

But there's hope for all disappointed vegetarians: some scholars now believe that the story about the Buddha and rotten meat is based on a mistranslation of a Pali text. Apparently, what the Buddha ate—and what eventually caused his death—was not any kind of meat. And it may not even have been rotten. Perhaps somebody plucked a wild mushroom in the forests of the Terai region and offered it to the Buddha by mistake. This story, if true, might explain the great man's death. Death from indigestion sounds a little weak. But death from mushroom poisoning sounds more probable.

I do not know which version of the legend is historically accurate. But for all foodies, religion is not the point of the story. The revelation lies in the mushroom.

If the Buddha was eating mushrooms several centuries before the birth of Christ, this proves that edible mushrooms have been part of the South Asian diet for thousands of years.

And yet, we still tend to disregard mushrooms as vaguely foreign in origin. We know the cultivated white mushroom as a Western import. And the black shiitake mushroom is something we only encounter at Chinese restaurants.

Even in those parts of India where mushrooms are a part of everyday cuisine, they are still regarded as leftovers from the Raj. And to some extent, this is true. I have just returned from Himachal Pradesh where they tend to use white mushrooms like any other Indian vegetable—cooking them with matar or in a curry—and where they are cheap and readily available. In Kasauli, for instance, you can buy lots and lots of mushrooms because they are cultivated in that region. But I seriously doubt if they are native to Himachal Pradesh.

As far as I can tell, the cultivated white mushroom was unknown in those parts until the British made Simla (now Shimla) their summer capital. Mushrooms are part of the Western culinary tradition and it was only after the sahibs discovered that they were easy to farm in the Himachali hills that they became a staple of local agriculturalists. The mushroom matar and masala mushroom on toast tradition is a relatively recent innovation—one reason why it is restricted to north India.

But if the Buddha was eating mushrooms when the Brits were still living in trees and had no concept of what a kitchen looked like, why don't mushrooms play a larger role in the Indian gastronomical lexicon?

There are two short answers to this question. The first is that though Indians do not usually like to accept this, the Buddha was not an Indian. He was, in fact, a Nepali. Or, to be more accurate, the region he grew up in is now part of modern Nepal.

And two: mushrooms are very much a part of the Nepali culinary tradition. Moreover, in some parts of India (Kashmir, for instance), people have eaten mushrooms for years.

The confusion emerges from our tendency to act as if there are only two kinds of mushroom: the white (dhingri) of modern north Indian cooking and the black of Chinese and Far Eastern cooking.

In fact, there are hundreds of kinds of mushrooms. And I can think of at least three that are native to South Asia. The first of these is the oyster mushroom, a cheap, relatively flavourless variety that is known in the West as the 'Weeper' because it lets out so much water when it is cooked. Nepalis still include the oyster mushroom in their menus, and it is not uncommon to eat a spicy oyster mushroom subzi all over Nepal. The white mushroom, on the other hand, is relatively unknown there.

The second South Asian mushroom is the morel, or the gucchi, found growing wild in Kashmir. This is the most expensive of all Indian mushrooms, largely because most efforts to cultivate it have failed. We are dependent, therefore, on foragers who scour the forests of Kashmir to look for fresh morels. After the trouble started in Kashmir, prices have gone up presumably because it's more difficult to go foraging when militants are trying to shoot you.

Frankly, I have never quite seen the point of the morel or understood why people are willing to spend such huge sums of money for it. Morels are mostly dry (I've seen fresh morels on sale, but only in Europe) and you have to rehydrate them in warm water before they can be used for cooking.

In north Indian cuisine, morels are cooked either with peas (gucchi matar) or with cream or used to flavour a pulao. In my view, there is no taste to a morel when you cook it as a subzi and all you get is a texture—which is reminiscent of a shrivelled-up old sock. They can flavour pulaos, but I do not believe that they contribute very much. Certainly, they have no distinctive smell or taste in the black-truffle league, and I think that the porcini (or cep) mushroom of Europe, which is far cheaper, is much more flavourful.

The third kind of South Asian mushroom is the girolle. At its best, this has a golden colour with a parasol-like shape. It has a delicate flavour that is destroyed by masala, and works best when fried in butter with a little salt and pepper. Girolles grow wild in the hilly parts of north India (Himachal Pradesh and Kashmir, for instance) but there is, at least as far as I know, no tradition of picking them commercially. At least partly this is because they only last for a day or two after you pick them, and if you dry them, they taste of nothing but sawdust when rehydrated.

Of course, there are the mushrooms that we all come across in our gardens and when we walk in the wild, especially after it has rained for a bit. For the most part, these are not edible, and we are rightly taught to beware of eating them when we are young. Despite the Buddha's unhappy experience, however, I doubt very much if they are potentially fatal.

But they can cause indigestion, which is probably why many Indians regard mushrooms as dirty, and approach them with so much suspicion. In Bengal, for instance, they are called *byanger chhata* (frog's umbrella), which I suspect may be a Bengali variation on the English toadstool. (The difference between a mushroom and a toadstool is that the latter is usually regarded as inedible.) As a general rule, wild mushrooms have more flavour than the cultivated variety; even a morel is much more flavourful than the white button mushroom you get in the shops.

Other rules: avoid canned mushrooms, they taste of nothing as much as brine; and remember that the smaller the cultivated mushroom, the blander it is likely to be. For instance, if you let white mushrooms grow to their full size, they can be much more flavour-filled than buttons, which have virtually no taste.

In an ideal world, we would only eat fresh mushrooms. But because of problems of geography, we are sometimes forced to eat the dried or preserved variety. Some mushrooms (morel, porcini or shiitake, for instance) have flavours that intensify during the drying process but the texture is completely altered. And some mushrooms simply cannot be successfully preserved: more delicate wild mushrooms must be eaten fresh, and most methods of preserving truffles damage the flavour.

It puzzles me, however, why we do not get more fresh mushrooms in India. Presumably, somebody cultivates the shiitake mushroom judging by the vast variety we see at Chinese restaurants. Yet, I am still to see a fresh shiitake mushroom on sale in India. All restaurants use the dried variety. But fresh shiitake has a delicate flavour that drying intensifies. And you cannot make a subzi or use dried shiitake in Indian cooking because the texture is all wrong.

Given that there now seems to be a vast market for cultivated white mushrooms in the cities of India, the logical next step would be for someone to sell other varieties of fresh mushroom in the shops. Shiitake is the obvious variety. And after that, I suspect, such European mushrooms as the porcini (which you could easily grow in north India) would find a ready market.

I don't know why nobody tries to capture this market. Could it be that we are still too gastronomically timid? Or could it be the traditional Indian aversion to mushrooms and the fear that unfamiliar fungi are poisonous?

But look at it this way: The people of the Far East thrive on mushrooms. The Japanese and the Thais eat dozens of varieties, for instance. And it doesn't seem to have done them any harm. So, if Buddhists can flourish on the vegetable that may have harmed the Buddha, why should the rest of us be so terrified?

Just Chilli

≈

About the only foodie-related fact that annoys Indians more than the origin of the samosa (we did not invent it, the Middle East did) is the suggestion that chillies are a colonial contribution to our cuisine.

When you tell people that there were no chillies in India till the Europeans got here, they look at you disbelievingly. And when you point out that as chillies were only discovered in the Americas, they could not possibly have been an indigenous food group, they ask the obvious question: If Europeans gave us the chilli, why are there no chillies in European cuisine?

Well, it is not as though all European cuisine is chilli-free. When Indians say 'chilli', we think of the hot red chilli that is a distinctive feature of our cuisine. But the chilli family is vast (there may be thousands of varieties), so it extends far beyond the red chilli.

You will find so-called 'peppers' (near to what we prefer to call capsicum) in Italian cuisine. The Hungarians are proud of the paprika, the chilli that is the mark of their cuisine.

The Spanish love chillies. The Pimiento de Padrón—a bright-green chilli from the town of Padrón in north-west Spain—has travelled around the world in recent decades as part of the global tapas craze.

But yes, it is true that Europeans tend not to like very hot chillies. Food writer Colleen Taylor Sen suggests that 'a taste for spices evolved over the centuries in hot climates because they contain powerful antibiotic chemicals that can kill or suppress bacteria or fungi that spoil foods . . . The antibiotic effects are even stronger when ingredients such as chillies, onion, garlic and cumin are combined.'

So, people in hot countries like hot food, while those in cold countries like blander food.

If we took to the chilli because, like residents of other hot countries, we like spice, what did we do before the Europeans discovered the New World?

Well, that's easy to answer. In Indian food (if it is done right!) the chilli is just one of the many flavouring ingredients. All of our other spices are native to India. Centuries ago, we were especially proud of our pepper. Not only did it provide the heat in Indian cuisine, it was so popular in Europe that we would export it to Rome, Venice and other European trading centres where it fetched an enormous premium.

When Christopher Columbus set sail, he was not looking for America, but for India and its spices. When he landed in what we now know was South America, he was so confused that he called the people he encountered 'Indians'. He also thought that the chilli they used in cooking was a kind of pepper, creating a second confusion in nomenclature that persists to this day.

Even food historian K.T. Achaya, who usually managed to find south Indian origins for all of the world's foods, was forced to concede that till Columbus got to America and thought that he had discovered a new kind of pepper, nobody in India had the slightest idea what a chilli was. 'There is no mention whatsoever of the chilli in Indian literature before the sixteenth century,' he noted, perhaps a little sadly.

As Achaya also pointed out, no Indian language had a word for chilli, and when it did finally reach our shores, we fell back on Columbus-like confusions with pepper: mirch in Hindi and milagu and milagai in Tamil, for instance.

Nobody has any exact record of the arrival of the chilli in India, but it is believed that the Portuguese fleet commanded by Vasco da Gama brought seeds for the plant to Goa. This is where they were first planted, and they then spread to Bombay where they were called Gova mirch.

Lizzie Collingham, the noted food historian, says that one mark of how quickly Indians accepted the chilli was the alacrity with which

Ayurvedic physicians, usually unwilling to accept any ingredient that had not been around in the Vedic age, incorporated chillies into their system of medicine.

Within a hundred years of Vasco da Gama's arrival in India, we had cultivated the chilli so successfully that India actually became a net exporter of chilli powder and dried chillies. Traders began to take Indian chillies to the West along with our pepper, nutmeg and other spices. (This ingenuity may explain why India was one of the world's richest countries in the pre-colonial era.)

According to Collingham, the chilli export was controlled by the Turks who bought chillies from the west coast of India and took them to Black Sea ports and their own country and from there, to northern Europe—Germany, Holland, etc., and to England.

This is what led many Europeans to regard the chilli (which is actually a vegetable) as just another Indian spice—a belief that still persists. Moreover, says Collingham, the Turks introduced the chilli to Hungary when they conquered it. So the famous paprika of Hungary is really an Indian chilli. (In botanical terms, it is closely related to the Kashmiri mirch or the Bedgi chilli of south India.)

So, while colonialists may well have introduced a South American flavour to our cuisine, the genius of India lies in the way we made it our own and gave it to other cuisines, to countries where nobody had heard of Columbus or Vasco da Gama.

Where else did we take it?

That's the big issue. The official version, found in every textbook, is that the Portuguese took it around the world. There is the example of the peri-peri chilli, which they planted in their colonies in Africa and which led to the creation of the famous hot sauce and, later, to Nando's and Barcelos. In Goa too, the peri-peri masala is the building block of the Catholic cuisine.

The Thais also use a variation of the peri-peri chilli, though it tends to be called a bird's eye chilli. (Birds play a large role in its dispersal.) Did they get it from India? After all, we were cultivating it all over the country. The conventional wisdom is that they did not. Apparently, the Portuguese sent an envoy to the ancient Thai capital of Ayutthaya soon after Portugal captured the port of Malacca (now in Malaysia). We are expected to believe that this short-lived, and minimal Portuguese presence in Thailand was enough to convert the Thais to the joys of the chilli.

There is a similar problem with the chilli and China. It is hard to think of Sichuan cuisine without the chilli. But who brought the chilli to Sichuan? One theory is the standard 'European traders brought it with them' version, but Sichuan is not on the coast. So, which European traders got there, and how and when? A second theory is that it reached overland, perhaps via Burma (now Myanmar), which, to me at least, seems a little more convincing.

The Spanish have their own theories about the arrival of the chilli in East Asia. They dispute the version that involves the Portuguese getting the plants from Bolivia and taking them around the world. They point out that they had strong links with Mexico (ruled by Spain) and the Philippines (also ruled by Spain). They say that they brought Mexican chillies to the Philippines and that it was from there that the chilli spread to the rest of Asia.

I don't see how we can rule this out. But we are still left with the bhut jolokia problem. Of late, this chilli has been much in the news for its potency: it can repel elephants, fell terrorists, etc.

But I have never read a good explanation of how it got to Nagaland and the hills of the north-east. There are no stories of colonialists taking it to those regions, which were cut off from the rest of India in that era.

Nor is it likely that the few missionaries who braved the journey carried a Bible in one hand and a chilli in the other. Moreover, the Naga chillies are part of the botanical species *Capsicum chinense*, not *Capsicum annuum*, like most other Indian chillies.

So how did this breed develop? And how did it grow wild and to such potency in those hills, a long, long way from South America or even Goa?

We don't know. Like many things about the spread of the chilli, this one too is a mystery. But what is clear is that the history of the spread of the chilli in Asia has, so far, been written by self-glorifying Europeans.

Perhaps it is time for us to do some research of our own.

Fruit

All About Fruit

≈

Many of the fruits we regard as Indian are all imports.

I often hear people complaining about the modern tendency to buy avocados and other expensive fruit.

'Why must you spend so much money on foreign fruit?' they say. 'What's wrong with good Indian fruit? Why go for imported fruit?'

The problem with these sentiments—as laudable as they are on the grounds of thrift—is that they refer to something that doesn't really exist. What are Indian fruits, anyway? The truth is that many of the fruits we regard as our own were never ours to begin with. They were all imports.

Indian fruit has long been unfairly judged. When the Mughals got here, they were appalled by the limited variety of fruits available in the market. Worse still, many of the ones they had some familiarity with were—or so they claimed—remarkably feeble in their Indian avatars.

Both Babur and Humayun often wrote about missing the sweet melons of Samarkand, and it is the Mughals we must thank for importing fruit seeds from Central Asia and expanding the range of local fruits available.

But the Portuguese and the British were even more influential than the Mughals. The sad—and shocking—reality is that were it not for colonial conquerors, India would be one of the worst places in the world to eat fruit.

Of course, we do not realize this. Each region of India has one or two varieties of fruit that it regards as its very own. In fact, rarely is this true. In nearly every case, the fruit was originally not native to India, let alone to that region.

Let's start with the one fruit we regard as indispensable to many kinds of cuisine: the imli or tamarind. We think of the tamarind as being not just Indian but uniquely Asian. Tamarind is an integral constituent of many South-east Asian cuisines—among them Thai and Malay.

Well, chew on this: The tamarind is not of Indian, or even Asian, origin. It originated in Africa and was brought to Asia by traders.

Records show that the tamarind was used all over North Africa long before the birth of Christ. It was even known to the ancient Egyptians. It is still used in many parts of Africa, including Malawi.

But the name tamarind—by which no Indian knows the plant—is Arabic and is, bizarrely enough, of Indian origin. An Arab gave it that name after he saw the plant in India. The 'tamar' in the name is Arabic, meaning a dry date fruit. And the 'ind' comes from Hind. The Arabs called it the tamar of Hind!

Let's take the custard apple. Gujaratis regard the fruit as their own personal property. Sitaphal (which is what we call custard apple) ice cream is a great Gujarati dish.

But the custard apple is as Gujarati as Viv Richards. It is a West Indian fruit that only got to Africa in the seventeenth century. It made its way to India sometime after that—at which stage, presumably, it was adopted by Gujaratis.

Or take Goans and the cashewnut. If you listen to Goans talk about the quality of their kajus or praise their feni, you would think that they had known the cashew for millennia. But, as you may have guessed, the cashewnut is of Brazilian origin and was brought to Goa by the Portuguese. (Interestingly, the Goans, like the Brazilians, prize the nut, while in the rest of South America, it is the outer cashew apple that is the delicacy.)

Tropical America (comprising the northern states of South America, Central America and the southern part of Mexico) provided many of the fruits that we regard as peculiarly Indian. The guava also comes from Brazil and was brought to Asia by the Portuguese. In Malaysia, it is called Jambu Portugis.

The papaya also came to India with the Portuguese who probably found the first papaya plants somewhere in the Americas—Mexico is one possibility.

So it is with the pineapple. Christopher Columbus found the plant in the Americas and brought it back to Europe where it was known as 'the noblest of all the fruits of India'. (The twits thought that Columbus had discovered a new sea route to India, not realizing that he'd ended up in America.)

The Spaniards and the Portuguese stuck for a while with the name given by Columbus—the pine of the Indies—before settling on 'apple' rather than 'Indies'. In many parts of India (and the rest of Asia) we still use names derived from the original Brazilian ('anana'), and current European names are variations of the Brazilian term.

Even those of us who are not entirely surprised to learn that the cashew and the pineapple came from the Americas may be startled to discover that even the kaddu or the pumpkin has a Central American origin.

The plant was discovered by Spanish conquistadores in Mexico and taken back to Europe along with other members of the same family (squash, marrow, etc.). It has never really caught on in Europe, but it is a favourite in North America (where they make pumpkin pie for Thanksgiving dinner) and in much of Asia.

Of course, not every fruit came from the Americas (though sometimes it seems that way). Many came from Africa and West Asia and reached India centuries ago. Take the pomegranate that was well known in Europe centuries ago. (Romeo's nightingale serenaded Juliet in Verona under a pomegranate tree.)

We know that the pomegranate was eaten by the ancient Egyptians and the Romans. Who brought it to India? There are many theories, but we have eaten it for over a thousand years—and have now forgotten that it was ever an import.

Say this for Indians though: Once we are shown a good fruit, we take it to our hearts. Many of us think of the lychee as being a Chinese fruit—which of course it is—because of the enthusiasm with which Chinese restaurateurs put it on their menus.

Fair enough. The lychee left China relatively late and only reached India in the eighteenth century. Nor did the lychee appear in its canned form in world markets till 1945.

But, guess what? India is now the world's largest producer of canned lychees.

All this may leave you wondering: Are there no Indian fruits at all? Is everything of foreign origin?

Actually yes, there are Indian fruits.

The most famous of these is the mango. It is a purely Indian plant even though it is now cultivated in many other parts of the world. There were mangoes in India over 4000 years ago and it crops up in ancient Sanskrit texts.

Even the Mughals had to drop their sniffiness after tasting the mango. Emperor Akbar planted 1,00,000 mango trees all over India— one reason why the mango's popularity perhaps extends to every part of the country.

There are other Indian fruits too. The king of the bunch is probably the banana. Many countries lay claim to the banana—the name itself comes from the local name of an African plant. And in South-east Asia they argue that the plant is native to Malaysia.

But the oldest reference to the banana, going back 2500 years, mentions India. Alexander the Great's army first encountered bananas in India in 326 BC and by then, his people were familiar with Iran and North Africa where they had seen no bananas at all.

Unlike many other fruits that were discovered in America, then taken to Europe and eventually made their way to Africa and India, the banana followed the opposite route. It was found in India, went to Africa and the Middle East, from there to Europe and then to North America. It was the demand for bananas in North America that led to the growth of banana plantations in Brazil.

Also, entirely Indian in origin is the coconut. You find palm trees all over tropical coasts, but the earliest records of the coconut fruit exist in Indian literature. It was Indians who learnt how to use the by-products of the coconut—coir, oil, milk and water. And the coconut seems to have been a part of Hindu rituals almost from the time such rituals began.

Speaking for myself, I am not a great fruit eater and so, unlike the Mughals or other imperialists, I have no problem with Indian fruits. I am happy to accept that we only discovered the guava, the papaya, the pumpkin or the pomegranate when foreigners brought them to our shores.

But give me a coconut or a banana and I will be more than happy to let you keep your cashews and your guavas.

Indian fruits may not have been the most exotic. But like India itself, they are solid, timeless and always reliable.

The Magnificent Mango

≈

The only place that really smells of mangoes is India.

It is a measure of how possessive we Indians are about the mango that whenever I hear of mangoes in other countries, I feel an entirely unreasonable rage. For instance, the Thais have their own mangoes, which they sell on the streets and incorporate into their salads.

They are so keen on regarding the mango as their own that Bangkok is often referred to as the Big Mango (which is also the title of a Bangkok novel by Jake Needham).

Now, I don't mind that the Thais know how to cultivate the mango, but I do resent the way in which they try to claim it for themselves. Everyone should know that the mango belongs to us and that if any city deserves to be called the Big Mango it is Mumbai.

So it is with the Egyptians. Some years ago, Hermès sent the master perfumer Jean-Claude Ellena to Egypt to create a fragrance that captured the aromas of the Nile. Like everyone else, I expected some heady Middle Eastern fragrance to emerge. Instead, Ellena returned with a slightly fruity fragrance, which, he said, was based on the smell of the green mangoes that grew around the Nile. Mangoes and the Nile?

Mangoes and Egypt? Unbelievable! It's a perfectly good fragrance but I can't get excited about it because I know that the only place that really smells of mangoes is India.

So irrational is my possessiveness about the mango that even when I see the mango fruit motif in fabrics, I expect it to be regarded as an Indian pattern. It annoys me to hear it referred to as 'paisley', and I am incredulous when people describe it as a traditional English motif or when such dodgy Italian fashion houses as Etro try and make it their trademark. The English can create roast beef motifs for all I care, and the Italians can paint pizzas on their ties. But the mango is Indian and should be acknowledged as such.

Even if my possessiveness has a slightly lunatic edge to its extremism, the reality is that the mango is not only Indian, it is as old as India itself. The virtues of the mango were noted in the *Brihadaranyaka Upanishad* in 1000 BC (i.e., a full millennium before anyone had heard of Jesus Christ or the Western civilization itself) and some authorities would argue that the reference to Saha in the Rig Veda is a reference to the mango. These mentions in ancient literature reflect the respect Hindus have for the mango. It is a transformation of Prajapati, the creator of all creatures, and its flowers symbolize the darts of Kamdev, the god of love and sex.

Even Buddhists respect the mango's sacred origins. The Buddha would rest in a mango grove. And according to one story, the Buddha once ate a mango, planted the stone and then washed his hands over it. 'A beautiful white mango tree sprang forth bearing flowers and fruit.' (The quote is from K.T. Achaya, who was almost as possessive about the mango as I am.)

Nobody seriously disputes that the mango is of Indian origin. Some people say that it was first cultivated in the subcontinent around 2000 BC and then spread from our shores to the rest of Asia. Contrary to what you and I may think, the mango is not a north Indian tree. It originated in the north-east, probably around Mizoram. Despite its religious significance, it soon became the ultimate Indian fruit appealing to people of all religions. When the Mughals first came to India, they complained bitterly about the poor quality of our fruits ('what? No Samarkand melons?' etc., etc.). But they soon realized that the mango was superior to many of the fruits they were used to. Mughal emperors took to planting orchards and in the sixteenth century, Akbar planted 1,00,000 mango trees at Darbhanga in Bihar and called the orchard Lakh Bagh.

By the time the Europeans got here, the mango had already spread to the Middle East (and to Egypt where, no doubt, it grew quietly, awaiting the arrival of Jean-Claude Ellena) but was still largely unknown in the West. The Portuguese took it to Africa and then to Brazil. By the eighteenth century it had reached the West Indies and, a few decades later, it turned up in the US. It is still cultivated in Florida and Hawaii and enjoyed by thousands of Americans who are entirely unaware of its Indian origins.

To be fair to the Europeans, they contributed to the development of the plant. It was the Portuguese who used grafting techniques to create new varieties. The most popular mango in Western India, the Aaphus, owes its name to a Portuguese grower called Nicholas Alfonso. The Indian word, Aaphus, is a corruption of Alfonso, though fancy people like referring to the variety as the Alphonso, thereby misspelling poor Nicholas Alfonso's name.

One reason why we regard the mango as so special is that it has a unique aroma and taste. But we sometimes do not give it the credit that is due for its sheer versatility. In Gujarat, where I come from, it is common during the mango season to make a thick pulp from the mango (*kairi no rus*) and to eat it with hot puris in the course of the meal. I can think of few other fruit that can be enjoyed in this manner. We also find many uses for the unripe mango. It becomes a flavouring agent in our cooking, and our most distinctive pickle is made from mango. How many fruits do you know that can be used as desserts, as a pulp to be enjoyed with hot breads and as the basis for a tangy pickle?

Nor are Gujaratis alone in our love of the mango. All over south India, mangoes are used for flavour, and the best Kerala curries use raw mango. This tradition dates back to ancient times: the Mahabharata describes a dish of meat cooked with mango pieces. The Gujarati mango pickle may be the best, but mangoes are pickled in different ways all over India, from Punjab to Tamil Nadu. Murabbas are also ubiquitous throughout the country, and their slightly sweetish marmalady flavour made them great favourites among Raj-era Brits. The mango chutneys that are still sold in Britain were a colonial variation on the traditional Indian murabba.

Despite the Thais, the Americans and even the Egyptians, India is the world's largest producer of mangoes. Though domestic demand is enormous, we manage to satisfy it from our own production and even have mangoes left over for export. And yet, if you tell a Frenchman or an Englishman or even a Chinese person that there is no fruit that is the equal of the mango, they will look at you with mild curiosity and open astonishment. Check the fruit juices on sale in the West and you will find that mango juice is not among the top sellers. Go to an ice-cream parlour and check the many varieties available. The chances are that you will not find a mango ice cream at an American parlour or an Italian gelato shop.

I can never work out why this should be so. Partly, I guess it is because the mango has an assertive flavour and cannot be mixed easily. Try making a mango cocktail and you'll face the same problem every time: too much mango and the drink will taste of nothing else and too little mango will mean that the cocktail has no point.

So it is with ice cream. There is only one kind of ice cream you can make with mangoes. The flavour is so instantly recognizable that there is very little you can do with it, and there is virtually no other ingredient (chocolate, raisins, nuts, etc.) that you can mix it with.

Then, there is the availability factor. In India, we are used to the idea of seasonal eating. Once the mango season starts, nearly everyone I know goes on eating as many mangoes as he or she can find because we all know that the season will soon end and no mangoes will be available till the following year.

In the West, on the other hand, they are less happy to accept the rules of seasonal eating. They like fruits that are available all the year round and find it difficult to get excited about the mango, only to see it disappear from their shelves in a couple of months.

My view is that this is the West's loss. The fewer mangoes they eat abroad, the more we can eat in India. So, go out and buy a mango. Cut it open and bite into the smooth, firm flesh. Feel that unmistakable flavour flood your taste buds. Inhale that delicious aroma.

And know that this is the taste of India through the millennia.

Strawberry Fields Forever

≈

Have you noticed that there seems to be a glut of strawberries in the market these days?

At nearly every restaurant and pastry shop, the chefs seem to be churning out strawberry pastries and tarts. At traffic lights (especially in Mumbai) hawkers come up to you with reasonably priced baskets of strawberries. Fruit sellers urge you to buy freshly grown strawberries.

It was all very different when I was growing up in Bombay (as it was then called) in the 1960s and '70s. In those days, we thought of strawberries as something that went into jam or flavoured ice cream. Fresh strawberries were expensive and hard to come by unless you went to the hill station of Mahabaleshwar where they were grown. For many people of my generation, a trip to Mahabaleshwar was no more than an excuse to eat lots of strawberries.

But now, you get so many strawberries at prices that are surprisingly affordable that chefs put them on everything. Nearly every dessert at some fancy restaurant will have a strawberry garnish. And the new generation of Indian pastry chefs does not grant strawberries the respect and reverence they were once accorded. For them, the strawberry is just another seasonal fruit.

But of course, the strawberry can never be just another fruit. For a start, there are all the pop-culture associations. It's not just the Beatles (though I gather that 'Strawberry Fields' was a lunatic asylum and John Lennon was not thinking of the fruit when he wrote the song) but it is also *Pretty Woman*. Who can forget Richard Gere ordering a bottle of champagne and a bowl of strawberries as he escorts Julia Roberts to his suite for the very first time? (The strawberries bring out the flavour of the champagne, he explains.)

And then there are all the glamorous associations. Anybody who has read about Wimbledon will know that spectators spend the entire tournament gorging on strawberries and cream. And small wild strawberries have long fascinated gourmets (and Ingmar Bergman, the Swedish film director).

Intrigued by the strawberry glut, I did some checking. It turns out that the strawberry is not native to India. (No surprises there.) But it is one of those rare fruits that was already reasonably well known in Europe (though mostly in its small, wild form) when it was found in the Americas.

The strawberry that we know today, however, is a hybrid. It was created from the American variety in the nineteenth century when British gardeners cross-bred strawberry plants to create the 'Keens Seedling' (one of the gardeners was called Michael Keens), which was a large flavourful strawberry of the sort we eat today. Since then, scientists have spent a lot of time and money developing other varieties, and there are hundreds of kinds of strawberries available today. (Though the European wild strawberry was first cultivated as early as the fourteenth century, it is so small and the yield so low that you only ever find it at gourmet markets these days.)

Some accounts say that the British brought the strawberry to India at the end of the nineteenth century (i.e., shortly after the hybrid version had been created) but the plant seems to have reached Mahabaleshwar in the 1920s. Ever since then, Mahabaleshwar has been the strawberry capital of India. It dines out on that reputation, organizing strawberry festivals, demanding a GI (geographical index) certification (like, say, Darjeeling tea) for its strawberries and claiming to account for over 80 per cent of all strawberries produced in India.

The current glut has its origins in a change in strawberry farming styles in Mahabaleshwar. An Australian high-yielding variety of strawberry was introduced to Mahabaleshwar in 1992 and production began to shoot up.

Some accounts say that Sharad Pawar, who ran Maharashtra in the 1990s and is a farmer himself, ordered the planting of the new strawberry breed. Since then, Mahabaleshwar's production has multiplied, and in other parts of Maharashtra, farmers have been encouraged to grow strawberries. This has contributed to the lowering of prices.

Since the boom of the 1990s, strawberry cultivation has spread to other parts of India. The strawberries we get in Delhi are often sourced from Himachal Pradesh and Punjab. They grow strawberries in Bengaluru. And even Meghalaya has a strawberry-growing tradition now!

Strawberry farmers believe that with the general drop in strawberry prices, the fruit will become more popular as it becomes more accessible. Though we no longer regard the strawberry as rare or exotic, we still don't buy many strawberries for home use, preferring to eat them when we go out. Strawberry farmers believe that once we start bringing them home, the demand will shoot up and the market will increase.

They are probably right. The thing about strawberries is that even those of us who hardly ever eat fresh strawberries are familiar with the flavour. We know it from strawberry ice cream (even though much of it uses synthetic flavouring), milk shakes and desserts. We have all eaten strawberry jam at some stage, and we recognize the distinctive taste of the fruit.

So why shouldn't we eat it at home?

My guess is that one of the things holding us back is that Indians like to wash and (perhaps) peel their fruit and then eat it raw. That's how we eat oranges, apples, guavas, lychees, and nearly all other fruits.

But this approach does not always work with strawberries. The truth is that most fresh strawberries available in India are simply not sweet enough. (Forgive me, farmers of Mahabaleshwar!) When we bite into them, we recognize the flavour but find that it lacks the sweet taste we associate with strawberry jam or strawberry ice cream.

This does not worry chefs or patissiers who know how to combine the strawberries with sweet ingredients (chocolate, most often) or poach them in sugar syrup or serve them with ice cream. (You can't really enjoy strawberries and cream with Indian strawberries unless you sprinkle them with lots of sugar first.) But it does make a difference to us at home because—unlike in the West—we eat our fruit neat and not as part of some dessert.

The strawberry farmers need to find some way around this. My guess is that if they start marketing their products as best eaten with ice cream (in which case, the acid of the fruit provides a counterpoint to the sweetness of the ice cream), they may have greater success in penetrating the home market. I can't see strawberries working well with most Indian sweets. (Strawberry jalebis? Strawberry gulab jamuns? Nah!) But you could, I guess, make strawberry shrikhand or strawberry kheer. (OK, not really, either.)

I know Richard Gere likes his champagne with strawberries (or not—from what I remember of *Pretty Woman*, Gere's character did not drink, so the champagne was for Julia) but in my experience champagne does not really go with strawberries and the claim that the strawberries bring out the flavour of the grape is bogus. But drink a sweet fizzy wine (say a sparkling moscato) and the combination could work. On the other hand, my friend Deepak Ohri served Perrier Jouet rosé champagne with sweet Korean strawberries at the bar at Bangkok's Lebua and the combination worked brilliantly. However, given that you and I, unlike Deepak, have no access to Korean strawberries, or bottles of Perrier Jouet rosé, I think we are still best off avoiding the champagne-and-strawberry combination.

But some flavours do go well with strawberry. Vanilla is one. Balsamico is another. It is an easy test. Put some strawberries in a wine glass. Top with good (i.e., not synthetic) vanilla ice cream and then pour a little balsamic vinegar on top. It makes for a surprising and very grown-up dessert.

If your strawberries are dry or not sweet enough, cook them with a little balsamico or Grand Marnier (which combines the flavours of brandy and oranges) on a very low flame for a longish period. The strawberries that result will taste great in any dessert.

Remember also that strawberries hide their flavour inside the fruit. (Those things on the outside of each strawberry are the seeds—strawberries tend to work inside out.) You can tease out the flavour either with sugar or with acid (hence the balsamico), but for texture, it often helps to add a bit of biscuit (shortcake?) to any strawberry dessert. Nuts work well too, but my favourite combination of strawberry, vanilla ice cream and balsamico can be best enhanced by adding sliced almonds, which not only add texture but also have a flavour that complements strawberry.

Many people like chocolate and strawberry but I find that the pairing only works when one of the components is not sweet. Use dense, dark chocolate with strawberries poached in something sweet, and the dessert will take off. Or use a sweetish chocolate to counteract the acid of the strawberries.

What you do is really up to you. But when strawberries are so plentiful and so reasonably priced, it is a shame not to take some home and experiment with the flavour.

AvocaDo
You Good

≈

Should you join the avocado craze?

Do you know what an 'English vegetable' is? No? Well, it took me a while to figure it out as well! An 'English vegetable' is not necessarily one that English people like but one that our local subziwallahs regard as strange and alien to Indian cooking. So asparagus is an 'English vegetable'. So is baby corn. And mushrooms. And so on.

The distinction is not as bizarre as it sounds. Even those of us who eat saag at home don't use pak choi for Indian food. We may eat lauki or doodhi but we have little experience of zucchini. Lettuce has been around long enough to be a staple, but rocket is still a novelty.

On the whole, 'English vegetables' are bought by restaurants or hotels. This is partly because restaurant chefs have different needs from ours at home. And partly it is because they have the 'vegetarian problem'.

This problem is easily stated. Meat and fish cost more than vegetables. Yet restaurants like to make the same amount of money from vegetarians as they do from non-vegetarians. Given that many vegetarians are canny eaters, drawn from India's commercially minded communities, pricing is always a tricky issue. Guests know how much tomatoes cost. They know that gobi costs less than chicken.

So, how can a restaurateur persuade vegetarians to pay nearly as much for a vegetarian meal as other guests are paying for meat and fish?

One way is to upgrade the vegetables. A vegetarian will not object to paying through the nose for a salad if he or she is told that the cherry tomatoes were flown in from Amsterdam.

The other is to pack the menu with so-called 'English vegetables' whose novelty value will distract the vegetarians from the grim reality that in nearly every Indian restaurant, the guys eating the vegetarian dishes are subsidizing those eating the lobster.

And let's be honest, even vegetarians don't like the idea of going to restaurants to eat bhindi or baingan. They want unusual vegetables that make the meal seem more special. For a long time, terrible canned button mushrooms packed in brine were regarded as glamorous. Soggy, stringy, tinned white asparagus was given pride of place. And artichoke hearts were the ultimate luxury.

Many of these so-called 'English vegetables' are now available at metropolitan subziwallahs, so they have lost some of their glamour. And chefs and vegetarians alike have searched for new exotic vegetables to focus on.

Himanshu Taneja, who won my Chef of the Year award in 2016, leads the kitchen team at Mumbai's St Regis and keeps me informed of the food trends he has noticed. When I was briefly visiting the St Regis, Himanshu asked me why I had not written anything about avocados.

Avocados? Why would I write about avocados? I was curious that Himanshu regarded this as a subject worth covering. 'It is the new hot food,' he said.

Himanshu always has his finger on the pulse of the market, so I made him tell me why he thought avocados were so hot.

His answer had to do with demand. It started, he said, with the craze for avocado toast—a global fad that I am familiar with.

'Nutritionists' have encouraged people in the West to give up on eggs for breakfast and eat avocados on toast. As is true of all fad foods, a variety of health benefits have been claimed for the avocado. ('It will make your skin glow. It is good for your heart. You will get an instant energy boost. The opposite sex will find you irresistible.' Oh, OK. I made up the last one. But you get the drift . . .)

But now, says Himanshu, guests at upmarket hotels and restaurants demand avocados on everything. They want avocado tacos. They want avocados in kulchas. They want avocado sushi rolls. How about avocado tartare? Avocado mash? They love avocado chaat. They even enjoy avocado tiramisu. (Yes, really!)

Himanshu is a super-talented chef, so he has no difficulty in creating new avocado dishes, especially for banquets and buffets. But even he is startled by the way in which the avocado craze is sweeping Mumbai.

On the flight back to Delhi after my encounter with Himanshu, I kept trying to work out why the avocado was such a big deal. My previous experience of avocados was limited to avocado vinaigrette, a starter popular in restaurants in the 1970s. Chefs loved it because all you had to do was cut the avocado in half, throw away the stone and fill the cavity with vinaigrette. And then, of course, there was guacamole, the ancient Aztec dish based on mashed avocados, tomatoes, onions, coriander and chillies, which has travelled the world as a dip and bar snack.

But, as far as I remembered, the 1980s orthodoxy was that the avocado was not particularly healthy. It was one of those fruit that people were told to avoid if they did not want to put on weight.

So when I got back to Delhi, I did little digging. Yes, the avocado is a member of the pear family (*Persea americana*) and has been cultivated in South and Central America (and the islands off the coast) for thousands of years. There are three principal kinds of avocado: Mexican, which is small and was named ahuacatl by the Aztecs because it looked like an ahuacatl (or testicle); the Guatemalan, which is darker in colour; and the larger West Indian. Now, of course, there are hundreds of hybrid varieties.

People will tell you that they like the avocado for its taste, which, frankly, is a load of ahuacatl. People like the avocado because of its fleshy texture and because it has a mild flavour that lends itself to most kinds of seasoning.

The secret of the avocado's popularity, however, is its fat content. Up to 30 per cent of each avocado is oil or just fat. This is a huge proportion—olives, for instance rarely have more than 15 per cent fat.

Most cooking uses of the avocado have focused on the fat content. When you make trendy avocado toast, for instance, all you are doing is replacing the butter on your toast with avocado fat. In California, they started putting avocado in sushi rolls in the 1970s to mimic the fattiness of the more expensive tuna belly. When people put avocado into kathi rolls, as is now fashionable in Mumbai, what they really want is a roll filled with fat. The flavour comes from the other ingredients.

So why is the avocado a health food?

Well, because doctors keep changing their minds. In the 1970s they told us to steer clear of fats, and as the avocado was the fatty of the fruit kingdom, it fell into disrepute. Then, the orthodoxy changed again. Doctors began to advocate vegetable and fruit fats over animal fats. So butter fell out of favour and olive oil became the rage. Clever marketers tagged the fat content of the avocado into the olive oil category. It is also an unsaturated fat and was said to be healthier than dairy.

You can, if you choose to, believe all the health claims made for the avocado. But there are two things you should know. The first is that doctors have, once again, changed their minds about dairy fat. Now they say that it's not bad for you provided you don't overindulge. And the second is that any fat—whether good, bad, animal, fruit, dairy, etc.—is still fat. So, if you think that avocados will keep you slim, you might want to rethink your diet.

It is worth mentioning also that avocados are not cheap. There are local suppliers (I have seen them on sale in Bengaluru as far back as the 1980s) but restaurant chefs complain that quality can vary and supplies can be erratic. Himanshu imports his avocados and pays around Rs 200 per avocado. That is a lot of money—and he gets a wholesale price. High-quality imported avocados can be even more expensive in the shops.

So, should you join the avocado craze?

Well, it is entirely up to you. If you like them and can afford them, there is no reason why you should not eat avocados.

But if you are eating them thinking that they are a super food or that they will make you healthier, tread cautiously. Fads come and go. And this one will follow the same pattern.

Eventually, I suspect the avocado will go back to the status it once enjoyed: as an 'English vegetable' that we may consume occasionally (like, say, asparagus).

Super foods can lose their super powers super fast.

Meat

The
Way of
All Flesh

≈

There is a strong intellectual case for vegetarianism. But in India, it is too closely linked to religion. Rare is the vegetarian who refuses to eat animals on ethical grounds.

The fuss over eating beef offers some indication of how important dietary habits are to Hindus. At some level, we still view eating meat as less holy than vegetarianism. We will not serve meat on a day when there is puja. Dedicated non-vegetarians will turn vegetarian for Navaratri. And Brahmins will have contempt for the Brahmins of Kashmir and Bengal, regarding them as bogus Brahmins because of their non-vegetarianism.

I have no problem with religious restrictions on food even if they seem illogical in this day and age. We don't worry too much about the Jewish refusal to eat lobster or the Muslim unwillingness to eat pork—even though the reasons for these prescriptions are no longer valid—because we accept that religion is not necessarily logical.

But it intrigues me that even those Hindus who make a fetish out of vegetarianism (there are loads of them) are unable to offer any coherent defence of the vegetarian principle. I'll respect somebody who says, 'Look, it is my religion and that is all that matters,' or somebody who says that perhaps, because of childhood conditioning, he or she cannot bring himself or herself to eat meat. Similarly, it is fine to say that you don't like meat or to say that no matter how illogical it seems, you won't eat duck because you always think of a row of ducks you saw crossing the street or that you won't eat snails because you once had a pet snail. (Think about it: Would you eat a dog? That's just as illogical.)

But there is a strong intellectual case for vegetarianism. It goes like this: Let's take the basic equality principle, which says, 'All men are created equal.' When we say that, what do we mean? All men are not equal. Some are cleverer. Some are fatter. Some are darker. (It's interesting that the framers of the US Constitution kept slaves and did not regard blacks as 'men' in the full sense of the term.) And yet, the basis of a liberal society is that we are equal before the law, equally able to elect a government (one vote each), etc.

That's because the equality principle is not a statement of fact. Rather, it is a moral assertion. What we are saying is that all men (and women, who, by the way, were also denied the vote by those high-minded framers of the US Constitution) are deserving of equal treatment and consideration. Thus, you may be smarter than me but you still have the same one vote that I do. You may be the son of a millionaire or a minister but if you commit a murder, you will be treated like anyone else (in theory, anyway).

So far, so good. Now, extend the equality principle to animals.

I see you protesting: But animals are different.

Are they? In what way? That they are not as intelligent as we are? Perhaps. But intelligence is not a relevant characteristic while using the equality principle; we treat those of varying intelligence on a par. To quote the vegetarianism advocate Peter Singer: 'If possessing a higher degree of intelligence does not entitle one human being to use another for his or her own ends, how can it entitle humans to exploit non-humans for the same purpose?'

You could argue that this is not just a question of intelligence. There are many other differences between animals and humans. But the vegetarian lobby grants that. We don't say that animals are the same as humans, it argues, or that they should be treated the same way. For instance, your son needs education. So you'll send him to college. But your dog does not want or need a BA degree, so he can stay at home.

But there is one thing that your dog and your son share, and that is a desire to avoid pain—this desire is common to all sentient creatures. So all that the vegetarians ask is that, in this one important respect in which we are all alike, we grant animals their desire to be free from pain (and of course death—rarely do sentient creatures desire death).

To some extent, we already accept this. Why else would we have laws preventing cruelty to animals? Why do we have a Society for the Prevention of Cruelty to Animals (SPCA)? The problem is that we restrict this—illogically—to certain animals, such as dogs, horses, cats and those we encounter in our daily lives. Why shouldn't we extend it to all sentient creatures?

It's a difficult argument to refute. We can say that animals are incapable of reason. But then, so is an infant. But we wouldn't let him be killed. Almost any argument of animal incapacity can be refuted by pointing to the handicapped and the demented—all of whom we regard as worthy of keeping alive.

The only way out is to make an arbitrary distinction. We can say we have decided that our laws about avoiding pain and preserving life apply only to humans. And that's it.

Well, yes and no. That's what the framers of the US Constitution and the Bill of Rights did. When they said 'All men are created equal', they really only meant white men. They excluded women. Slaves were beyond any consideration at all. And as for Americans Indians, don't forget that all this talk about equality preceded and followed a genocide of Native Americans.

If we are to make these arbitrary distinctions, how are we any better than people who denied rights to women, to blacks and even, in the case of the empire, our own ancestors? Arbitrary distinctions are all very well but they are morally dubious.

This is such a strong philosophical case for vegetarianism that it is almost impossible to refute. You can argue that animals kill each other all the time; this is the natural order. Sure. But do you want it said that you base your moral code on the animal kingdom? Because if you do, not only are you no better than an animal but also lots of other things—murder, assault, rape, incest, polygamy, etc.—would be okay.

Plus, there's one other factor. Ours is a species that can survive without eating meat. A vegetarian tiger would soon be a dead tiger. A vegetarian human being might become an L.N. Mittal or an Anil Ambani.

So, if we don't need to eat meat to survive, what possible moral justification can there be for causing pain and death to other sentient beings? Just the fact that we like the taste of tandoori chicken is not really good enough.

It's such a substantial philosophical case that it surprises me that so few of our home-grown vegetarians bother to make it. Instead of arguing for vegetarianism at the level of the mind, they base their arguments on woolly-headed religion or dubious nutrition.

Of course, there are problems with vegetarianism in real terms. The biggest one is that even if you never eat another sentient being again, you will still be responsible for loss of life. The wheat and vegetables you eat will have been grown in fields where pesticides are used. The whole point of pesticide is to kill living things. God knows how many 'pests' died for your chapatti. When the wheat was being harvested, the combine shredded any field mice that happened to live on the farm, and the tractor wheel crushed countless other animals.

The reality is that the process of creating food—even through agriculture—involves some loss of life, no matter what you do. To say that as long as you don't eat the flesh of the animals and birds that died, you are pious, is silly. If you eat the grain and vegetables that came out of this murder, you are just as much of a murderer.

But assume that, in theory, you grow your own food entirely organically and are sure that no animals died along the way, would you be keeping to the motto that all sentient beings are created equal? I reckon you would.

So why don't we spend more time on the intellectual case for vegetarianism? I suspect it's because, in India, vegetarianism is too closely linked to religion. Rare is the vegetarian who refuses to eat animals on ethical grounds. And when you find such a person, he or she turns out to be an animal rights activist.

I'm not a vegetarian—or rather, I am one only on Tuesdays. But I can see the arguments for vegetarianism. And I wish we would debate them more.

For more on this and similar subjects, I recommend interested readers to Michael Pollan's *The Omnivore's Dilemma*.

Fowl Play

≈

The bird of Meluha. Why do Indians love chicken so much? Or is it just north Indians who can't seem to get enough of the bird?

I know of several chefs who have been warned that they need to change their menus if they are to succeed in Delhi. One chef at a leading hotel chain was told that his Delhi non-vegetarian menu would have to be 60 per cent chicken (if not 70 per cent). Everything else (fish, mutton, pork, duck, tenderloin, etc.) could not exceed 30–40 per cent of the menu.

Even as I've assured chefs that this is not true—the people of Delhi do eat other meat—the evidence around us has suggested the exact opposite. Take the hamburger. All over the world, the patty is made from beef. In India, public and religious sensitivities may mitigate against beef burgers, so it should be possible to make the patty from buffalo (tenderloin) or goat. But no, most Indian hamburgers are made from a breaded chicken patty. It doesn't taste anything like a real hamburger—it tastes revolting, actually—but, hey, it sells.

Or take a more mysterious example: the sausage. In most of the world, sausages are usually made from pork and perhaps from beef (or from a mixture of beef and pork). Once again, I can understand why a beef sausage might be unacceptable in India, but what's wrong with a pork sausage? In fact, until about a decade ago, most sausages served at restaurants were made from pork. But now, even deluxe hotels, which should know better, serve chicken sausages. People even put chicken sausage on top of pizzas or make hot dogs with it. Ninety-nine per cent

61

of the chicken sausages I have tasted in India are tasteless. Chewing on one is like eating a slice of rubber tubing filled with goo. And yet, the mysterious popularity of the chicken sausage continues to grow.

One possible explanation for the popularity of chicken as a meat of choice is that we invented it.

The domestic chicken (the bird we eat) seems to have been first bred in the Indus Valley at least 4000 years ago. DNA analysis suggests that the ancestors of the chicken were the grey jungle fowl of south India and the red jungle fowl, whose habitat stretched from north-east India to the Philippines.

These two wild species begot the modern chicken, whose greatest appeal to early man was that it could hardly fly, making it perfect for breeding purposes. Archaeologists have recovered chicken bones from Lothal, an Indus Valley site, and it is believed that our Indus Valley ancestors exported chickens to the Middle East. Cuneiform tablets from ancient Mesopotamia refer to 'the bird of Meluha', which was their name for our Indus Valley Civilization. ('Bird of Meluha' sounds like the title of an Amish Tripathi novel, doesn't it?)

The chickens travelled from Mesopotamia to ancient Egypt (where they perfected the art of getting them to lay eggs on a daily basis) and then to Rome, from where they landed on the European table. As time went on, the West forgot that the chicken was actually an Indian bird and soon came to regard it as its own.

It is tempting to argue that if the chicken first emerged in the Indus Valley, it must be a Punjabi bird. After all, the cities of Harappa and Mohenjo-Daro are now in Pakistan, and the boundaries of the Indus Valley Civilization were thought to cover only modern Punjab and Sindh. But recent archaeological evidence suggests that the Indus Valley Civilization actually covered a much larger area and Lothal —where the first chicken bones have been found—is near present-day Ahmedabad. (That's one slogan Gujarat Tourism will not use: 'Ahmedabad: The Original Home of the Delicious Chicken'.)

And yet, for all its early glory, the chicken only came into its own in the twentieth century because of a triumph of breeding technology. The popular image of the chicken roaming around a farmyard used to be accurate. Chickens need vitamin D, which they synthesize from sunlight. But farm breeding was a time-consuming process that did not allow for economies of scale.

In the twentieth century, it became possible to fortify chicken feed with vitamins and antibiotics. This meant that chickens no longer needed sunlight and could be kept indoors. And that's how the battery hen was born. Chickens began to be bred in factories. They were packed tightly into wire cages so small that they could not even spread their wings. Large windowless buildings that could house 20,000 to 30,000 chickens at one time were constructed all over the world.

In the old days, it took a chicken around three or four months to become large enough to slaughter. Now, chemically fed battery hens reach five pounds in weight in just six weeks. That means that a) the cost of feed halves along with the chicken's life and b) turnover doubles because the chickens grow to a slaughter-able maturity twice as quickly as they used to. And they need less feed, pound for pound, than pigs or cows.

Once you understand the economics of modern chicken breeding, it is easy to see why the fast-food industry loves it so much. When you buy in bulk from a chicken factory, chicken is the cheapest meat that a fast-food chain can purchase. So why bother to make anything (a hot dog, a hamburger, a kebab, or anything at all) with expensive, good-quality meat when you can simply use cheap, industrial chicken?

But of course, there is a price to be paid for preferring factory chickens. Most chickens used in restaurants these days are bland, flabby and tasteless. You can get away with this in a curry because the spices mask the taste of the chicken, but a tandoori item depends on the quality of the bird. A few places insist on buying free-range chickens (the so-called country chickens), which are full of flavour, but most chefs don't like them because they can be tougher and smaller than the rubber-soft, large broiler chickens they pull out of the deep freeze.

Oddly enough, it is the stand-alones and the older restaurants that hold out for real chickens. Too many five-star hotels save money by using industrial broilers. The chefs claim that people really can't tell the difference and that it's not worth spending the extra money on real chickens. Perhaps they are right. But in my experience, guests can taste the difference even if they can't put it into words.

Why, for instance, is the tandoori chicken at Bukhara so popular and so tasty? The answer lies in the chicken: the Bukhara chefs use a smaller, free-range bird. Guests are happy to pay Bukhara prices for the chicken because they know that it is special, even if they haven't worked out that the difference in flavour is because of the quality of the chicken.

Many foodies believe that the myth of India's fondness for chicken is a bit of a chicken-and-egg (sorry!) story. Do we really like industrial chicken that much? Or have we just got used to eating chicken because the big food companies make their money by getting us to eat it? At least one knowledgeable person in the food business has told me that he doesn't think it is a coincidence that so many politicians are into chicken breeding or that big chicken breeders have such strong political links.

What is clear is that our food businesses are more chicken-centric than those in other countries. India must be the only market where fast food is focused more on chicken than on other meat. And we are certainly the only country I know of where even top chefs are happy to use broilers—birds that would not make it past the kitchen door in most Western restaurants.

Which is bizarre. It is America that invented chicken factories in the twentieth century. But American chefs are turning away from industrial chickens and finding free-range birds with real flavour. On the other hand, it is India where the free-range chicken first made an appearance 5000 years ago.

And guess what? Our chefs are in thrall to the factory bird.

It's not just a betrayal of the traditions of our ancestors. It is also a sad commentary on the palate of a nation.

Mutton Dressed As Lamb

≈

Why are Indian chefs so embarrassed about serving goat meat?

Just as every MP begins his or her career with a lie—by saying that his or her total electoral expenditure was under the limit—so also every chef or restaurant manager who writes a menu usually starts out with a lie of his or her own. The lie consists of a description of the red meat that is used in the kitchen. Often, the menu will simply say 'mutton'. This is a term widely used in the culinary world to describe meat from a sheep. The term 'lamb' is restricted to young sheep. If the meat comes from an older animal, 'mutton' is used. It is the sort of distinction embodied by the phrase 'mutton dressed as lamb' that is commonly employed to describe older women who try to dress young.

The problem, of course, is that the kitchen does not use mutton, no matter what it says on the menu. The chances are that the chef is using goat—a meat for which the term 'mutton' is never used outside of India.

Some chefs and menu writers go further with their evasions. In the descriptive line below such menu staples as seekh kebab and raan, they will use 'lamb' instead of 'goat'. So, a seekh kebab will be described as 'minced lamb cooked on a skewer in the tandoor', and a raan as 'leg of lamb'.

65

Even as the menu is being written, the chefs and managers will know that they are telling big fat lies. But they will rationalize it, arguing, just as our MPs do when they file their election expenses, that everyone does it, so it is perfectly acceptable to engage in such evasions or misstatements.

The one time Indian chefs don't lie about the true nature of the meat they are using is at restaurants abroad. Indian restaurants in London will usually substitute goat with lamb, so when they say that their seekh kebabs are made with minced lamb, they are not lying. But the consequence is that their meat dishes hardly ever taste exactly the same as the original dishes do in India—how could they, given that they are using a completely different animal?

Two mysteries remain. First, why do chefs in India use goat rather than lamb? The answer is simple enough. The dishes were invented for goat meat, not for lamb. Besides, many Indians much prefer the taste of goat to that of lamb. Indian chefs sometimes complain that lamb can be too fatty, and customers occasionally protest that dishes made with lamb smell all wrong.

The second mystery is the more profound one. Given that the cuisine of the subcontinent has developed around the meat of the goat, why are our chefs and managers so embarrassed to admit this? Why do they feel obliged to lie?

One answer, usually offered by chefs, is that the term 'mutton' means goat meat in India. Well, yes, it does now after decades of misuse, but you can't arbitrarily rename an animal or a bird or its meat. You can't say that it is perfectly legitimate to refer to a 'duck' as 'chicken' in India because that is how we use the term. So it is with mutton and goats.

The second answer—and I would argue that this one makes more sense—is that chefs treat this as a harmless evasion. Most Indians know that the meat they are served at restaurants (or the meat at home) is goat regardless of how it is described on the menu. So, when we order a seekh kebab at a restaurant, we expect to get goat meat even if the menu promises lamb.

Foreigners are not so understanding. There is no real tradition of eating goat in much of the Western world. You find goat in Jamaican, Mexican and African food and some Greek dishes require goat meat. But in most of Europe and America, the idea of eating goat is as repugnant as the idea of eating horse or fox would be to you and me. (The French and the Italians are quite happy to eat fox or horse, or even donkey; so their objection to goat is strange.)

I sometimes wonder if our chefs are being too careful about offending foreigners. Goat meat is actually gaining in popularity in the West. It is still hard to find, but shops that do sell it often charge more for goat than they do for lamb, treating it as an exotic and hard-to-find meat.

What's interesting though is that nobody in the West regards it as a simple substitute for lamb. Most Western chefs and food writers argue that the meat is very different. I was reading about the rising popularity of goat in the *Wall Street Journal*, and it intrigued me that the writer was struggling to describe the flavour of goat to American readers. As the journal said, 'Goat is the ultimate mystery meat for American home cooks . . . it's just not part of our food culture.'

A cookbook writer is quoted by the *Journal* as saying that goat tastes like a cross between dark-meat turkey and pork. Other descriptions suggest that it is a cross between veal and lamb.

American chefs also treat goat as a meat that is difficult to cook. Many suggestions are offered for softening the meat and taming what is described as its strong, gamey flavour.

Indian chefs have long recognized that goat requires special attention—that is one reason why marination is such an important part of the Indian culinary tradition. The process involved in making a raan, for instance, is so long and complicated that many Western chefs, used to simply roasting a leg of lamb, would faint at the prospect of turning a leg of goat into a melt-in-the-mouth dish.

But what's interesting—and I didn't realize this till I read the *Journal* story—is that goat is being promoted as the healthy and environmentally friendly alternative to beef, lamb and pork.

Bill Niman (the founder of Niman Ranch, whose meat products are famous the world over) recommends goat because it is a sustainable meat from animals that thrive on pasture. The health argument is also compelling. A pound of goat meat has two-thirds the calories of a pound of beef. And this is the astonishing bit: goat has half the saturated fat of chicken. So, all those Indian doctors who read American textbooks that tell people to give up red meat and switch to chicken for the sake of their hearts may be making a mistake. The American textbooks use red meat as a synonym for beef. But the red meat we eat, goat, is actually better for your heart than chicken.

As goat becomes the trendy meat, Western chefs are creating a caste system for goats similar to the one that is already employed for pork, chicken and beef. Most people in the food business know that blackleg chickens or those from the French town of Bresse are the best. There is a classification of pork as well. Near the top of the heap is Berkshire pork. (Berkshire pigs, bred in Japan, produce korobuta pork, which is also highly regarded.) When it comes to beef, such breeds as Angus are highly prized, and beef from the Japanese town of Kobe can be among the world's most expensive meats.

The same sort of thing seems set to happen to goat meat. Chefs look for goats from the Spanish, Kiko or Boer breeds. Goats from lesser breeds command a lower price. They insist that a goat should not weigh more than 60 pounds. If it is older than nine months, its meat falls in value. Female goats are preferred to male goats because their meat is tenderer.

Much of this will not surprise India's Qureshi chefs who come from a long tradition of butchers and understand the goat best. The Qureshis even understand goat fat, choosing the fat from particular parts of the animal for each dish. (For instance, while the meat for a Kakori can come from different parts of the goat, the fat must come from the kidney area.)

But Indian restaurants and hotels are reluctant to even admit that they serve goat, let alone brag about the expertise of the chef in choosing the right part of a goat from the best breed of a certain age and under a certain weight. So while American and European chefs celebrate the goat and turn it into a trendy gourmet delicacy, our contribution to eating goat meal is to call the animal 'lamb' even though we know we are lying.

But as the goat craze catches on, perhaps Indian restaurants will finally overturn the lies and evasions of so many decades.

Raaning
Out of Time

≈

The raan is so spectacular a dish that every modern Indian chef has his own version.

The raan is one of those spectacular restaurant dishes that always create a stir when served at the table.

Usually described as a whole roast leg of mutton, it should be vast and impressive—lots of red meat with a texture that is soft and melting.

The way the raan is often described, you would think that it is the Indian equivalent of British roast lamb—the same dish but with Indian spices. And indeed, when restaurants abroad serve the raan, this is how they describe it. And even on Indian menus, it is often called a leg of lamb even though this is usually a barefaced lie.

In reality, a classic raan is never made with lamb. Most traditional Indian recipes call for goat—which is the point of the dish.

A goat has four legs. The front two—often called the dast—represent the choicest part of the animal. Most Indian goat recipes use the front part of the animal. The meat at the back, including the two hind legs, is regarded as inferior.

The point of the raan is that it comes from the hind legs. Because this meat is tough and difficult to cook, it is usually minced and used for keema. The trick with the raan is to take the toughest meat in the goat and to make it so tender and succulent that you should—in the words of that famous cook Digvijaya Singh, the late maharaja of Sailana—be able to eat it with a spoon.

I've been looking at raan recipes, and though I have found versions from Avadh, from Hyderabad (in Pratibha Karan's definitive cookbook) and from Kashmir, the consensus is that the raan is a rustic dish that does not come from any of these regions. It has nomadic origins and probably developed in campfires and military kitchens in Central Asia as an item of food for warriors and tribesmen. Manjit Gill, ITC's corporate chef, thinks that the first raans were not made with the domesticated goats of today but with mountain goats and sheep.

The challenge for a modern chef is to take the tough meat and make it palatable while still maintaining the simple appearance of the dish. Though restaurants act as though they simply stick the leg into the tandoor, the reality is far more complicated. Take the hind leg of a goat, shove it in an oven and you will end up with a dish that nobody can eat.

Marut Sikka, the restaurateur who runs Kainoosh in Delhi, says that the problem with many restaurant raans is that chefs go berserk with papaya and other tenderizers that interfere with the taste of the dish. Actually, only slow cooking gives you the right tenderness. In Pratibha Karan's recipe, the meat is fried in masala for a few minutes but is then covered with water and then cooked for ages ('until the meat is tender').

As Marut says, the English roast is a precision-controlled dish with a fixed cooking time in the oven at a certain temperature. An Indian raan—at least one made with goat—cannot be made that way and there is nothing precise about our cooking techniques.

Of all Indian hospitality companies, it is ITC that has probably done the most research into creating the perfect raan. Even today, most ITC hotels serve two different raans: one at Bukhara (or Peshawari) and the other at Dum Pukht. Of the two, the Bukhara raan conforms to the traditional recipe while the Dum Pukht version is a reinvention.

I asked my old pal Gautam Anand, who has spent his life with ITC chefs, what the secret of the perfect raan is. Gautam believes that the raan has its origins in frontier cuisine. His Hindu Punjabi grandmother wrote out a recipe for her kitchen in Peshawar in 1932, and it does not conform to most modern styles.

His grandmother's secret was to take half a seer (about 475 gm) of mutton and then cook it in half a seer of chhaach or buttermilk. It was the slow cooking in chhaach that broke down the tough membranes and softened the meat.

Gautam thinks that the modern raan is a combination of home-style Peshawari cooking and the influence of the British Raj. His view is that the raan became popular not in the era of the nawabs but during the British Empire when Brits longed for a meaty, not particularly spicy, dish. Why else, he asks, would so many modern recipes use malt vinegar, hardly an integral part of Indian cooking but a staple of the Raj kitchen?

The most famous raan in India and the one most copied by other restaurants is the Bukhara version. ITC is notoriously secretive about its recipes, but all of us know enough chefs who have worked in their kitchens to get an idea of the basic methods. The Bukhara raan uses one mutton leg (with bone) weighing about 1.2 kg of meat. The crucial part of the recipe consists of trimming the white membranes around the leg that make the meat tough. Then, the raan is marinated for a couple of hours with lots of malt vinegar, salt, red chilli, ginger, garlic. Whereas papaya would pulverize the meat, the malt vinegar tenderizes it and contributes to the flavour.

Then, the raan is seared for a few minutes, braised in a little water, put in a convection oven for an hour and twenty minutes and then basted with ghee and finished in the tandoor for twenty minutes. It is a long and complicated process. Restaurants like to give the impression that they begin cooking the dish when you order it. Actually, nearly everything is done before service begins. Only the finishing in the tandoor is done à la minute or once your order is in.

Even the Dum Pukht raan is enormously complicated. ITC's problem was that if you already serve a world-famous raan, how can you compete with your own speciality? Though this is not the company's own view, I suspect that Imtiaz Qureshi, the chef who originally created the Dum Pukht version, decided to go more Western with his recipe.

The Dum Pukht raan—and again, I'm going by hearsay because the official recipe is secret—is made with half a kilo of baby leg, off the bone. The chef sautés pickled onions, garlic, mint, etc., in a pan and then stuffs all this into a raan. It is tied with a thread and marinated for two hours with salt, ginger, garlic, etc., and—of course—malt vinegar to break down the fibres.

This is followed by a second marination in hung curd, red chilli, brown onion, star anise, other spices and pastes and lots of rum. After two marinations, the raan is braised on hot charcoal till it is al dente and then finished off in the tandoor. The original Imtiaz recipe called for the dish to be served under a pastry sheet as a sort of Goat Wellington. This pseudo-Western presentation was a little poncy and has now been dispensed with.

Because the raan is so spectacular a dish, modern Indian chefs have experimented with variations. Recently, at Davos, Manjit Gill wowed them with a gin-marinated raan with juniper berries. Marut Sikka uses the techniques of modern Western cooking to tenderize his raan. He first brines the leg (puts it in salt water) for eight to ten hours. Then he cooks the raan sous-vide (vacuum-packed in a water bath) for three to four hours at a consistent temperature of 60 degrees Celsius.

Other chefs—and especially those who cook at Indian restaurants abroad—use lamb rather than goat. This is easier to pull off because lamb is softer and fattier. The dish that results is not a traditional goat raan, but many foreigners prefer lamb much to goat anyway.

The best lamb raan I've had is Manish Mehrotra's version at Delhi's Indian Accent. Manish uses New Zealand lamb braised for two-and-a-half hours and finished with a few minutes in the tandoor. One of Manish's chelas cooked a great version of this raan for me at Saket's Punjab Grill. It's not traditional, but it's good.

When you see the effort that goes into the cooking of a raan, you realize how complicated fine Indian cooking can be. When the raan arrives on the table at Bukhara, it is just a leg of mutton with a great texture and a fabulous taste. You may be forgiven for thinking—as so many of us do—that it's just a simple roast leg of lamb.

But nothing in classic Indian cuisine is ever easy. The genius of our chefs lies in their ability to spend hours in the kitchen executing a series of long and complicated manoeuvres to produce dishes that seem straightforward and tasty.

It's easy to show off about being complicated. It's far more difficult to make the complex seem so simple.

So You
Think You
Know Sausages?

≈

It is virtually impossible to buy good sausages in India.

Ask me what my favourite convenience food is and I'll tell you that it is the sausage. At any given time, my fridge is full of sausages. I have all kinds: spicy Italian sausages, meaty-but-sweet Chinese sausages, pimenton-packed chorizo from Portugal, little cocktail sausages which my wife wraps in rashers of bacon and then fries, Goan sausages full of vinegar and masala, and slice-able Thai sausages from Chiang Mai, waiting to be cut into chunks and eaten with garlic and peanuts.

Ask me what my least favourite convenience food is and I'll tell you that it is . . . the sausage.

Yup. Because in most of India, the good name of the sausage has been dragged through the mud and then attached to the tail of a chicken. It is virtually impossible to buy good sausages in India.

I know because I have tried. The biggest problem is that an increasingly large number of sausages in the Indian market are made from chicken. This is worse than terrible; it is also bizarre. Rare is the nation that bothers to make its sausages with minced chicken. As we all know, chicken is not the most flavourful meat and it is particularly

73

unsuited to sausages. And yet, manufacturer after manufacturer will finely mince poor-quality, industrially reared chicken and then shape the meat into a nasty little torpedo. (I guess that some manufacturers use the disgusting bits of the chicken that they can't sell on their own.)

Oddly enough, the worst sausages in India are served at so-called deluxe hotels. Most hotel chefs prefer chicken sausages—positive proof, if any were needed, that they have no clue what a sausage should taste like.

Why do they do this? I am told that in the old days, chefs were taught to be careful of all pork because it went off easily and sometimes carried parasites. So, chicken seemed safest even if it was tasteless. The problem is that even now, when it is easy to source pork that is hygienically reared, chefs still stick to chicken sausages.

While researching this piece, I wandered around cold storages and grocery stores in Delhi, buying up whatever Indian sausages were available.

Every single sausage (including those recommended by chefs in five-star hotels as 'great pork brands') was utterly revolting. All were tasteless and some had a nasty synthetic texture as though someone had filled a length of pipe with a rubber solution (or Fevicol or Quick Fix) and allowed it to solidify. (If it is any consolation, the ham was even more disgusting.)

As I went from one tasteless rubber torpedo to another, I thought back to my childhood. The sausages of my memory were flavourful and juicy, made with pork fillings that had texture and taste. How, in this age of globalization, was it possible that sausage quality had actually dropped all over India?

The answer seemed to be that in the pre-liberalization era, Big Meat had still not arrived. It was a time when chickens were free range, and when small piggeries raised their own animals and either made the sausages themselves or gave their pork to butchers to make small batches of sausages by hand. There was no mechanization and the meat processing industry had not taken off.

Now, in the age of Big Meat, manufacturers care more about increasing their profit margins than they do about taste and quality. The only people who could demand that they made a better sausage are chefs—the restaurant and hotel sector accounts for a large chunk of the business—and the chefs either don't know or don't care. (Purchase departments are also very cosy with Big Meat . . .)

It is interesting that at some hotels, where the kitchen is run by quality-conscious chefs, the sausages are either imported or made on the premises. For years, I went to Celini at the Mumbai Grand Hyatt for the sausages because they were made in-house. At the Gurgaon Leela, Ramon Salto, the son of a butcher, would not use any chorizo-style sausages he did not make himself. At the Taj Land's End in Mumbai, the single best dish on the menu of Maritime (now closed, sadly) was the Italian sausage, which the chef Anirudhya Roy imported. Manu Chandra makes his own merguez and chorizo for his restaurants.

And then there is the example of the Oberoi chain. Two decades ago, fed up of questions about the provenance of the charcuterie and weary of the crap sausages available in the market, the Oberois set up their own deli unit.

To this day, they import pork from Australia and Holland, their chefs chop it themselves and the Oberois then make the best artisanal sausages in India from high-quality pork. It's meant not only for their own restaurants but also for retail sales at the delis in their hotels.

All of which begs the question: If the Oberois can make their own sausages and if many individual chefs have identified the problem, why are the majority of the chefs in India's hotel sector content to serve rubbish industrial sausages?

I cannot be certain what the answer is. But I'm pretty sure it does not reflect well on India's five-star chefs.

So what do you do if you want to eat good sausages in India? Well, there is always the Oberoi option. Some food stores will sell imported sausages. And if you know a good artisanal sausage maker, you will be fortunate enough to be spared the plastic torpedoes of Big Meat.

Alternatively, you can look for the delicious Goan chorise (a descendant of the Portuguese chorizo), which is always made by artisans, and which more and more chefs seem to be sourcing. Thomas Zacharias gets it for the Bombay Canteen and O Pedro. Manu Chandra serves the real thing at many of his restaurants (though Manu may well be making his own). So do many others.

If you can get your hands on good sausages, what should you do?

Well, speaking for myself, I nearly always look for something interesting to do with sausages. This is a lesson I may have learnt from my mother who, though she was hardly a passionate cook, had perfected an Indian-style curry made with chunks of pork sausage sourced from a local cold storage in Mumbai.

Of late, I have been experimenting with the use of sausages to flavour rice. Most Goans are familiar with the idea of a chorise pulao (though they may call it something else) in which the white rice is streaked red from the vinegar as it escapes the sausages in the pan and in which the fat from the chorise coats each grain of rice even as the masalas flavour the pulao.

The Goan idea comes from southern Europe where sausages have been used to flavour rice for centuries. But there is also an oriental equivalent. It is not difficult to find slightly sweet Chinese sausages in most metropolitan Indian cities now. These sausages work better as a condiment than on their own. I chop them into little dices and stir-fry them with rice and chopped black olives, with just a little soya. You get a perfect fried rice with virtually no effort.

If you are fortunate enough to gain access to more unusual sausages, the possibilities are endless. One of the advantages of going to Bangkok so often is that my wife and I are able to buy Thai sausages fairly regularly. There is one sausage in particular—easily available at branches of the Tops supermarket chain—called a northern Thai sausage that we always bring back. (This is a fresh sausage, unlike the salami-style Chiang Mai sausage that I also like.)

The northern Thai sausage is not much good on its own—it oozes liquid when you cook it—but it is terrific in a curry because it imbues the gravy with the flavours of its stuffing: coriander seeds, makroot, lemon grass, etc. And four sausages are enough to make a brimming pot of curry.

I have no idea whether it was because she heard me babbling about my mother's sausage curry, but my wife makes a killer Thai curry with these sausages. As with all improvised dishes, I am sure it is not authentically Thai, but it is truly delicious.

The only special ingredient you need is the sausage. Everything else is easily available in most large Indian cities. And after much persuasion, I persuaded my wife to part with her recipe for the quick and easy Thai sausage curry.

You should try it.

Seema's Sausage Curry

Ingredients

Oil: 4 tablespoons
Thai sausages: 4
Thai red chillies: 3
Green onions: 1 small cup, chopped small
White onions: 1 small cup, chopped small
Garlic: 1 whole bulb, chopped small
Thai galangal: 3 tablespoons, chopped small
Lemon grass: chopped into big chunks (easy to remove later)
Kaffir lime leaves: 6
Kaffir lime: half
Coconut milk: 1 can
Green curry paste: 1 packet
Krapow paste: 1 packet
Fish sauce to taste
Basil leaves: a handful

Method

Let the oil heat in a large pan. Make a vertical cut in the chillies and fry in oil. Add kaffir lime leaves and allow them to crisp up. Add ginger and garlic, and sauté. Then add the green and white onions and cook until translucent. Chop the sausages into rounds. Add them to the pan and cook until they are browned. Then add the curry paste and krapow paste and stir. Once the paste has coated the sausages evenly, add the coconut milk. Let the curry boil for a couple of minutes and then reduce the heat so that the curry simmers.

Add fish sauce and lime to taste. Garnish with fresh basil leaves, roughly torn. Serve with sticky rice.

Vegetarians can substitute shiitake mushrooms and baby corn for the sausages and use the same recipe, using soya sauce instead of fish sauce. The recipe works with most artisanal sausages if you can't get your hands on the Thai sausage.

Seafood

Seafood

Fish
Out of Water

≈

No matter how clever Indian chefs try to be with their fish dishes, fewer and fewer of us are ordering them. (We're not wild about the smell.)

I know we are supposed to be living in a brave new world where everybody eats healthily, but here's something I keep noticing whenever I go out: less and less people seem to order fish.

This is distinctly odd. We are into an era of expensive restaurants and celebrity chefs, and so our experience should mirror that of the West where something like 40 per cent of the menu of any fancy restaurant will comprise fish. Partly this is because customers are health-conscious but partly it is also because chefs feel that the delicate flavour of fish gives them more opportunities to experiment and to show off their recipes. After all, there's only so much you can do with a piece of beef or a lamb chop. But with good fish, the possibilities are endless.

In India, however, my friends seem less and less willing to order fish. When they do look at a seafood option, it tends to be shellfish—prawns or crab, mainly. If they go for a fish, they like it cooked as indelicately as possible: fried or coated in masala.

I've taken to asking people why they are so reluctant to order fish. Usually, after they have hummed and hawed a little, they come up with the same answer: it smells.

Now, there are—in my experience—two kinds of fish eaters. There are those who enjoy everything that goes with the seafood option. The Thais, for instance, are fastidious to the point of intolerance about smell. In Thailand, even a small child can detect a noxious smell at fifty paces. But they seem strangely immune to fish smells. All of their food is flavoured with *nam pla*, a delicious condiment made from dried fish that betrays its provenance with every sniff. The simplest dishes (pad Thai noodles, for instance) get an extra zing from the liberal additions of fistfuls of dried fish. And no matter what drying method you use, dried fish will always smell more pungently than fresh fish. But no, the Thais seem not to mind the smell at all.

So it is with Bengalis. They may be justly proud of their cuisine (fish, poppy seeds, mustard oil, lots of deep-frying and more fish), but go to any Bengali home when dinner is being cooked and your nostrils will be assailed by the unmistakable smell of fish sizzling in mustard oil.

The Bengalis don't seem to mind it at all. I have seen grown men in Kolkata weep with joy at the sight of a smelly ilish that has come over the border from Bangladesh, even as I hold my breath and try not to inhale. They also love the bits of fish that the rest of us throw away. The point of a prawn, they will tell you, is the brain, especially when the cerebral juices have been congealed through skilful cooking. They will eat the boniest fish imaginable and then spit the bones out without any embarrassment.

That kind of fish eater—what we might call the True Fish Lover—is not put off by the smell of fish. Except that the True Fish Lover is usually unwilling to spend much money on fish at fancy restaurants, arguing that his wife or mother cooks it much better at home at much lower cost.

That leaves the rest of us: the Regular Fish Eaters. We have nothing against fish, but we are not wild about the smell and we find a very fishy taste off-putting.

My guess is that the Regular Fish Eaters are growing in number even as the True Fish Lovers are in decline. No matter how clever Indian chefs try to be with their fish dishes, fewer and fewer of us are ordering them.

The restaurant trade tells me I'm quite wrong. Fish consumption is actually on the increase. There was a time when Norwegian salmon was considered an expensive luxury. Now even stand-alone restaurants make their fish tikkas with Scandinavian imports. The Chilean Sea Bass is a staple of menus everywhere. Nobu's famous Black Cod in Miso has a way of turning up at the unlikeliest of places. Once scallops were unknown. Now, everyone serves them.

I don't dispute all of this. I just think that it explains exactly what the problem is.

At all the great fish restaurants that I have eaten in (and the two best are One-O-One in London and Le Bernardin in New York) the fish does not smell at all. Part of the appeal of each dish is the freshness. Every oyster tastes of the sea. Every trout reminds you of streams and running brooks. As chefs will tell you, fresh fish will rarely smell. It is only as time goes on that bacteria begin to break down the amino acids in the fish and the odours develop. What we call a fishy flavour is never found in fresh fish. It is a consequence of bacteria action. There are times when cooks need fish to be fermented (in Far Eastern cookery, for instance) but the rest of us have no great love for the stench of rotting fish.

Sadly, most Indian restaurants have stopped serving fresh fish. There was a time when chefs would go to the fish market early in the morning to buy the day's stock. If the fish ran out in the course of the service, the dish was taken off the menu.

Now, alas, in the era of imported supplies and inventory control, chefs no longer bother to go to the market. Instead, they want the market to come to them. So, hotels and restaurants contract suppliers who fly in consignments of frozen or refrigerated fish. The chefs keep the fish in their cold storages and take it out when they need it. The good thing is that they never run out of fish. The bad thing is that it is never really fresh.

In a perfect world, even refrigerated fish can taste fresh. The Japanese, for instance, import refrigerated tuna from North America and still manage to make sashimi that tastes entirely fresh from it. But sadly, we do not live in a perfect world. Often, the refrigeration does not work throughout the transportation process and the bacteria begin their work. Sometimes, restaurants' cold storages are faulty. And inevitably, the fish begins to smell. Chefs argue that a smelly fish may not be a fresh fish but it is still not a spoilt fish. And, of course, they are right. But ask yourselves this: Do you really want to pay huge amounts for a smelly fish that was caught miles away a month ago? Wouldn't you rather eat a much less fancy (and less smelly) fish that somebody caught nearby a couple of days ago—if not yesterday?

The change in the supply chain has meant that much of the fish we get is frozen. And freezing usually destroys the texture of a fish. Much of it is farmed—like the ubiquitous Norwegian salmon that is dyed pink so that it looks like wild salmon. And farmed fish rarely has much flavour, which is why the giant prawns that hotels love taste of nothing at all.

My feeling—entirely unsupported by any empirical evidence at all—is that more and more of us are getting tired of the uncertainty that accompanies the ordering of fish: Will it taste too fishy? Will it smell? Will it be like cardboard to touch? People will take a chance on prawns because they rarely smell. Crabs are usually okay because they are often transported alive. But order anything else, and you are playing Russian roulette.

Perhaps it's just my friends and I. Maybe the restaurant trade is right and the number of fish eaters is growing.

But, try a little experiment. The next time you go out, check how many of your friends order fish (as distinct from prawns). And ask those who do take the fish option if they find it a little smelly.

I have a hunch that you'll discover more fish resistance than the trade is willing to admit.

Hooked on Fish

≈

Fish lands itself much more easily to displays of culinary ingenuity.

Food and clothes have something in common: both are subject to the dictates of fashion—often in ways that you don't expect them to be. Take clothes for example. We all know that fashion changes with the season and that trends tend to be global: a shorter hemline at the Paris collections will be echoed in the shops in New York.

But what we don't realize is that even if we claim to be determinedly unfashionable, to be completely unaffected by what the designers dream up, we still cannot entirely escape the effects of global fashion.

Some examples from men's clothing: if Giorgio Armani is dispensing with big shoulders, if designers are cutting narrower ties, and if lapels are widening, no matter how unaware we are of these trends, they will find their way into our wardrobes.

Wherever we go, the only ties on sale will be narrow. All suits, even the cheapest, most unfashionable ones, will lose the padding in their shoulders or sport broad lapels. We will have no choice but to purchase them. And in doing so, we will buy into the global fashion conspiracy.

So it is with food. Some chef will set off a new trend in New York and though we may read about it in the papers, we will act as though it has nothing to do with us.

But, of course it does.

Once the trend takes off, it will appear on many American menus. Then it will cross the Atlantic. Next, the global hotel chains will pick it up. Bright chefs in every country, eager to be ahead of the curve, will seize on the trend for their menus. Soon, customers will develop a taste for it and start demanding the dish in question for themselves—forcing other, non-trendy restaurants to follow suit.

Even if you regard yourself as completely uninterested in food fads and immune to food and beverage trends, all this will change the way you eat and drink.

For instance, ask yourself these questions (especially if you are under forty): Is vodka your hard liquor of choice? Do you like red wine? Do you prefer good coffee (say, the kind they serve at Barista) to instant coffee?

If you answered yes to any of these questions, you too—no matter how un-foodie-like you think of yourself as being—have fallen victim to the trends of the last decade. Just look at the contrast with what your parents drank. The chances are that they preferred whisky to vodka, drank no red wine and were quite happy with Nescafé.

One of the compensations of a life of seemingly endless travel—once you've got past the jet lag, the queues at immigration, the uncomfortable seats and the frequent delays—is that you realize quite how international the food scene is now. Frequently, you'll notice a trend just as it is taking off in New York only to discover a year later that it has reached Bangkok and will soon hit Mumbai.

Here, in no particular order, is a list of food fads and restaurant trends that I have noticed over the last couple of years.

The Rise of Fish

This goes back a decade or so, I think, but it became truly global only three or four years ago. Like many food trends it originated on American menus.

There was a time when the balance of nearly all menus would be tilted in favour of meat and chicken. You'd find steaks, lamb cutlets, veal escalope and such traditional dishes as chicken cooked with wine (coq au vin) or a navarin (a sort of stew) of lamb.

But now, something like 50 per cent of all main course options at many restaurants all over the world will be fish. The main reason is, I suspect, health. In the 1990s, Americans gave up on red meat and looked for low-cholesterol alternatives. A second reason is that fish lends itself much more easily to displays of culinary ingenuity—there's only so much you can do with a lamb chop or a steak. A third reason is that both supplies and delivery systems have now improved. There was a time when chefs were unwilling to put fish on the menu for fear that they might not find it in the market every day and because they were scared that it spoilt too easily.

Now, however, chefs no longer need to set out for the market every morning to buy fish for the day. The supply chain has developed to the extent that nearly every restaurant—and not just the expensive ones—can count on fresh fish that has been flown in from far away.

At its most exotic level, you see it in such top-end restaurants as Wasabi in Mumbai where the oysters come from the Pacific Ocean, or at Sakura in Delhi where the fish comes from Tokyo. But even the less expensive places rely on prawns, lobster and crab from Kochi. If you've enjoyed the crab at Swagath in Defence Colony, Delhi, you should remember that it was minding its own business a few miles off the coast of Kerala before they drowned it in garlic butter for your delectation.

Often this makes for unusual juxtapositions. At a traditional English oyster house in London I enjoyed the oysters (from Colchester, from Cornwall and from Brittany) before being served a plate of prawns. And which side of the Channel did they come from, I asked.

'The Maldives,' was the reply.

Indian seafood suppliers still emphasize quality but the fish boom has had several other consequences—some happy, some not so happy.

Rise of the Bogus Fish

Fish farming is a big business globally, so the chances are most of the fish you eat anywhere in the world will have swum no further than to the edge of its tank and back. (This is why foreigners get so excited when they see freshly caught fish in India.)

As a general rule, farmed fish does not have the flavour of the wild version, but it is a good deal cheaper. One reason why salmon turns up on so many menus (even in India five-star hotels use it for deluxe fish tikka) is that farmed salmon (unlike the hard-to-find wild fish) is relatively inexpensive. Sadly, it can also be bland and tasteless. Even the pink colour does not come naturally to farmed salmon (and this includes so-called 'organic' salmon), so a food dye is used to colour the fish.

In America, the rise in the use of farmed fish has been accompanied by a preference for bogus fish. Take that staple of most US menus in the 1990s: the Chilean Sea Bass. It is nothing like a real sea bass. In fact, it isn't a sea bass at all, but a completely different species that should properly be called the Patagonian Tooth Fish (doesn't sound quite so appealing, does it?). Or take Nobu's famous Black Cod in Miso. Great dish but wrong fish. The Black Cod is not a cod at all.

Frozen Fish

For years, chefs lusted after the scallop because of its remarkable flavour and great appearance—in the centre of a seashell so perfect that it almost seemed fake. Though the scallop is a cold-water fish, it was quickly adopted to oriental cuisines: Chinese restaurants steamed scallops in the shell with ginger and soya or black bean sauce, and such Indian restaurants as London's Bombay Brasserie cooked them in the tandoor.

Then, as the supply chain developed, it became easy and cheap to farm and freeze (or refrigerate) scallops.

Now, you find them all over the Orient where chefs ignore the bland flavour of frozen scallops to stir-fry them, put them in salads or to serve them as starters. A refrigerated scallop may well be better than no scallop at all, but the world is now full of chefs who think they know what a scallop tastes like without ever having enjoyed the full flavour of a wild, hand-dived scallop.

With crab, the situation is even worse. All oriental restaurants will serve some variation of the crab stick. Problem: not only is the stick frozen and then brought back to room temperature, it is not usually—even when it is served as part of nigiri sushi—made of crab at all. Nine times out of ten, a cheap fish is minced, and colour and flavour are added. Bizarrely, nobody seems to mind that crab sticks contain no crab.

Twenty-first-century Fish

Can you think of a fish that costs more than lobster or crab?

It's tuna.

By any standards, the tuna is the fish of the twenty-first century. Forget about the canned rubbish you feed your dog or put into a salade niçoise. The trendy tuna is toro, fatty meat from the stomach. This is so expensive that even the Japanese close their eyes and breathe deeply before ordering toro.

But there are lots of other kinds of tuna. Any good sushi place will offer three different kinds of tuna sashimi, all of which will taste entirely different.

Chefs like tuna because you can treat it as you would treat red meat: tuna steak, lightly seared tuna or even tuna carpaccio—all of which can be paired with red wine.

In the Raw

When it comes to fish, the basic rule of current cooking is that less is more.

Tuna carpaccio is just one example, but broadly, the trend is to serve fish as raw or lightly cooked as possible. Chefs, eager to make some use of frozen scallops, will often add a slice of scallop sashimi to other dishes. Fish tartare (in the style of steak tartare—raw and spicy) is a menu cliché—ranging all the way from Nobu and Wasabi's Toro Tartare to a more inexpensive Salmon Tartare on many coffee-shop menus.

In the process, chefs care less for fish that require too much cooking: raw oysters will always be preferred over Moules Marinière (mussels steamed with cream and wine).

The
World Is
Your Oyster

≈

Oysters are now easily available here. But unfortunately, Indian oysters are not terribly good.

It is a measure of how quickly food habits are changing in metropolitan India that many of the things I wrote about a couple of years ago and treated as though they were unusual or, at the very least, not readily available, are now easy to find at your local restaurant.

Oysters are just one instance. I have been an oyster fanatic for years, and my friends continually make jokes about my ability to consume several dozen at one seating. But oysters have always been hard to find in India.

For some reason, Arabian Sea oysters seem rarely available on the west coast. Twenty years ago, I heard about a man who supplied a limited quantity of fresh oysters to top Mumbai hotels. But the more I probed, the more elusive the fellow seemed to be. Eventually, I just gave up.

Then, I tried looking for oysters in Goa. The secret of fresh seafood in Goa is—are you ready for this?—that there usually isn't any. Because international prices for fresh (or refrigerated) shellfish are so high, much of the catch is simply exported. Those hotels that sell you giant tiger prawns rarely sell you the local wild produce. Quite often, they simply fly it in from farms in Kerala. So it is with lobsters and many other exotic fish. The only really fresh local fish you get tends to be the humble stuff that you net quite near the shore. The expensive stuff is almost always not local, though, of course, the hotels would rather die than admit this to guests.

Sadly, because there seems to be no Indian tradition of oyster dishes, the only places that have ever bothered to try to source oysters are the hotels. You can go from shack to shack in Goa, and though they will offer you squid, mussels and crabs, they will make it clear that oysters are simply not on the menu.

I heard that the Bay of Bengal was a better source of oysters. Over a decade ago, I was told that fishermen roamed the beach at Gopalpur-on-Sea in Odisha, offering to sell oysters by the bucket. Perhaps this was true once upon a time. But I've yet to taste a single Odisha oyster.

Likewise at the beach on the way from Chennai to Mahabalipuram. Anyone who has done that stretch will know that the water is a clear blue (unlike the dirty grey of the Arabian Sea) and that the beach, though rocky, offers a measure of privacy—so rare for an area that is an hour away from a metropolitan city.

Naturally, I hit all the small restaurants looking for fresh oysters. They had fish. They had lots of crab. They even had shark. But oysters? Forget it.

When I did find oysters, it was only because the chef at the Fisherman's Cove knew how to source them. Once again, I was convinced that the only place to find oysters was a hotel. When I first wrote about oysters in my column, I was pretty sure that they would remain a hard-to-find food that would be too expensive for most readers. Wait till you get abroad, I advised, because they can be relatively cheap and plentiful in many foreign countries (in America and Australia, for instance).

Fate has a way of slapping over-smart columnists on the face. Within four months of that piece, every Delhi hotel was offering fresh oysters on the half-shell. In no time at all, fresh oysters became a staple of Sunday brunches at most hotels. Then, the stand-alone restaurants got in on the act. And by the end of that year, anybody who wanted to try an oyster knew how to get one.

What had made the difference? The hotels say that enterprising shippers from Kerala (from Kochi mainly) who had, so far, been content to put crabs into refrigerated containers and fly them all over India suddenly discovered that there was a market for oysters.

Mumbai, where the crab–lobster stradition is much more established than landlocked Delhi, was the first port of call. But the Malayali fishmongers worked out that Delhi was only two hours away and decided to hit the Punjabi market, previously regarded as too boring and unadventurous.

Restaurants helped by recognizing that guests would not necessarily order fresh oysters from the menu. So they put them on buffets and encouraged guests to try one. If diners liked the taste they could have more at no extra charge.

In the beginning, I was delighted by the oyster revolution. Everywhere I went—and at lunchtime every Sunday—I would down my standard quantity of several dozen oysters. Then, about a year ago, oyster fatigue set in.

I still eat oyster on occasion but I am much less of a fanatic than I used to be.

Is it a question of being over-tired of the great harvest I myself desired?

Partly. But it is also that—and I'm sorry to be so unpatriotic—the Indian oysters, which these nice Malayali gentlemen ship to every part of the country, are not terribly good. They don't have the complex briny taste of the Atlantic or the Pacific oysters and, for most of the year, they seem undernourished and weedy. (Oysters are a fish, so they vary in size from month to month.)

No doubt this is just a phase and within a couple of months I will be back to devouring the usual two or three dozen. Certainly, they are the one fish you can eat with a clear conscience. Ideally, you eat them raw with just a little bit of lemon, so there is no fat content at all. And the oyster itself is mainly water, so it's largely calorie-free—the oceanic equivalent of Diet Coke.

If you haven't already been seduced by all the oysters on offer at restaurants in Delhi and Mumbai, here are a few tips.

1. Oysters are best eaten raw. This is not to say that you cannot cook them. But their iodine-tinged marine flavour can be masked if you

use too many other ingredients. Plus, an inexperienced chef will simply turn them into rubbery bits of rubbish during the cooking process.

2. If you are eating them raw, on the half-shell, there are many things you can do to compliment the flavour. The first and foremost is to drink a good wine with them. In an ideal world you would drink white Burgundy (Chablis, Montrachet, etc.) but most Chardonnay-based wines (if they aren't too sweet and oakey) should go with it.

3. Other tricks of the trade include a dash of lemon that makes the oyster come alive. Some people like Tabasco, and Americans make a concentrated Bloody Mary–style cocktail sauce to go with them. More traditional is a vinaigrette of some description.

4. My favourite way to introduce the flavour of the sea to oyster virgins is to do the following: Take a good warm crusty bread roll (or baguette) and tear off a chunk. Smear it liberally with a good butter—ideally, the bread should be warm enough for the butter to melt and suffuse some of it. Squeeze a little lemon on an oyster, separate it from its shell and put it on the bread. Then, take a small piece of a good, cooked sausage (i.e., chorizo or Cumberland rather than Milano salami) and put it on top of the oyster. By now, the entire package will have begun to look a little unsteady so quickly rush it into your mouth and start chewing. As the flavours begin to subside, wash them down with a sip of cold white wine.

5. There are Indian oyster recipes and they're worth a try (basically, they are prawn and mussel recipes where oysters have been substituted for the main ingredients), but masala rather destroys the point of an oyster. If you want a more chatpata dressing for your oyster, I suggest you make small juliennes of garlic and onion and fry them very quickly till they are brown and crisp. Put them on top of the oyster along with the lemon and then eat as you would normally.

6. Most Western oyster recipes are rubbish. The most famous is Oysters Rockefeller, which is basically oysters baked with spinach. I am not a great fan. The French cook oysters in a creamy stew, and the English put them in pies, but frankly, I can't see the point. The only memorable cooked oyster dish I have ever eaten consisted of gently poaching the oysters in a seawater emulsion. It worked because both the water and the oysters tasted of the sea and because

a brilliant chef was doing the poaching. Sadly, this dish was available only in a restaurant in the French village of Chablis, and I have never found anything like it anywhere else.

But of course you'll get all kinds of variations on the cooked oyster, including oyster tempura, oyster pakoda (they call it 'deep-fried oyster' on the menu, which sounds better but it is the same thing) and oyster croquette. Eat at your own peril.

And finally, if you do like the magic of the Malayali oysters, remember that there are many varieties of oyster that are much tastier, and so, if you go abroad, order the local oyster. The potential for surprise in endless. Recently, I loved an oyster on a mixed platter in London. It was not, as far as I could tell, a Whitstable native or the French Belon. So I asked what I was eating.

It turned out to be an oyster from the Duchy of Cornwall, from an organic oyster farm run by Prince Charles.

A dozen more of those and I'll forgive him for all his mad conversations with trees and his dodgy taste in women.

Dairy

Dairy

Don't Say Cheese

≈

For the French, cheese is humankind's greatest invention. The English are proud of it. For the Italians, it's an important part of cooking. But Indians have no real understanding of it.

If you are French, you think of cheese as one of the greatest inventions in the history of humankind. You cannot imagine life without cheese and you judge restaurants by the quality of their cheese trolley. If you are English, you are much less adventurous than the French but still proud of your cheese and fond of drinking port with your Stilton. If you are Italian, you recognize that cheese is an important part of cooking, whether it is the mozzarella on your pizza, the mascarpone in your pudding or the Parmesan on your pasta.

But if you are Indian?

Well, if you are Indian and of my generation, cheese means the following things to you: (a) a yellow substance that comes in a circular tin, (b) a wonderfully plasticine-like object that is sold in individually wrapped foil squares, (c) thin slices of something that you use for cheese toast.

Yes, it's sad but true: Indians have no real understanding of (let alone love for) cheese. We don't even know what the bloody thing really is. We are revolted by the disgusting smells like body odour that emanate from some cheeses. We loathe the strong tastes of the cheeses that get the French going. And we are suspicious of blue cheese—are there maggots hiding in those purple veins? (Answer: yes, there are—in a manner of speaking.)

I try my hardest to be international in my food habits and to like other people's food. But when it comes to cheese, I am resolutely Indian. I treat the cheese course in a set meal as a complete waste of time. I encourage them not to grate Parmesan (or Parmigiano Reggiano or whatever they are calling it these days) on my pasta. I hate cheesy risottos. And I have very little patience even with the one cheese that most Indians will eat—processed cheese of the Kraft/Amul variety.

When I was growing up in Bombay, nobody had heard of Buffalo Mozzarella. (And even now, I'd rather eat the buffalo than the mozzarella.) We couldn't give a monkey's about the difference between a Brie and a Camembert. (Still don't, actually.) And as for blue cheese—sorry, but that was too yucky. ('Do you know that this cheese moves on its own because of the live maggots inside it?'—I was informed as a schoolboy. It isn't true. Or is it? Who knows?)

In that era before Amul became ubiquitous, we relied on canned Kraft processed cheese that seemed miraculously to be available at most grocers' shops. Kraft had a pleasant, non-assertive taste and we would come across it everywhere. It would go into omelettes. It would be cut into cubes and paired with chunks of canned pineapples on toothpicks (each skewer artistically finished with a tinned cherry on the end) as a cocktail canapé. It would be sliced to go into cheese sandwiches. It would be grated, mixed with bits of chicken and then turned into a chicken-and-cheese toasty. It would go into 'baked dishes' at Gujarati and Marwari homes.

Sophisticated people told us that Kraft was processed cheese and therefore not of very high quality. Far better, they would insist, was real cheese. In that era this meant huge wedges of a crumbly cheese that was supposed to come from various Raj hills stations. One day we would be told that it was Ooty (Udhagamandalam) cheese. At other times the same cheese was said to have travelled from Kalimpong. In reality, I suspect it always came from the Aarey Milk Colony, then located near the lakes on the outskirts of Bombay (where Film City now stands).

Truth be told, I had no time for Ooty/Kalimpong/Aarey cheese. I wasn't even very keen on the Kraft version. When local companies (I think one was Dippy's) produced a canned cheese spread (I shudder to think what cheese they used), I was put off by its lack of 'flavour'.

But in that era, we had to adapt. The gastronomic riches of the world were not available at every grocer's (as they are today) and we took what we could get. So, even I learnt to find uses for cheese.

The key to making processed cheese palatable, I decided, was to introduce stronger flavours. At boarding school, we used a simple trick. We would scoop out a third of a can (or jar) of cheese spread and fill the newly vacated space with a mixture of tomato ketchup and Chinese chilli sauce. Then we would mix the cheese with the sauce by twisting a spoon in and out of the jar (or perhaps we just used a pencil) till the cheese became infused with the tomato–chilli flavour. Finally, we would smear this tarted up cheese spread on Monaco biscuits. You may laugh, but I reckon we were on to something: a wheat base, cheese, tomatoes, chillies. Doesn't that sound like a primitive pizza? (Oh all right, be like that.)

At home we grappled with ways of making cheese toast seem tasty. There is a considerable body of literature on the perfect cheese toast. (Which cheese do you use? Which is the right bread? Do you add cream to the cheese? What about mustard? When do you remove it from the heat? . . .) But we were happily unaware of this. In any case, all we had access to was Britannia bread (white and sponge-like) and Kraft cheese. So our solution was to grate the cheese, add chopped green chillies and perhaps the stalks of kothmir (coriander leaves). It gave the cheese a much-needed kick and even Britannia bread tasted good. (This variation still survives in many avatars in Mumbai.)

Then, slowly, other cheese became available. Like all non-cheese lovers, the one I really took to was garlic Boursin. I liked it because it did not taste like proper cheese (which it is not, strictly speaking; so fair enough!) and because I will eat anything if you put enough garlic in it.

After I tired of spreading Boursin on biscuits and toast, I decided to use it as a dip, inventing a Boursin-olive dip that I still make when I'm bored. It's very simple. You open a packet of Boursin and put it in a bowl. Add lots of finely chopped green olives (and a few capers if you like). For more flavour throw in some Mediterranean-type spices (basil, oregano or pre-mixed Herbs de Provence) and a dash of Tabasco. Add olive oil, bit by bit, stirring the Boursin with a fork as you do so. You'll get an emulsion rather than a paste (which means it won't last very long and you'll have to beat it up with a fork again as the ingredients separate) but it is quite delicious. Everyone I know has loved it and I've dined out on the recipe for years, even getting it published in a cookbook.

I didn't realize that cheese was meant to be taken seriously (i.e., no tomato ketchup) till the early 1980s when I began drinking wine. There was a phase when I actually enjoyed it. For nearly four years, I threw a wine-and-cheese party at home in Bombay every April, buying my cheese abroad and learning how to tell a ripe Camembert from an industrially produced unripe one. I experimented with wine–cheese pairings and I loved the sheer hedonism of eating a rich Brie with figs and walnuts.

Alas, it was not to last. In no time at all it became clear that I was a child of 1960s Bombay, and my affair with cheese ended as quickly as it had begun. If you offer me a great cheese, I'll probably try a bit out of curiosity or politeness, but I doubt if I'll enjoy it very much. (One exception: at Vinitaly in Verona I was introduced to Taleggio served with marmalade, and I loved it. For a full month. After that, it was back to no cheese again.)

As for cooking, I'm determinedly on the side of the 'no-cheese, please' lobby. I'll never order a Caprese or any dish that depends on mozzarella. I hate people grating any kind of cheese on my food. (Though I'll confess to a weakness for deep-fried Parmesan with red wine, but only in moderation.) Show me one of those pizzas where the cheese comes apart in thick ribbons, and I'll run the other way. And I won't even eat paneer if I can help it.

Does this make me a freak? Can you really claim to be a food writer if you loathe cheese, which is such an integral part of European cuisine?

Who knows? What I do know is this: If I never eat another piece of cheese for as long as I live I won't really miss it.

Since this article was originally published, I have grown up and changed my mind. I now love cheese, the smellier and bluer the better!

Golden Days

≈

Butter is such a special food that it is an adjective by itself. Ignore those killjoys who decided that if it was so good, it must be sinful.

You know a food is special when it does not need an adjective to describe it. And you know that it is truly extraordinary when it becomes an adjective by itself.

I refer, of course, to butter.

Think about it. What adjective could you possibly use to describe butter? Golden, perhaps, because that captures the visual element. But in terms of taste? Nothing that I can think of.

Now consider how often we use butter as an adjective. When we want to describe something as being comforting and rich, it is butter that we fall back on. Mashed potatoes can be buttery. So can sweet wines. Or scrambled eggs. Or great pasta.

Even when we talk of things other than food, the butter image keeps cropping up. Skin and complexions can be buttery. Fine leather has a buttery finish. Something soft is characterized by 'a knife cutting through butter'. And so on.

Is it any wonder that the greatest Indian food-advertising slogan of the twentieth century was Sylvester daCunha's immortal Amul line: Utterly Butterly Delicious.

That's the point with butter. If you want to say how good it is, the best thing to do is to describe it as, well, butter.

It is a measure of how wonderful butter is that some decades ago the killjoys decided that if it was so good, it must be sinful. Or that it would kill you.

Fortunately, this bit of gastronomical/nutritional nonsense has now been convincingly debunked. But for many years, we were made to eat disgusting substitutes for the real thing.

For instance, nutritionists told us in the 1950s that margarine was better than butter. We know now that this is nonsense. Margarine is actually much more of a killer than butter ever can be. Commercial margarine can be full of trans fats (which are now banned in New York City restaurants and will eventually be banned in most of the world, I guess) and its nutritional value is negative.

Then, they told us that butter would clog our arteries. What they did not tell us was that you would need to eat industrial quantities of butter (which is an animal fat) for these effects to occur. For decades now, the nutritional establishment has completely failed to explain why the French, who put butter in everything, have rates of heart disease that are significantly lower than those of Americans who are used to eating processed foods that conspicuously eschew butter.

The so-called French paradox is sought to be explained by the bogus 'olive-oil explanation'. Broadly put, this states that French people have fewer heart attacks because they use olive oil, which contains flavonoids. In fact, olive oil is only popular in the south of France. The parts of France with the lowest rates of heart disease are in the north where not only do they not use olive oil but they also cook everything in butter, lard and goose fat.

Some conclusions are obvious. Of course, too much butter is bad for you. Of course butter is a fat, so it is laden with calories. But it is not poison. It is foolish to avoid it on some dubious health grounds. It is madness to prefer some nasty synthetic industrial butter substitute like margarine. The chances are that it is the substitute that will kill you (one reason why Americans are so fat and the French so thin is that Americans eat lots of processed food made with industrial substitutes) while butter, eaten in moderation, will keep you healthy.

Having got that off my chest (and if you are some cardiologist who wants to dash off an angry letter to my publisher, dear reader, forget everything they taught you in your dire medical college and try to keep up with the research on the subject), let me now praise the virtues of butter.

If you grew up in India as part of my generation, you divide the world into BA (Before Amul) and AA (After Amul). In the days before we Gujaratis colonized the butter world with our Kaira District Cooperative (but pronounced Kheda—the anglicized spelling is all wrong), each town had its own local butters. Usually, they were small artisanal produce from a nearby dairy that did not have the benefit of Amul's access to modern technology.

In Bombay, we had Polson, frequently sold in tin cans (you needed a can opener to get at the butter) and now remembered chiefly for the name rather than the quality of the butter. (Because the Bombay film industry set the standard for the colloquial, Polson became a synonym for makkhan as in makkhan lagana.)

At school in Ajmer, we had a local butter that was incompletely churned, so rather than being an even yellow, it had little chunks of cream. Such was our desire to get 'real' butter that we petitioned for the mess to arrange for supplies of Amul. Looking back, I guess we were not foodies in those days. Serve the same butter now and you can pass it off as an artisanal product that is so fresh that you can actually taste the cream.

Amul succeeded in equal parts because of Dr Kurien and Sylvester daCunha. Kurien's contribution lay in organizing the cooperative that churned international-quality butter of a consistent standard. Sylvie's contribution was to make Amul India's first great food brand. His slogan and the fat boy and girl who dominated the hoardings all became an integral part of Indian popular culture. In the process, Amul became synonymous with butter. (Funny business that a Gujarati butter should have been promoted by a Malayali and a Goan, no?)

Since then, other dairies have begun producing international-quality butter. But on the whole, they have been content to reproduce the taste of Amul. Do a blind tasting of four widely available butters, and you will be surprised to find that they're all broadly similar because market research has told manufacturers that Indians think that the true taste of butter is the one that Amul perfected.

Fortunately, there is now some experimentation in the market. You can buy commercially manufactured white butter, which tries to mimic the taste of home-made makkhan. And the easing of import regulations has allowed us to try a variety of European butters, many of which are excellent.

Butter can be a complicated business, so I'm wary of making recommendations. But remember that there are some things for which no butter other than Amul will ever do. One of these is pao bhaji, another great Gujarati invention.

According to legend, pao bhaji was invented in Bombay near the Cotton Exchange. In those days, Gujarati cotton traders would wait for the New York cotton figures to come in. Because of the time difference, it would be early morning in India by the time trading would end on the New York exchange.

Having made their deals on the basis of the new prices, the weary traders would head for their homes. But as their wives were unlikely to wake up and make theplas at that unearthly hour, they would look for sustenance on the roadside.

The first pao bhaji stalls developed in the Cotton Exchange area. Somehow, it did not seem right to serve bhelpuri at that hour of the morning. So a new snack was developed which involved mashing vegetables on a tawa with a seasoning that consisted largely of garlic (I don't suppose the Jain traders ever admitted eating pao bhaji to their wives) and chilli. The dish was made rich and filling by the addition of copious amounts of butter.

Even now, pao bhaji is essentially about butter—not about the bhaji or the pao. And if you are to make it right, you can forget about poncy Normandy butters. Nothing but that most Gujarati of butters—Amul—will do.

Which is not to say there is no room for poncy butters. You can't bake properly with Amul. You need a slightly sweeter, unsalted butter to cook with. And very good bread demands the best butter you can find.

But for most purposes—smearing on sliced bread, melting over waffles, using as a sauce for garlic crab or merely spreading on a hot naan—you can't beat Amul. It's utterly butterly Indian and it's the butter we grew up on.

Curd Is Crucial

≈

Do Indians need Greeks to tell us how to enjoy yoghurt?

Most Indians take dahi for granted.

At my home in Mumbai, I paid little attention to the process of setting the dahi every night and treated it as something that was entirely normal and unexceptional. Had I been a little brighter or more inquisitive as a child, I would have asked how the milk turned into dahi or why we needed to add a little bit of the previous day's dahi to the new lot.

But because we ate so much dahi—Gujaratis eat dahi with theplas, use it in cooking, make kadhi out of it, etc.—I treated what should have been a magical and fascinating process as just something that everybody everywhere did every day.

It was only during a trip to London, where my parents spent part of the year, that I began to notice things. First of all, my mother would not make dahi. She would buy it from a shop. It came in a plastic tub with a tin-foil top and was called 'yoghurt' and not 'curd', which I had been told was the English name for dahi. My mother was not much help. When I asked her what yoghurt was, she answered shortly, 'It is the English name for dahi.' And that was that.

But she kept complaining about English dahi. It had no taste. The consistency was nothing like real dahi. And why was it so expensive?

It took me years to figure out why we were the only people in that English grocery shop who bothered to buy yoghurt. (Brits did not eat it those days.) And it took even longer for me to figure out that the key to yoghurt was bacteria. As for the name, well, dahi is yoghurt. The term 'curd' refers to the solids in the yoghurt, not to dahi itself.

As you probably know, yoghurt is the child of the marriage between milk and bacteria. Our bodies contain millions of bacteria, most of them beneficial. In fact there are more bacteria in the human body than there are cells. These bacteria perform a variety of functions, but one of the most crucial is the role that gut bacteria play in the digestive process.

Certain strains of bacteria have the power to transform milk. Some bacteria assist in the making of cheese. And a more common bundle of varieties turns it into dahi. The reason we add a little bit of old dahi to milk when we need to make some more is because we want the bacteria inside the old dahi to act on the milk.

There is evidence to suggest that the bacteria in dahi are good for our digestion. And so, over the last two decades, yoghurt has come to be regarded as a miracle food and westerners are suddenly buying millions of little plastic tubs of yoghurt.

This marks a change from the old days. Any yoghurt my mother used to buy had been processed to kill all bacteria, so it had no health benefits at all. Now, food companies try to ensure that the bacteria stay alive because that is the principal selling point of yoghurt in the West.

But, I wondered, was my mother right to complain about how bland and tasteless the English packaged yoghurt was?

It turned out she was right, after all. The manufacturing process for nearly all commercial yoghurt relies on introducing bacteria into the milk, not in the form of old dahi, but as a ready-made bacteria powder. Because many different bacteria can turn milk into yoghurt, the chances are that commercial bacteria powder used micro-organisms that were quite different from the ones we found naturally in India, which gave our dahi a slight khatta taste. Plus yoghurt is not meant to set into a smooth semi-solid. It should be like home-made dahi with a little water in the bowl. But industrial yoghurt manufacturers use chemicals to thicken the yoghurt and give it that smooth consistency and texture.

So could my mother have made her own dahi in London? Yes, she could have, but only if she had taken a little Indian dahi with her to add to milk to start off the next batch of yoghurt. She couldn't have used commercial yoghurt for that purpose because it had no active (still alive) bacteria in it. And even then, it may not have tasted the same.

As bacteria begin to act on milk, they also attract other micro-organisms, which are in the atmosphere. So, when the dahi is finally set, it is thanks to the work of the original bacteria in the dahi starter and the effect of atmospheric micro-organisms. And because these micro-organisms vary so much from location to location, the taste they impart to the dahi can vary considerably.

You don't have to go abroad to test this hypothesis. A bowl of dahi made in a home in Thiruvananthapuram will taste different from one that has been set in Delhi or Shimla. Commercial yoghurt manufacturers discovered this the hard way when they tried to reproduce Bulgarian yoghurt in the US and the UK. No matter how hard they tried (the same milk, the same ambient temperatures and a starter culture of yoghurt that had set in Bulgaria), it just would not taste the same. You simply could not reproduce the micro-organisms in the Bulgarian air in America or England.

While America only discovered yoghurt a century ago, our ancestors knew all about it and its healing properties 500 years before the birth of Jesus Christ. That's when we find the first references to dahi in ancient Indian texts. And many medicinal writings from the ancient period suggest yoghurt as a remedy for stomach ailments. One theory is that the tradition of including yoghurt in an Indian meal (as a raita, chhaach or on its own) was a way of ensuring that there were enough good bacteria in your system to fight off infections. Our forefathers did not know the science—there are no writings about bacteria in ancient Indian texts—but they understood the efficacy of yoghurt.

The other people who recognized that yoghurt was good for health were eastern Europeans (like the aforementioned Bulgarians). It is possible (and the Turks say it is certain) that Greece learned how to make yoghurt from Turkey and other Middle Eastern cultures. But the Greeks made it their own and Greek yoghurt is now a global rage.

The term 'Greek yoghurt' sounds fanciful but it actually is no more than ordinary dahi that has had the water drained away so that the milk solids remain. It is a process that will be familiar to all Indians because we hang dahi in muslin before making such desserts as shrikhand.

Thick Greek yoghurt is now a hot property in the US. Over the last five years, the growth in the yoghurt market in the US has come almost entirely from Greek yoghurt. And India may follow the global trend.

I came across Epigamia yoghurts almost by accident when the manager of my local Nature's Basket in Defence Colony suggested I try some. Though I am normally sceptical of packaged yoghurts, I took Vaibhav at his word and bought a few.

Within a day, I was hooked. Then, I launched a very public search on Twitter to find out who made them (because I had never heard of Epigamia). Twitter has a way of delivering, so I got my answer in minutes. Rohan Mirchandani and his two partners (Rahul Jain and chef Ganesh Krishnamoorthy) started out with ice cream, then moved into this untried segment because they had dairy experience. The success of Epigamia has taken them by surprise and their biggest problem is keeping up with the demand, which is roughly twice their current manufacturing capacity.

Rohan has positioned his yoghurts as a solution for the 'choti si bhook' problem. So when hunger strikes, and you don't want to eat something heavy like a samosa, a small tub of Epigamia should do the trick. According to Ganesh Krishnamoorthy, who is responsible for the great taste of the product, the challenge was to make Indians rethink our attitude towards yoghurt. We are used to dahi—hell, we practically invented it!—but we treat it as a side dish or an accompaniment (like raita). The trick was to make yoghurt the star of the show—something we ate by itself.

The success of Epigamia suggests that we are willing to look at yoghurt differently, though Indians have not yet bought into the good-health hype that is an integral part of yoghurt marketing in the West. Apart from the probiotic benefits, Greek yoghurt is rich in protein and has half the carbs of normal yoghurt. These health benefits are slightly compromised if you add lots of sugar to it, so Epigamia will probably branch away from its fruit flavours (strawberry, mango, banana, etc.) and also try a savoury line.

Speaking for myself, I like unflavoured Epigamia yoghurt, which you can use for cooking in place of normal dahi or as a snack on its own (I add a little honey).

But do Indians need Greeks to tell us how to enjoy yoghurt? I guess not. We should treat it not as some fancy foreign product but as our very own dahi, just strained to remove the water.

Eggs

The Real Chicken- and-Egg Story

≈

There is only one good reason for not eating eggs and that's if you don't like them. All the other reasons are incredibly unconvincing.

I can never understand vegetarians who claim that they don't eat eggs for religious reasons. As far as I can tell, the basis of vegetarianism is that you don't like to eat living things (and for the purposes of this argument you have to pretend that plants and bacteria are not really living things). But how is an egg a living thing?

I don't want to restart the old abortion debate (at what stage does the fertilized ovum constitute life, etc.). But the simple truth is that the eggs most of us eat are unfertilized eggs. This means, for all of you who missed biology class in school, that the chicken lays them without ever having been, ahem, fertilized by a rooster. Even if you were to let the egg remain uneaten, it would not hatch into a chicken. (Some Indians like to eat fertilized eggs, in which case of course, the standard vegetarian arguments would apply, but 99 per cent of the eggs you and I are likely to encounter will be unfertilized.)

Vegetarians retort that even if eggs do not constitute life, they are still animal products because they have emerged from a living thing (i.e. the sadly unfertilized and still frustrated chicken). This is not a bad argument until you realize that the basis of most vegetarian cuisines is another animal product: milk.

In many ways, eggs are the bird kingdom's equivalent of milk. Birds produce them anyway just as cows continue to give milk even if there are no cows to be fed. I can't understand how vegetarians can drink milk, eat yogurt, enjoy paneer and cook in ghee and still claim that they are avoiding animal products. (In the West, there is a category of vegetarian called vegan consisting of those who avoid dairy products, but the distinction seems to have eluded Indian vegetarians.)

So, if the vegetarian argument against eggs is bogus, that leaves only the many health arguments. Foremost among them is the old cholesterol-is-a-killer theology. It is true that egg yolks can raise the levels of bad cholesterol in the blood. But there's no evidence that this happens if you are content to consume the occasional egg. And besides, there is my very own challenge to the medical orthodoxy: Russi Mody.

As is well known, the charismatic former head of Tata Steel specialized in eating fourteen egg omelettes. Yet, each time anxious doctors sent him off to look for signs of heart disease, the test results confounded them. Old Russi's cholesterol was always within acceptable limits.

Why, I ask, if eggs are so bad for you, does Russi Mody continue to thrive? Russi is a symbol of a greater medical mystery. As we all know, most Parsis live to be 105. The average age of the community is something like sixty-five. (I'm not sure that's true—I made the figure up—but it does sound right, doesn't it?) And Parsis subsist on eggs. Most of us are partial to the odd omelettes but for Parsis, eggs are not a food, they are a religion. Apart from the most famous Parsi egg dish— akuri, basically bhurjee with spices—eggs crop up in nearly every nook and corner of Parsi cuisine. My favourite Parsi dish, after dhansaak, is the sauté potato-and-fried-onion concoction that they eat as a snack. I thought it was a wonderful concept till I realized that Parsis put eggs on everything. I love eggs but, frankly, a fried egg on bhindi is going a bit far—even for me.

But the challenge to medical orthodoxy endures. If eggs are so bad for you, why do Parsis live so long?

The other objections to eggs are silly. In the 1980s, there was a salmonella scare in the UK when it was discovered that some eggs had been infected with salmonella. If you cooked the eggs properly, there was no problem. But if you did not, you would probably get food poisoning.

Fears about salmonella may have been genuine, but I have a particular affection for the great salmonella scare because it marked the Waterloo of the second most obnoxious woman in British politics: the appalling Edwina Currie. Now best known as the writer of unreadable semi-pornographic novels, Currie used to be a publicity-loving minister who declared that most eggs in Britain had salmonella. She got the headlines she wanted. But she also got the sack because this simply wasn't true. Now she has confessed that she was bonking John Major (though perhaps not at the same time when she was steering clear of eggs), so all is explained.

(Second most obnoxious woman? Yes, of course. Who could be worse than the hateful Margaret Thatcher?)

A second and more recent category of medical objection has been the bird flu scare. Sometime in the recent past, all the five-star hotels in Bangkok posted little signs saying that they wouldn't serve chicken or any poultry product because of the health hazards. Some added disclaimers to the effect that they would continue to serve omelettes because these were made not from real eggs but from imported, reconstituted egg powder.

Reconstituted egg powder? Yup. Sad but true. All over the rest of the world, and now it seems in Asia as well, institutional caterers don't bother to use real eggs. Instead, they use this disgusting industrially manufactured powder to make omelettes, scrambled eggs and the like (only boiled and fried eggs cannot be replicated by a factory) because (a) it's cheaper and (b) they don't have to bother about the freshness of the ingredients. The salmonella scare gave a huge boost to the manufacturers of factory egg powder and, now, bird flu seems to have given them a huge export market. (For the record, the hotel in Bangkok was the Holiday Inn in Silom. Eat breakfast there at your own peril.)

In India, bird flu never really took off, but such was the scare that local hatchery owners quickly enlisted the aid of their celebrity friends to declare that eggs were safe. The Venky's people got Suniel Shetty and assorted movie stars to sing the praise of poultry products. And Perizaad Zorabian, whose father is in the chicken business, appeared at Crawford Market to entertain the media by doing bodily harm to a chicken leg. But these publicity stunts were not necessary.

Most Indians were not troubled in the slightest by the Asian bird flu scare. All the people I know realized that eggs could pose a health hazard only after they saw the pictures of movie stars on their front pages.

Alas, the Government of India is more stupid than the average Indian. The bird flu scare led to a ban on the import of all poultry products. This may have been reasonable if it had simply banned people from bringing dead ducks and live chickens from China or Thailand. But the law bans the import of anything that contains eggs from anywhere in the world.

This means that if you want to import a cake from Belgium, or if you want to bring a tub of Ben and Jerry's ice cream from America, customs will be well within its rights to seize the goods claiming that you are exposing vulnerable Indian public to the deadly dangers of bird flu.

I know it makes no sense. But that's how ministries function. No matter how illogical this sounds—if American eggs were tainted by bird flu, the streets of New York would be littered with corpses—once a babu takes a decision, no amount of logic can be allowed to intervene. (There's also an incredibly foolish ban on the import of meat products. This is extraordinary because Indian pork is clearly unsafe and yet the babus are preventing us from eating safer Parma ham or German sausage, all on health grounds. But don't get me started on the bureaucracy.)

A Rush of Brunch
to the Head

≈

A Sunday brunch is, at heart, a delayed breakfast.

As you may have noticed, Chennai is now the centre of India's hotel industry—it seems a new place opens every month. But I went to the Westin—a bright, cheery hotel with a young staff and a great vibe—because the general manager, Shrikant Wakharkar, has been a friend of mine for twenty years.

Shrikant plans to open an Oriental restaurant soon, but for now the property has only one outlet, a relaxed, sun-filled, cafe-type, all-day diner, which does a vast Sunday brunch replete with nearly every kind of food you can think of—from pizzas, appams, stews and sushi to north Indian curries, Middle Eastern rice dishes and teppanyaki ice cream.

Though the food was fine, we got to discussing possible innovations. In the West, a Sunday brunch is usually a bakwas meal at top restaurants, served on the head chef's day off, when assorted kitchen minions make eggs to order, add a couple of basic dishes (minute steak, French toast, waffles, etc.) and charge you a fixed price. Coffee and orange juice are always included in the rate.

In the Far East, however, the Sunday brunch is a big deal—a sort of bigger and better version of the normal lunch buffet, with free champagne thrown in and lots of luxury ingredients (foie gras, caviar, lobster, oysters, etc.) laid out on the tables. If you wake up hungry on Sundays, a brunch can be the best deal you'll get at any restaurant.

115

In India, we've tended to follow the Far Eastern model largely because the foreign chains that brought the concept to our hotels used expatriate chefs who had worked in East Asia. The La Piazza Sunday brunch at Delhi's Hyatt Regency was the pioneer, but nearly every restaurant or hotel now offer some kind of variation on the theme.

The one thing that remains constant at all brunches—whether in the West or in the East—is the idea that Sunday brunch is, at heart, a delayed breakfast. In the Indian context it should mean that restaurants serve parathas, theplas, idlis, vadas, dosas and the like. And indeed, some places do offer Indian breakfast specialities, but most restaurants stick with the global idea that as long as you have a live egg counter, with a chef churning out omelettes, fried eggs, etc., you are sticking with the spirit of breakfast.

Personally, I'm getting a little tired of brunches where the junior-most chef in the kitchen is sent to the restaurant to fry eggs because his top bosses are too high and mighty to make omelettes. Why can't Indian restaurants try to do something fresh and innovative with eggs at their Sunday brunches? God knows there are enough egg dishes in the world for the chefs not to have to rely on the same tired old mushroom omelette or fried eggs sunny side up formula.

Over brunch that Sunday, Shrikant and I sat down and made a list of things we would like to see on Sunday brunch menus—the kind of dishes that would make imaginative use of eggs. We decided that one could find enough good ideas within South Asia not to have to bother with elaborate soufflés or other European dishes. Here are some of the things we thought of.

Egg roast and Appam: I'm sure they will hate me in Kerala for saying this but, as much as I love appams, I loathe the boring white stew that is traditionally served with them. (And while we are on the subject, I'm not keen on idi-appams either. They taste like the sort of messed-up noodle dish an inexperienced cook in a bad Chinese restaurant in Ernakulam turned out by mistake . . . Okay, Malayalis: you can shoot me now!)

But the egg roast is one of the world's greatest egg dishes. It is not difficult to make and goes perfectly with appams. So, why can't we get egg roast and appams at Sunday brunches rather than boring ham-and-cheese omelettes?

Shrikant spent three years in Colombo at the Taj Samudra, so he is familiar with Sri Lankan cuisine. The Lankan version of the appam is called a 'hopper', a name that apparently originates from an English mispronunciation of the world 'appam'. (How can anyone, even a Brit, make appam sound like hopper? No idea. I find the story mystifying myself, but there it is . . .)

The Lankans fry an egg, sunny side up on their appams, and call them egg-hoppers. They can be delicious and are easy to find all over Sri Lanka. So why don't we serve them here at our brunches?

No matter what you call it, an anda paratha or a baida roti, the combination of paratha/roti and egg is a marriage made in heaven. It is the secret of a satisfying Nizam's roll (or a kathi, if you want to call it that). Every second roadside vendor in parts of Mumbai turns out the most delicious baida roti.

So, why in God's name are our hotels still serving us disgusting, pale, battery-chicken scrambled eggs on pheeka toast? Why can't we get anda parathas or baida rotis at our brunches?

The only Parsi dish that most Indians have heard of is dhansaak but no community uses eggs as imaginatively as the Parsis. They are so willing to fry an egg on top of anything (even bhindi) that I sometimes wonder if their ancestors escaped from Persia with all of that country's chickens.

One great thing about the Parsi love for eggs (Russi Mody used to brag about his fourteen-egg omelette) is that they all live to be a hundred or so. Remember that the next time a doctor tells you that eggs are bad for your heart.

The other great thing is that they have at least two wonderful egg dishes that make perfect brunch specialties. The first is reasonably well known in Mumbai—their akuri, which is a classier version of the north Indian ande ki bhurjee and tastes more delicious than any scrambled egg you will ever eat. (You can even buy an akuri powder in Bombay, or so I am told, which is the secret ingredient in many home-style akuris.)

The other wonderful Parsi egg dish, and my personal favourite, consists of perfectly fried eggs on top of a bed of sautéed potatoes and onions. You'll hardly ever see this on restaurant menus. But try it. I find it can be addictive.

We sometimes come across the Scotch egg, though the dish has generally fallen out of favour even in the West. In essence, this is a boiled egg encased in sausage meat, battered or breaded and then fried. I have too many unhappy memories of Scotch eggs from school to be nostalgic about them. But we have our own Indian equivalent, which is much tastier—the nargisi kofta.

This is a little like a Scotch egg but instead of the sausage meat, you use delicious, delicately spiced keema of the kind you would use for a kebab. Made properly, the dish adds a new dimension to the flavour of the egg by surrounding it with moist, juicy keema. And yet, I don't know of anybody who serves it for Sunday brunch at a restaurant in India.

These are just some of the ideas Shrikant and I came up with over brunch that Sunday. I'm sure you can think of even more interesting things to do with eggs.

Egg Akuri Style One

Ingredients

3 eggs
2 onions (chopped)
1 tbsp ghee
Salt to taste
3 cloves of garlic

Grind for masala

½ inch piece of ginger
2 tsp chopped coriander leaves
1 green chilli
1 tsp tamarind or a slice of green mango
1 tsp cumin seeds
1 tsp turmeric powder
½ tsp dhania and jeera powder combined

Method

Heat ghee, add the onions and masala and fry well till ghee separates. Remove from fire and cool. Mix eggs lightly, add salt. Add to the fried masala. Mix well. Put on fire and cook on medium heat, stir constantly till cooked like scrambled eggs.

Egg Akuri Style Two (Serves 6)

Ingredients

6 eggs
Salt to taste

¼ cup of milk
6 medium onions (sliced)
2 tbsp ghee
5 green chillies (chopped fine)
1 small bunch of coriander leaves (chopped fine)
1 tsp cumin seeds (fry for garnishing)
1 green chilli (chopped; fry for garnishing)

Method

Break eggs in a pan. Add salt and milk and mix lightly. Fry the onions, and when golden, add the chillies and coriander and cook for a few minutes. Pour in the egg mixture and stir constantly till cooked like scrambled eggs. Pour into a hot dish, garnish with the fried cumin seeds and chilli and serve immediately.

Eggs on Potatoes and Onions (Serves 6)

Ingredients

6 eggs
½ kg potatoes
2 tbsp ghee
¼ kg onions (sliced thinly)
2 green chillies (chopped)
¾ tbsp salt
1 tbsp chopped coriander leaves

Method

Cut potatoes into small cubes. Heat ghee and fry onions for two minutes. Add potatoes and cook both vegetables till almost done. Add salt, chillies and coriander leaves. Remove from fire and spread in a flat greased baking dish. Break six eggs on the potato mixture, sprinkle with salt, cover and keep on a low fire or in a slow oven till eggs are set. Serve hot.

Great Eggspectations

≈

The simplest egg dishes that we eat at breakfast are the hardest to make. And most Indian restaurant kitchens don't know how to cook them properly.

So I'm not the only one who loves eggs! When I lamented that Indian cooks were unfairly neglecting one of nature's great treasures, I portrayed the egg as a humble object, passed over by mighty chefs as they reached for the lobster, the lamb or even the chicken.

Not true, some of you have since told me. You like eggs as much as I do and wish more cooks would learn to cook with them. Moreover, most of you regret that the breakfast egg has now become a cheap and nasty dish, usually made by the junior-most chef in the kitchen, using the most inexpensive ingredients available.

What interested me was that (a) most of you still like your eggs done Western style and (b) you still think of them as breakfast items.

Okay, fair enough, but I have to warn you: Be ready to be disappointed. The simplest egg dishes of Continental breakfast cuisine are the hardest to make. Most Indian restaurant kitchens do not know how to cook them properly. And the ingredients used are often so substandard that the chefs should be ashamed of themselves.

Here's my own guide (based mainly on stealing other people's recipes—I am the world's worst cook, or so they regularly tell me at home) to getting a decent egg breakfast.

The eggs—I am sorry if I've become a bore on the subject of free-range eggs and sometimes sound like a shill for Keggs eggs—but you cannot make a decent egg dish with the nasty industrial eggs available in the market. You must use eggs that come from hens that have been allowed to run around, enjoy the fresh air, and have been fed a proper diet. My friend Tapas Bhattacharya served me fried eggs with hash browns at Machan, the restaurant where he is chef/manager. There was nothing wrong with the cooking, but the eggs were anaemic with yolks that were pale grey. Tapas took one look at the eggs, worked out what was wrong, disappeared into the kitchen and returned with another plate of two fried eggs, their whites gleaming and their yolks the colour of bright sunlight. The eggs had been cooked in exactly the same way—Tapas had just used free-range eggs instead of the industrial ones that most hotels use for their breakfast service.

So, with eggs, the quality of the ingredient is paramount. Even a great chef will fail if he uses an industrial egg.

As important is freshness. Some cooks believe that if you rub eggs with oil or butter (as the Irish do), you'll keep them fresher for longer. Perhaps. But food scientists say that an egg loses 4 mg of water each day of its life (even if it is oiled or buttered). As the egg's insides shrink, the air within the shell expands till ultimately you get rotten eggs. So eggs must be fresh. Anyone can check this. Put your egg in a bowl of water. If it sinks to the bottom, it is fresh. If it floats, it is old and full of air. Cook only with eggs that sink.

Some hotels use reconstituted egg, that is to say, an egg powder, which goes into scrambled eggs. Any chef who uses egg powder should first have his toque ceremonially confiscated.

Then, he should be smeared with egg yolk.

The Fried Egg

You only understand the principle of a fried egg if you realize that your purpose is not just to fry an egg but also to babysit a yolk. A fried egg cooked over easy or one with a coagulated yolk is a failed egg, a disgrace to the culinary arts. A proper fried egg should have a golden, runny yolk in the centre. The white should be solid but still shimmering and evanescent, fresh enough to pop in your mouth but soft enough to melt once it is inside, leaving behind a buttery explosion.

This is not easy to do; so chefs cheat. One trick is not to fry at all. Simmer some water in a pot. Place a serving plate over the pot. When the plate is hot, crack an egg on it. Cover with another plate and leave for four minutes. You'll get a fried egg—but one that's never been fried.

A poncier and needlessly complicated method attributed to Bernard Loiseau, the celebrated French chef who committed suicide because he thought he would lose his third Michelin star or because of the strain of inventing recipes like this one, is as follows: Preheat an oven to 245 degrees Celcius. Put a pan containing butter and a spoon of water (to prevent the butter from burning) over a flame. When the butter begins to foam, add just the white of the egg. Now, put the pan in the oven for ninety seconds. Take it out. Put a raw yolk at the centre. Put it back in the oven for two minutes, and voila! You have a perfect fried egg.

If you have no time for all this nonsense, remember that the basic dilemma with a fried egg is that the white is nearer the heat, but the yolk is further away. This is why many chefs cover the pan so that the heat is reflected back to the yolk. There are variations to this. You can put the eggs in a pan containing very hot fat and cover them. Then, turn the heat off. That should give you perfect, delicate fried eggs.

Scrambled Eggs

Unless you are making akuri, remember that scrambled eggs must be soft, creamy and runny. If you can eat them easily with a fork, you've probably screwed up. Either you eat them with a spoon or you pour them over toast, which serves as a sort of egg-plate.

How do you get them creamy? The usual trick is to use cream. But it is not so simple. The trick to a scrambled egg is a minimum of heat. You can do this either by using a very low flame or—as Gordon Ramsay suggests—by periodically lifting the pan off the heat to keep the temperature low.

The broad principle being low temperature, all chefs have their own ruses. Some pour the egg mixture into a pan containing a little fat and then, just as the egg starts coagulating, add cream. The cream will help with the consistency but because it is cold, it will also automatically lower the temperature of the pan and slow down the coagulation process.

There is, in most recipes, a point when you decide that you have to start stirring before you end up with shards of omelettes. Quite when the point is reached depends on your egg mixture: Has it been diluted with milk? Have you added cream? And so on. But there are those who say that you should never stir. Heston Blumenthal says there should be thickening for at least ten minutes if the flame is low enough. M.F.K. Fisher puts in lots of cream, uses a low flame and says that it should take half an hour, without stirring.

No matter which method you end up using, here are some tips: Try to use butter—it adds something to the taste. Do not bother to whip the eggs too much before cooking—it's no help. Remember that while you can season with herbs, salt and pepper are usually enough. And if your eggs are solid, you've done something wrong.

Accompaniments

Different people like different things with eggs. I believe that fried bread and the tomato, so beloved of the full English breakfast, are unnecessary. Nor am I keen on the blood sausage (black pudding, white pudding, boudin noir, etc.) that many Europeans prefer.

A good eggy breakfast should include bread (good-quality toast is enough), some pork, either in the form of a flavourful sausage or crisp good-quality bacon, and ideally, potato. Potato crisps may seem excessive first thing in the morning but a hash brown (now available frozen and therefore, easy to cook) is perfect. A more adventurous cook may want to try potatoes sautéed with onion but it's not really necessary. A perfect breakfast forkful should mix fried egg white with a little bacon and some potato dipped in the runny yolk.

Opinions are divided on baked beans. If your yolks are moist, you don't need them. Otherwise, they go well with fried egg, I reckon, but they are a waste with good scrambled eggs.

Some people say that coffee is the ideal breakfast beverage. I prefer Darjeeling tea, but no doubt you will make up your own mind. My general rule is that if you want to go all French you can have coffee, croissants and cigarettes for breakfast.

For the rest of us, tea and eggs should be good enough.

Eggs Kejriwal

≈

How was Eggs Kejriwal born?

Does Arvind Kejriwal lay eggs?

Yes, I know it is a silly question, but you would be amazed by how many variations on that theme I have heard over the last few years. The question stems from the new-found popularity of a fairly old dish: Eggs Kejriwal.

If you live in Mumbai, you may or may not have heard of Eggs Kejriwal. (I grew up in Mumbai and had never heard of the dish, by the way, for most of my life.) It was invented apparently at the Willingdon Club, one of the city's most exclusive (in the post-Independence period) clubs.

During the Raj, Indians were not allowed to enter the top clubs in every city. So any Indian would have been turned away at the gate of the Bombay Gymkhana (by another Indian, happy to work as a lackey for his British masters). Legend has it that Jamsetji Tata was sent back from the gate of the Royal Bombay Yacht Club for the crime of having a brown skin though he was a knight of the realm. Jamsetji vowed to build a grand hotel that would eclipse the Yacht Club, then the city's most exclusive spot. Which, of course, he did when the Taj opened.

When Lord Willingdon was governor of Bombay in 1917, he tried to take a maharaja to dinner at the Bombay Gymkhana and the Yacht Club only to be told that while His Excellency was most welcome, the brown fellow would have to eat somewhere else. A more decent and decisive governor would have forced the top clubs to end the colour bar, but old Willingdon took a different approach. Why not open another club where the white sahibs could mingle on equal (oh well, more or less equal) terms with the natives? And so, in 1918, he opened the Willingdon Club (named, modestly, after the great man himself) where Indians were allowed entry.

Over the post-Independence years, as pressure forced the Bombay Gymkhana, the Yacht Club (and eventually, even the notorious Breach Candy Club) to let Indians in, the Willingdon lost its special cachet. But its membership consisted of descendants of some of Bombay's top families, people whose ancestors had been rich and successful in the days when Mahatma Gandhi was still in jail.

Many of the members came from old Parsi and Muslim families (among the builders of Bombay before it became Mumbai). And the Willingdon has always had a fair number of bania/vania members from rich Marwari and Gujarati families.

Many of these members lived in joint families and ate satvik food cooked by maharajs in their mansions. But when they felt like a drink or a bite of something more daring, they scampered off to the Willingdon or later, to such Bombay restaurants as The Other Room at the Ambassador. Most of these rich Marwaris and Gujaratis were not averse to a Scotch or two. Some wanted special dishes made for them (for years, The Other Room kept a Chunni Cutlet on the menu for a rich patron called Chunnibhai) and often they hungered for something expressly forbidden at home.

Obviously meat was no-no at bania/vania mansions. But so were eggs. The story goes (and I warn you that it might be apocryphal) that a rich merchant called Devi Prasad Kejriwal would go to the Willingdon for his daily egg-and-toast. But because the food of the white sahibs could be a little boring, Mr Kejriwal got the club's cooks to tart up his eggs.

Thus was born Eggs Kejriwal. It consisted of a slice of toasted pao bread (some versions of the story say that it was plain white bread), some grated cheese (probably Kraft from tins; there was no Amul in those days), topped by a fried egg (or two eggs) with a garnish of chillies and kothmir (coriander).

Long after the original Mr Kejriwal has been forgotten, the Willingdon Club continues to serve Eggs Kejriwal as a sort of sad and weak-kneed Indian response to Eggs Benedict (invented by Delmonico's in New York for a rich patron using bread, eggs, Hollandaise and a slice of bacon) as a signature dish.

I doubt if Eggs Kejriwal would have travelled very far from the tables of the Willingdon if it hadn't been for Arvind Kejriwal. When Thomas Zacharias, Floyd Cardoz and the rest of the team were putting together the menu at The Bombay Canteen, which was to open soon, Arvind Kejriwal was in the news every day. Somebody remembered that the Willingdon had a dish called Kejriwal and wondered if they could do something witty with it.

Sameer Seth, one of the partners at The Bombay Canteen, told me the story. They had been working on a dish that never made it to the menu, and the chef, Thomas Zacharias (or Chef Zach as he is called by nearly everyone) had come up with a green chilli chutney that was terrific. They looked for uses for the chutney and thought that perhaps they could combine it with Eggs Kejriwal. There were some brioche rounds in the kitchen and they had the bright idea of throwing out the pao (or Britannia white bread, depending on which Willingdon recipe you prefer) and replacing it with brioche. They kept the grated processed cheese, used high-quality eggs, retained the chilli and kothmir garnish but elevated the dish with Zach's chutney, which gave it a zing that the boring Willingdon Club original sadly lacked.

According to Sameer, they put it on the menu when they opened the restaurant in 2015 because they thought the name Kejriwal would provoke some curiosity. The Bombay Canteen changes its menus regularly, so they believed that Eggs Kejriwal would be a novelty item on the first menu and would disappear after a few weeks. But Sameer and his partners were staggered by the response. It became one of the fastest-moving items on the menu and critics loved it. (I said at the time that it would become 'the restaurant's signature dish'.) Though the Canteen menu has been overhauled regularly, Eggs Kejriwal is one of the few dishes that they have never removed.

Marut Sikka opened his Delhi Club House with the idea of recreating the great dishes of Indian club cuisine.

It was not a concept I loved. (As you can probably tell from the sneering tone of this piece, I have no time for clubs that restrict admission on the basis of 'social acceptability' or colour, nor am I a member of any of these so-called elite clubs.) And in any case, club food has no great reputation for quality.

Marut started out by putting akuri on the menu to represent the egg dishes of clubland, but now, even Delhi Club House has its own version of Eggs Kejriwal. Like Zach, Marut was impressed by the idea behind the Willingdon Club dish but not overly pleased with the Willingdon's execution. He uses his own kind of brioche as the base for the eggs. A spicy chutney, while not the same as Zach's (which, with its coconut oil, is vaguely Malayali), is used to perk up the dish. It remains one of Delhi Club House's bestsellers, and that's no mean feat given that the rest of the food at the restaurant is of such high quality.

Both Zach and Marut have had the same basic idea. There are some interesting dishes out there in clubland but most of them work better as ideas than they do as complete dishes. A talented chef will take these ideas, use top-quality ingredients, and convert boring dishes into gourmet classics.

The secret of The Bombay Canteen's reinvention of Eggs Kejriwal lies in the quality of the bread and, more significantly, with the tasty, top-quality, orange-yolk eggs that Zach uses in his kitchen. So it is with the club dishes on Marut's menu: none of them ever tasted this good in the hands of club cooks.

Which takes us back to Lord Willingdon and Arvind Kejriwal. I am not one of those rename-everything maniacs, but I do find it offensive to celebrate anything with Willingdon's name on it. At one stage, all kinds of places in Delhi were named after Willingdon and his pushy wife— from Willingdon Airfield (now Safdarjung Airport) to Lady Willingdon Park (now Lodhi Garden) to Willingdon Hospital (now R.M. Lohia Hospital).

And as for Arvind Kejriwal, I know that the dish has nothing to do with him. But is there a lesson for him in its popular revival? Take the basic idea and start all over again with higher-quality ingredients and more imagination?

It's a formula that may work in politics too.

Nargisi Kofta

≈

Scotch Egg has nothing Scotch in it.

Over the last two decades, chefs in the West have taken relatively humble dishes and tried to turn them into something special. The hamburger is one instance. In the late 1980s and early 1990s, most American chefs did their own riffs on the burger, including, perhaps most influentially, Daniel Boulud's version at DB Bistro Moderne in New York. This used high-quality beef, foie gras and every other luxury ingredient Boulud had lying around in his kitchen.

Then, it was the turn of the boring old mac and cheese to get the haute cuisine treatment. These days, fancy chefs will add slices of black truffles to the cheese (the flavours go well) while lesser chefs will mistakenly believe that they are elevating the dish with liberal use of synthetic truffle oil.

British chefs took longer to catch on and when they did, the luxury updates focused on better cooking skills and ingredients: good fish and superb frying for fish and chips, triple-cooking of chips for the perfect texture, pigs-in-a-blanket or bangers and mash made with artisanal sausages, etc.

I like the idea of upgrading dishes, though, frankly, one often gets tired of the newer versions fairly quickly. I would never order a so-called gourmet burger, for instance. And very few of the upgrades actually last; most fade as new trends develop.

These are a few exceptions though. Joël Robuchon's pommes puree has become the benchmark for upmarket mashed potatoes. Anton

Mosimann's bread-and-butter pudding has transformed the way that old nursery favourite is cooked. And though Heston Blumenthal's triple-cooked chips are difficult to pull off (even the ones I had at Heston's own The Hind's Head were rubbish), that hasn't stopped chefs from using 'triple-cooked chips' as a menu cliché.

One such dish that has become a favourite of chefs who want to upgrade old comfort staples is the Scotch Egg. If you have tried one of the industrially manufactured versions in the UK, you will know how disgusting mass-produced Scotch Eggs can be. The meat component consists of cheap sausage meat, which is basically mince made from the parts of the pig that nobody wants to buy. And the inside is a tough, hard-boiled egg, laid by a battery chicken in an industrial operation somewhere.

So, it was relatively easy for chefs to upgrade the dish. All they had to do was to use good-quality free-range eggs and proper sausage meat.

As the remake grew in popularity, newer versions emerged. One obvious route—to indicate that the dish had been freshly made—was to soft-boil the egg (the original dish calls for hard-boiled eggs) so that a liquid yolk oozed out when you cut into it. A second was to change the batter. At one of Bruce Poole's restaurants in London (it may have been La Trompette), I had an interesting Scotch Egg over a decade ago—the egg was soft-boiled, the batter was panko (which is of Japanese origin) and they had used good-quality truffle oil to add another layer of flavour.

These days the upmarket Scotch Egg turns up again and again as a canapé. Chefs use quail's eggs, which are much smaller than hen's eggs, and you are encouraged to pop the whole thing into your mouth at one go.

Why should the fortunes of the Scotch Egg concern us?

Well, because it is an Indian dish.

Yes. Really.

This is not something Brits are ready to accept. The London store Fortnum and Mason even claims to have invented the Scotch Egg. And there have been many theories about the name because it is clearly not a traditional Scottish dish. One theory even has it that the recipe was first written down by the author of *Ivanhoe*, who was called Sir Walter Scott. And so, rather than call it the Ivanhoe Egg, they named it after the author—Scott became Scotch.

But I will go with the views of the late Alan Davidson, the greatest food historian of the twentieth century. Davidson says that British soldiers ate our Nargisi Kofta curry and loved it so much that they tried to recreate it at home. The original curry had a tomato gravy, and when this proved too difficult to reproduce in Britain, they started using a hot sauce instead. It was a small step from eating the koftas with a bottled sauce to serving them on their own and leaving it to individuals to decide which condiment they wanted to use.

That's how the dry Scotch Egg was created, and today its Indian origins are either forgotten or denied outright. I have read many outlandish theories about its origin. One states that it was invented as a fish-mince dish in Yorkshire by an establishment called William J. Scott and sons—hence the name Scotch Egg. Another ascribes Algerian origins to the dish, which might have been slightly plausible had Britain (rather than France) colonized Algeria or if there had been mass Algerian immigration to the UK.

We know that the first British recipe for a Scotch Egg turns up in 1826 and calls for the dish to be eaten with gravy. This fits in nicely with the Raj origin theory: all the we-Brits-invented-it nonsense works on the assumption that a dry Scotch Egg was the original. But as that early recipe proves, it started out as a gravy dish.

But where in India did the British find the original Scotch Egg/Nargisi Kofta?

One view is that it is a Hyderabadi dish, but I have met chefs from Lucknow who say that it is part of their tradition. And let's not forget that kofta is a Middle Eastern word. So my guess is that some enterprising Indian chef in the middle ages was experimenting with a new kind of kofta curry when he came up with this dish.

It could have been invented in north India and then travelled to Hyderabad, or the journey could have taken the reverse direction. Either way, it is hard to find a good Nargisi Kofta in either Lucknow or Hyderabad these days.

When the food writer Anissa Helou was researching for her masterly *Feast: The Food of the Islamic World*, I had dinner with her at the Maurya in Delhi. Though she enjoyed the Dum Pukht biryani, she told Ghulam Qureshi, the chef, that she had searched in vain for a good Nargisi Kofta in India.

Ghulam wandered off and then, towards the end of our meal, he returned with a plate of Nargisi Koftas. They were outstanding. Anissa loved them, and a recipe for Nargisi Koftas (and this story) ended up in *Feast*.

Long after Anissa had departed, I phoned Dum Pukht and asked Ghulam if he could make some Nargisi Kofta for dinner. And he was kind enough to do so. But this time he made the original dish: a curry.

This was the classic version, he explained. The last time around, he didn't have the keema required to make the koftas so he had used the mixture that goes into Kakori kebabs instead.

I am nobody to argue with one of the country's best Avadhi chefs but while his gravy version was terrific, I much preferred the improvised Kakori-mince version.

Ghulam's Nargisi Kofta is not on the Dum Pukht menu yet but he is working on putting the dish on his tasting menu. Let's see which version he goes with.

Sadly, even Manish Mehrotra has taken his modern Nargisi Kofta off the Indian Accent menu. Influenced perhaps by the Scotch Egg revival in the UK, Manish tried to create a kofta in which the yolk stayed runny. He poached the egg, threw away the white and put the yolk in the centre of the kofta.

Then, he found he had a problem. In the time it took to cook the mutton mince, the yolk solidified. So Manish decided to use chicken mince, which cooks much faster and lets the yolk stay runny. The dish was a great hit in its time, but Manish has now moved on.

Much of Manish's food has its roots in humble dishes that he modernizes and upgrades (the famous Daulat Ki Chaat, for example). Ghulam's food, on the other hand, is largely faithful to the Avadhi court cuisine tradition. But that's the beauty of the Nargisi Kofta. It works brilliantly as both a modern and a traditional dish. It is a true Indian classic.

As for the British Scotch Egg—they can keep it. We much prefer the original.

Spices

The
Spice Route

≈

Pepper—indigenous to India—is the original Indian spice and the basis of the hotness of authentic Indian cuisine.

There is one remarkable thing about pepper. And there's one very confusing thing about it. The remarkable thing first: hard as it is to imagine Indian food without chilli, the truth is that chillies were only introduced by the Europeans after the discovery of the New World. There are various theories about how chilli got here but the most commonly accepted version gives credit to the Portuguese (who also took it to their African colonies) though quite how Indians so readily accepted an essentially colonial food has never been satisfactorily explained.

So what did we do before the white man gave us the chilli? How did Indian food get its fiery hotness? Or did we eat a bland cuisine that we suddenly spiced up thanks to an American vegetable?

Judging by ancient texts, Indian food was always spicy. Accounts left behind by the first Europeans to reach our shores speak of the tongue-tingling spiciness of Indian food. But if there were no chillies, how did we introduce a teekha flavour to our cuisine?

The answer: pepper.

Even now if you try some of the south Indian curries that rely on black pepper for flavour, you realize that it can add a fiery hotness that is quite different from the teekha flavour of the chilli family.

135

Thus pepper—indigenous to India and not carried over two oceans from the New World—is the original Indian spice and the basis of the hotness of authentic Indian cuisine.

That's the remarkable thing about pepper.

The confusing thing is the name. When the Europeans got to the New World they were introduced to the spicy fruit of the chilli plant. Because their only experience of hotness consisted of the pepper that traders used to ship to Europe from India, they immediately concluded that the chilli was also a kind of pepper.

And so, we've had the endless confusion caused by two completely different kinds of peppers, neither of which has anything to do with the other.

For the record, the chilli plant and its relative give us the paprika, the green pepper, the yellow pepper, the pimento, the poblano, the jalapeño, the bird chilli and nearly every other kind of chilli that you can think of. Though these peppers tend to vary in hotness from the blandness of the yellow pepper to the fiery heat of the bird chilli, they are all recognizably part of the same family.

On the other hand, the vine that gives us whole peppercorns is completely unrelated to the chilli pepper family. You find it growing wild all over south India and the peppers of Kerala are justly famous throughout the world. Unfortunately, because we've all sold ourselves to the chilli pepper, we tend to ignore the solid and subtle flavours of true Indian pepper. Rarely will we use it to spice up a curry. Nor will most of us use fresh peppercorns as a seasoning in the way that the Thais do. And there are few classic Indian dishes that depend on pepper, unlike, say, the steak au poivre of classic French cooking.

Sadly, even though we grow the world's best pepper, we act as though it is no more than a Western-style seasoning to be sprinkled on our fried eggs along with a little salt.

And even then, most of us tend to use pre-packaged black pepper, which often has the dull taste of adulterated sawdust. (Because we have no sense of the true taste of pepper, it is not uncommon for unscrupulous traders to mix powdered date stones with pepper.)

The point of the pepper is that the flavour begins to deteriorate the moment you grind the peppercorn. Nevertheless, we are quite content to use ready-made pepper, which was probably ground several months before it came to our table.

In fact, it is the easiest thing in the world to grind pepper. All you need is a pepper mill, which is not expensive and is easy to find. As for the raw material, whole peppercorns of an astonishingly high quality are freely available in our markets. Ideally, you should fill your mill with whole peppercorns and grind the pepper over your food as you eat or as you cook. The difference in flavour is so astonishing that you begin to wonder why you never bothered to do this earlier.

There are different kinds of pepper; so you need to be sure of what you're getting. The best known is black pepper, which consists of the dried, shrivelled berries of the vine. The berries are picked before they are fully ripe and are then left out in the sun to dry for a couple of days. The black colour comes from the drying process.

Whole peppercorns are an important ingredient in many Indian dishes (chicken Chettinad, a south Indian curry that you will find on many menus, is based around whole black pepper). And should you decide to use the whole peppercorn for cooking, your best bets are the great peppers of south India: Tellicherry or Malabar black.

Even if you want ground pepper to season a dish, stick to one of the better grades. But remember that the point of black pepper is that it should release a fresh aroma when you grind it and it should manage to taste both fresh and, well, peppery in your mouth.

Less common is white pepper. This is the same thing, from the same vines, but the berries are not picked till they are fully ripe. The husks are removed and it is sun-dried for a little while.

In Western cuisine, white pepper is used largely for its appearance. It is added to sauces where specks of black pepper might seem unaesthetic. But it has a distinct flavour of its own. I find it less warm and slightly less spicy than black pepper.

If you've eaten an authentic Thai meal, you've probably come across fresh green peppercorns. These are the under-ripe berries and are picked when they are still green. In Thailand, you find little branches with the berries still on them at greengroceries and you are expected to add them whole to curries and stir-fries. They add a completely different flavour. There is the distinctive taste of pepper, but there is also the fresh tang of chlorophyll.

There's no reason why we shouldn't be able to get these in our shops, but I have rarely seen green peppercorns on sale.

Two other kinds of peppercorn also exist. In Provence, they pride themselves on their pink peppercorns, which are much used to flavour fish dishes. Though they look right, they taste all wrong without the hot tang of black pepper. There is a good reason for this: they are not peppercorns at all. They are berries of another tree and only look like pepper.

The other kind of false peppercorn is the so-called Sichuan pepper. Sichuan restaurants in most of the world (but not in India where we prefer chilli powder) use the local peppercorn to add hotness to the food.

I am sure there are compelling reasons for loving the Sichuan peppercorn—millions of Chinese cannot all be wrong—but I have to say that I am not a fan. The chief effect of the Sichuan pepper is to fool you. When you bite into it, nothing happens for a few seconds and you wonder what the fuss is about. Then the flavour suddenly overwhelms your mouth with a strong sense of menthol so that it puckers up everything that it comes in contact with. By the time you've had your second peppercorn, your mouth will be so numb and puckered that you won't be able to taste anything at all. Chinese people think that this is a wonderful sensation, but I'm not so sure.

My view is that we are best off if we stick with our local pepper. Avoid the Provencal and Sichuan versions and go out and buy lots of black peppercorns. If you don't have a pepper mill at home, grind it like a masala with a mortar and pestle. Sprinkle the freshly ground pepper on practically anything: on creamy scrambled eggs, on a thickly buttered toast or a lightly fried fillet of fish. Almost from the time the subtle aroma assaults your nostrils and even before the taste reaches your tongue, you will realize what the fuss is about.

After all, long before the misguided Christopher Columbus turned up in America and thought it was India, traders had carried the peppercorns of Malabar and Tellicherry across the oceans. In the great cities of Europe, these peppercorns had commanded roughly the sort of prices and esteem that black truffles command these days. When the East India Company first set sail for our shores, pepper was one of the riches of India that the Brits so eagerly lusted after.

What a shame then that we should have lost sight of one of our country's great treasures. And what a shame that we should be content with the nasty, pre-packaged, pre-ground, polythene-packed version.

It's time to bite into the spice that made India famous.

Some Like It Hot

≈

All of us have different levels of chilli tolerance: Some people (like Europeans) can only take bland food. But others, like many Indians, enjoy their food only when it's spiced with chillies.

How can you tell if there is too much chilli in the food? Hard to say because all of us have different levels of chilli tolerance. But I find that as a general rule, it always pays to watch your scalp. If you can feel the sweat streaming out of the pores and causing your hair to limply plaster itself close to your skin, you know that the chilli level is in the higher reaches of the Richter scale. (Though, if you are interested in this sort of thing, there is actually a scale by which you measure the capsaicin level—the level of pungency of capsicums—or for that matter of any variety of chilli or pepper, and this is used to grade each chilli by its hotness quotient. It is called the Scoville scale.)

Indians have a relatively short but, nevertheless, quite complicated relationship with the chilli. It is not native to our shores. It was brought to the subcontinent by the Portuguese who knew it as a New World vegetable, found by Christopher Columbus and his men in South America. But, like residents of Portugal's African colonies (Angola, Mozambique, etc.) we quickly made the chilli our own. And though history suggests that the Aztecs and the Mayas used the chilli pepper primarily as a garnish and a vegetable (the much less hot Shimla mirch or capsicum is a member of the same family), colonial people began using it as a spice.

But because we've made the chilli a part of our cuisine for a few centuries now, we are no longer impressed by its mere hotness. The key to most good Indian food is the harmony of the spices—and, as far as we are concerned, the chilli is just one of the spices. For instance, we use Kashmiri red chillies for colour rather than taste and even Goa's peri-peri masala is far more sophisticated than the peri-peri mixes of Africa (based on the same Portuguese-introduced chilli) that emphasize the chilli over everything else.

There are Indian cuisines that make great use of the chilli—Andhra food, for example—but most Indian food (especially in north India) need not be particularly hot. In fact, we are civilized enough to offer diners the chutney–achar option so that they can add spiciness to their food should they want to.

Which is not to say that we like bland food either. Rare is the Indian who, confronted with particularly flavourless European food, will not ask if there is any Tabasco available. When we eat Chinese, we like it tangy and the condiments must always be hot; the vinegar should contain sliced chilli and chilli-garlic is now the favourite table sauce of most Indians.

Many of us will even carry our own chilli. Zubin Mehta used to carry a small gold box full of chilli powder to formal dinners in Europe and America so that he could tart up the food. Camellia Panjabi would do the same—she once caused horror and outrage at a dinner to mark the launch of *The Official Foodie Handbook* in London in the early 1980s by sprinkling red chilli over the meal, which all of Europe's great chefs had laboured to create.

All this means that the average Indian has much higher tolerance for chilli than say, the average Frenchman. (And some of us can be chilli-obsessives.) But it does not mean—as westerners sometimes believe—that we can all eat very hot food.

Speaking for myself, I am always careful to avoid the small deadly chillies (called mouse-shit chillies by the Thais in an uncharacteristic lapse of taste) that are scattered around Thai dishes in the manner of tiny time bombs. I find the new style of Sichuan cooking (now catching on in America) where much of the food is served on a bed of chillies profoundly hazardous. I will always tell an Andhra cook to go easy on the chillies. And I regard with suspicion those people who treat an ability to consume hot chillies as proof of virility. (Have you ever heard a woman say of a sweaty, chilli-sodden Lothario: 'Gosh, he's so hot?')

But that, alas, is what the whole chilli-eating phenomenon has become—in the West. It began in the Bangladeshi curry houses of England where hordes of novice Bengali cooks, fresh off the plane from Sylhet, invented a range of hot curries for English yobs. As none of the cooks had been south of Dhaka, they had no idea what Indians actually ate so they made up names of curries based on hotness: a patia (no relation to the Parsi dish of the same name) was slightly sweet; a vindaloo (no relation to the Goan dish) was hot; a Madras curry (which any self-respecting Tamil would throw up all over) was very hot; and so it went.

Over the last decade or so, Indian food in the UK has followed the class divide of Chinese food: the middle classes try to eat the real thing while the yobs treat eating a Madras curry, downing eight pints of lager and insulting the waiters as an integral part of the experience. Madras curry and vindaloo (reinvented via Bangladesh) are the sweet and sour and chop suey of Indian food.

But, with so many white people craving hot food, it was inevitable that a whole industry would grow up around the very hot chilli. And while the Brits were content to mix their chicken tikkas, vindaloos, pulao rice, fried papadoms into a single dish, the Americans wanted a more, well, American approach.

And so began the hot sauce industry. Figures tell us that salsas now outsell tomato ketchup in the US (though this is misleading because the term 'salsa' seems to cover everything that is not ketchup). There was a time when this meant such sauces as Tabasco (spicy but not terribly hot) but now chilli fanatics have created sauces that make regular salsas taste as bland as mayonnaise.

The basis of measurement for the new sauces is the Scoville scale, which measures hotness. Tabasco scores 2500 on Scoville, less than many Indian achars. The hottest chilli in the world is the Mexican Red Savino Habanero (though I have even heard similar claims for a chilli from north-east India), which scores 500,000 on Scoville. In my view, you'd have to be an idiot to eat something that hot.

But obviously there are bigger idiots. A famous American hot sauce is called Dave Insanity and is made by a man called David Hirschkop. Insane Dave's ambition (this guy appears on TV wearing a straitjacket—

seriously!) was to invent a sauce that was hotter than the Mexican Red Savino.

Dave's Insanity comes in at over a million on the Scoville scale. (Yes, the guy is nuts.)

Why, you may well ask, should anybody want to make a sauce that is so hot that it is almost impossible to eat?

Good question.

I have no bloody idea.

But consider this: the vast majority of people who consume very, very hot sauces (and the range usually begins at 500,000 on Scoville and can go up to several million) are not people with any interest in food. These are hamburger-and-fries guys (the sauces are very popular in the American Midwest and South) who like food that you can't actually taste.

My guess is that their love for hot sauces is either a virility thing ('my sauce is hotter than yours') or some kind of chemical dependency (their own explanation). Fans of really hot sauces claim that the chilli rush comes from the release of endorphins and adrenaline. Others say that they are addicted to capsaicin in the manner that junkies are addicted to heroin.

I am not convinced by the pseudo-chemical explanation. My view on eating chilli is that there are four kinds of people. Group one is those who can't take much chilli (most of the Western world.) Group two is people like you and me who can eat more chilli than the Europeans, but who like it as part of a meal. Group three is people who really enjoy chilli (my ultimate boss at the *Hindustan Times*, for instance, will eat no onion or garlic, but will add red chilli to his food) and can enjoy its flavour. And group four is the studs: the people who like Madras curries and Dave's Insanity because it makes them feel more like men. (I've never known a woman to be part of this group.) They don't care about the food. They just want to prove that they like it hot.

I've always felt sorry for the first group—Europeans who can only eat bland food are really missing out. But the ones I really feel sorry for are the ones in group four.

Get a life, guys! Don't get your kicks from a sauce bottle.

The Great
Coriander Leaf

≈

For many years I believed that kothmir was a Gujarati speciality, our little secret.

Ask any Gujarati what his favourite herb is, and after humming and hawing—'we don't use herbs in our cooking, we use spices', etc.—he'll probably admit that if Gujaratis do have a favourite herb, it is kothmir. This is not a name most people in north India will recognize because the same herb is usually referred to as dhania (or more properly, as dhania patta, to distinguish it from its seeds) in the north. But whatever name you use, there's no doubt that most Gujaratis will find it difficult to live without kothmir. We use the leaves as a garnish for many dishes, we add it to bhel for an extra zing and most often, we pound it to make fresh kothmir chutney, a staple of most Gujarati kitchens—guaranteed to enliven any meal or rotli, thepla or puri.

For many years I believed that kothmir was a Gujarati speciality, our little secret. Even when I came across the dhania patta of the north (and let's be honest, even I am not chauvinistic enough to deny that north Indians do use a fair amount of dhania), I continued to believe that only we Gujaratis actually knew what to do with kothmir.

It was only in the mid-1980s that I came to the reluctant conclusion that far from being a Gujarati secret, it was actually a very international herb. And that when most people wrote about kothmir, Gujarati cuisine rarely merited more than a footnote—if at all that.

First of all, the name kothmir is bogus. It is a corruption of the English word, coriander. It comes from the classical Greek *koris*, meaning bedbug. The ancient Greeks (and many contemporary Europeans) believed that coriander leaves smell like bedsheets infested with bedbugs. Hence the name, and hence the reluctance of Western Europe to bother with the herb.

But coriander has another name: cilantro. This is of Latin American origin and while the usual debate rages about whether it was Europeans who introduced the plant to South America or not (there's a similar controversy about oregano, but Mexican oregano is actually a member of the mint family and not the stuff Italians put on pizza), there's no doubt that Central Americans claim it as their own.

In the mid- to late 1980s, a new generation of American chefs discovered cilantro and attempted to find uses for its flavour. Some of the new dishes worked: cilantro pesto, made using cilantro rather than basil, tastes good, but Indians may think it is a poor man's version of the Gujarati kothmir chutney. Alas! American chefs are relentlessly trendy, so cilantro was quickly discarded in favour of some new flavour of the season. It survives though, in the names of restaurants.

It is a general rule of thumb that unimaginative restaurateurs use the names of vegetables and herbs for restaurants. Thus, the first Sichuan restaurants all had such names as Red Pepper. Indian restaurants try to use the variations of chilli or mirchi in their names. Thai restaurants are stuck with basil or lemon grass. Indian restaurants abroad use some variation of saffron. Italian restaurants tend to be called Olive or Pomodoro (for tomato). And Cilantro survives as an all-purpose name for multi-cuisine restaurants and coffee shops run by hoteliers who know that guests will be put off if the restaurant is called Dhania or Kothmir.

Latin American cilantro dishes rarely make it to international menus these days. When kothmir does turn up in Europe, it is as an ingredient of Portuguese cuisine. But even the Portuguese get it from their African colonies and are conscious of its ethnic origins.

It is a funny thing but as far as I can tell, rich countries don't like kothmir; they find the smell too common. But in most poor countries, it invariably becomes a favourite. You find it in India and South America, for instance. You find it in Africa. You find it in West Asia (yes, I know they are rich now but they started using the herb long before they struck oil). And you find it in much of South-east Asia but not, interestingly enough, in Japan, which has always been rich and where wealthy Japanese turn their sensitive noses up at the smell.

What the connection between kothmir and wealth is, I do not know. But it is hard to deny that it exists.

Nevertheless, no matter what you call it—kothmir, coriander, dhania, cilantro, etc.—this is a herb that adapts itself to many cuisines. In India, we use the seeds for garam masala and the leaves for a variety of other uses. But the Arabs also use coriander leaves (as flavouring and as a garnish) so freely that the herb is often called Arab parsley. In South-east Asia, it is traced back to its Chinese origins (it was probably introduced to Thailand by the Chinese, for example) and is known as Chinese parsley. In fact, coriander/cilantro/kothmir is not a kind of parsley (*Petroselinum crispum*) at all but is a plant by itself (*Coriandrum sativum*).

If I have a criticism of the way we use it in India it is that all too often we are content to use it as a garnish and miss the flavour of the leaves or the texture of the stalks. Many years ago, at a Chinese restaurant in Bangkok (called, I think, Water 1999—but it was a long time ago), I had an amazing dish of beef with kothmir stalks. Because there were so many crunchy, stir-fried stalks, the flavour of the kothmir enveloped the pieces of beef and showed me what could be done with the herb if we used it as more than a mere garnish.

I've never found the dish again but I make my own variation, using beef, lean pork or good lamb. You need to cut the meat into thin strips as you would for any Chinese dish. And you need a mountain of cilantro stalks.

My recipe is very basic. Stir-fry finely chopped shallots and garlic over high heat. When they begin to turn opaque, add the meat/pork/ whatever and cook quickly for a few minutes. (The exact time will depend on the level of the heat and the size and the quality of the meat.) Towards the end of this process, add a little light soya, an equal amount of dark soya and a dash of nam pla. When the dish seems to have about a minute or so to go, add the stalks and stir vigorously. Then, put off the gas, cover the pan and wait for another three minutes for the kothmir flavour to permeate the meat. Serve with rice. (If you need more gravy, you can add a little stock when you add the soya sauce.)

I'm sure that the original dish had a far more sophisticated recipe but my simple version has the advantage of ensuring that no other flavours interfere with the kothmir.

Of course, most Gujaratis would faint if they learnt that one of the best ways of enjoying the unique flavour of kothmir is to cook it with meat. In north India, we do use it with meat but it is rarely more than a garnish. Only the Thais know how to use its flavour to enliven fish soups and curry pastes.

Nevertheless, there are many vegetarian recipes too. When I get too many olives in gift hampers, for instance, I put masses of them along with fistfuls of kothmir, handfuls of garlic, hefty doses of Tabasco and a spoonful of sugar into the food processor and blend like crazy. The puree that results makes a perfect sandwich spread and can be used as the basis of a good vegetarian, masaledaar (and thus, inauthentic) pasta sauce.

Healthy Haldi

≈

The haldi fad has been raging in the West for a while, but the only person who really benefits from that turmeric latte is the guy who makes money selling it to you.

Who would have thought that one day haldi would rule the Western world? It is now much more than just the yellow stuff we use to add colour and flavour to our food. It is a global craze, much sought after because of its alleged properties as a super food or miracle spice.

So you have turmeric lattes, turmeric teas, turmeric cookies, turmeric cold-pressed juices, turmeric shakes, turmeric spreads and God alone knows what else.

And what is turmeric supposed to do?

Well, it improves your memory. It lightens your mood. It makes your skin glow. It helps you live longer. It fights arthritis. It can delay the onset of diabetes. It can protect you from cancer. It detoxifies your liver.

The list goes on and on. The only claim not made so far is that it improves your sex life. But I am sure that is coming too.

The turmeric fad has been raging in the West for about four years now and I reckon it has spread to the rest of the world by now. As is true of all such fads, it is hard to tell where it began or how. But it follows the standard pattern of all health fads.

1. Somebody starts throwing health data around and quoting so-called scientific studies to 'prove' that a particular food has miraculous properties.

147

2. Health freaks, and what I call the 'goji-berry set' (people who like to think they have discovered ancient remedies that modern medicine has suppressed), start talking to each other about the miracle ingredient.

3. The fad spreads from those who stock their larders with chia seeds and other such nonsense to the public. Suddenly, everyone begins serving some kind of product based on the alleged super food.

4. The ordinary person, outside the goji-berry set, hears about the so-called miracle herb/food/spice and starts subscribing to the fad. By this stage, it is no longer necessary to explain why the super food is so super. A herd mentality takes over. If everybody says it is so wonderful, well, it must be!

5. The fad fades. A new super food is discovered, and a new fad begins.

At present, we are at stage four where the herd mentality has set in. The advocates of turmeric no longer need to explain why it is supposed to be so good for you. All they have to do is invoke the Mystic East, talk about Ayurveda and the Indian connection.

However, this approach does not work that well in the actual Mystic East because we don't regard haldi as a strange and formerly unknown magic ingredient. We have grown up eating it. We know that it is often used in Ayurveda. But Indians recognize that Ayurveda makes use of most herbs and spices in one way or another. So we don't treat any one spice as a super food.

Moreover, the Indian Ayurvedic tradition is more scientific than the American fad tradition. So we know that certain herbs are used to treat specific ailments or conditions. There are no works-for-everything super foods or magic spices.

As Marryam Reshii tells us in *The Flavour of Spice*, turmeric is the most elemental of Indian spices, and, yes, it is truly Indian, being native to south India. It has now spread all over the world, but India is its main producer, growing 80 per cent of the world's turmeric. Not only is it used in Ayurveda (it is believed to have antiseptic properties), but it is also regarded as auspicious by Hindus.

Oddly enough, Muslims in north India do not use turmeric as much. Reshii points out that turmeric hardly turns up in Avadhi cooking, and when it does, it is used mainly for its colour. Kashmiri Muslims, on the other hand, use a lot of turmeric both for reasons of taste and health.

Our view of haldi's benefits differs from the West's and is more limited. We value it, but we do not ascribe miraculous properties to it. The American turmeric fad is based on scientific research allegedly carried out on turmeric. This can sound convincing till you realize that the scientists were not really testing turmeric. They were testing and researching curcumin, a compound found in turmeric.

Many of the claims made for curcumin are not without a foundation. It does contain antioxidants and anti-inflammatory properties. And there is some research that suggests that people with Alzheimer's disease can benefit from curcumin.

But there are many problems with the 'curcumin is good for you, so you must have a turmeric latte' school of fad medicine.

Firstly, curcumin is remarkably hard for our bodies to absorb. We can use only 25 per cent of what we consume.

Secondly, turmeric is not the same as curcumin. Yes, it does contain curcumin. But only 3 per cent of turmeric is curcumin; 97 per cent is composed of other things.

When you consider that only 3 per cent of turmeric is curcumin and that you will only absorb about 25 per cent of the curcumin you consume, you begin to wonder about the logic behind this fad.

How much haldi do you need to eat to get the benefit of curcumin? And aren't there more efficient ways of finding the antioxidants you need?

These are questions that are never asked, let alone answered, by health faddists.

Basically, Ayurveda had it right. Haldi is good for you. But, no, it is by no means an all-purpose super food.

The curcumin fallacy should remind us of the dangers of believing all the fad health reporting you may read. Faddists will nearly always lie (or not know the truth) about the food they are promoting. They will pretend that turmeric was unknown in America till they discovered it. In fact, the food industry there has long used turmeric as a colourant. The colour of the mustard sauce you see on a hot dog comes from turmeric. But nobody who has eaten a lot of hot dogs has felt healthier because of all that turmeric!

And then there is the quantity con. Faddists will deliberately confuse a small amount of a beneficial ingredient found in a food with the food itself. Let's take chocolate for example. I like dark chocolate and I eat a little nearly every single day. But I eat it because I like the taste, not because it is good for my health.

However, over the last two decades, we have been bombarded with reporting that tells us how chocolate is good for our bodies. Eat some chocolate, we are told, and you will avoid getting a heart attack.

The chocolate-is-good-for-you campaign is based on the effects of chemicals called flavanols. Research suggests that flavanols are linked to reductions in blood pressure. Other research suggests that flavanols possibly improve insulin sensitivity and help with your lipid profile.

There are problems with some of the studies from which this research is derived—they might have been funded by the chocolate industry—but all the reporting misses out on one vital distinction. These health benefits don't come from chocolate. Even if the studies are right, what is being studied is flavanol. Not chocolate.

And yes, flavanol may indeed help with blood circulation. Except that chocolate is not all flavanol. In fact, flavanol is not even the main constituent of chocolate.

The Observer (London) looked at the studies and discovered that the amount of chocolate you would have to consume to get the benefits of flavanol is massive. 'For example, the blood pressure study involved participants getting an average of 670 mg of flavanols. Someone would need to consume about twelve standard bars of dark chocolate or about fifty bars of milk chocolate every day to get that much,' the paper reported.

It is the same curcumin fallacy at work again. Yes, there are many compounds that might be good for us—curcumin and flavanols, for example—but we should never be misled into confusing them with actual foods as they contain too little of the beneficial compounds to make any difference.

One study, for instance, showed that there might even be more flavanols in salami than in chocolate. But you don't see anyone advising you to eat salami to live longer.

Whenever people talk about super foods, just use common sense. Do you know any particularly healthy people who subsist on a diet of chocolate cake? Are Indians, who have grown up on turmeric, the healthiest people in the world?

The answers are self-evident. So throw out those goji berries, chia seeds and all the other so-called super foods. And live a little.

The Secret Ingredient

≈

Dishes like pilaus may have come to us from West Asia, but it was India's spice magic that raised them to another level.

Many years ago, I wrote that some of the food of Central Asia and the Middle East was a rough draft for Indian cuisine.

This led to (understandable) outrage and claims that I had ignored the contribution of foreign visitors to our cuisine.

What about kebabs? I was asked. Weren't they a Middle Eastern invention? What about the samosa?

Arabs brought it to India and variations of the original samosa (under such names as sambusak) can still be found all over West Asia.

And then there was the big one: pilaus.

Didn't I realize that the first pilaus came from Turkey and other Middle Eastern countries? Why was I going on and on about biryani's Indian flavours when it was clear that the dish came to India with Arab armies? And so on.

My answer has always been that while I have huge respect for the cuisines of West Asia, they have always struck me as lacking the depth of Indian cuisines. (Yes, yes, I concede that I haven't travelled through the whole of the Middle East and that, as an Indian, I am not exactly an unbiased or disinterested observer.)

I do not dispute that samosas, kebabs and pilaus came to India from the Middle East. (Though biryani, I think, was our own creation.) But I

151

believe that these dishes were raised to the next level of complexity and sophistication because of India's secret ingredient: spice.

Any Indian who eats a Middle Eastern kebab or pilau will find it bland and unsophisticated because it will not have the complicated spice flavours that are the hallmark of good Indian food. My view is that yes, these dishes came to us from West Asia but it was India's spice magic that raised them to another level entirely.

Great Indian food is all about spices. Do you know of any other country where so many of the great chefs will refuse to part with the secret spice mixture that goes into each dish?

It's not just kebabs and pilaus. Go to any traditional restaurant anywhere in India and you will never be able to get the chefs to reveal what the exact proportion of masalas is. When fancy restaurants hire traditional chefs, they are shocked to discover that the chefs will make their masala mixes at home and will come to the kitchen with little packets of ready-made spice mixes.

Nor is this restricted to north Indian food. I once shot a TV programme at Muthu's Curry, the famous fish-head curry restaurant in Singapore. It turned out that only a few members of the founding family knew the exact proportion of masalas that went into the curry. Each morning, a family member would come and make the curry masala in secret. The cooks would have to use that masala and would never learn what it was that made the famous curry so special.

Take away the spices and most Indian food loses its distinctive identity. The reason why a Turkish pilau pales before a Lucknawi pilau is that the man who made the Lucknawi dish used spices. Compare any minced-meat kebab from the Middle East to a shami kebab (let alone a galouti or a Kakori) and the Indian kebab will always have a more complex taste because the Indian kebabchi has used complex spicing.

Many people in the Middle East (and the West) disagree violently with me. Some suggest that I am making too much of the spice factor. If a pilau has meat and rice, surely it is the same dish everywhere, even if the Indian version has a little more spice, they argue.

So I was relieved to meet up with Ganesh Bagler who has spent many years researching the science of Indian food along with many enthusiastic and gifted students and collaborators.

'It is the flavour molecules that determine the taste. And the spice mixes in our kebabs and pilaus are uniquely Indian,' he says.

Bagler specializes in flavour molecules. This is an area of great interest to the food industry, though not one that interests most chefs. But the chefs who have studied it (such as Heston Blumenthal) have come to some interesting conclusions.

When we taste, say, a strawberry, we actually taste hundreds of different flavour compounds that combine to give the strawberry its characteristic taste. This fascinates the food industry, which tries to isolate the molecules that make up these compounds. Then it merges many of these molecules in a lab to create the strawberry flavour that goes into, say, your strawberry ice cream.

Some of these molecules are at the heart of what we regard as strawberry flavour. For instance, if you mix ethyl butyrate, cis-3-hexenol, furaneol and gamma-decalactone, these four molecules will give you the essence of a strawberry taste even though a real strawberry has many more flavour molecules. (OK. No more technical stuff after this, I promise.)

All ingredients can be broken down into flavour molecules. Research suggests that most Western recipes combine ingredients that contain common flavour molecules. For instance, asparagus and butter go well together because they share many flavour molecules.

Often these similarities extend to ingredients that would appear to have nothing in common. Modern chefs make dishes that mix strong blue cheese with chocolate, a combination that sounds wrong at an intuitive level. In fact, the two ingredients share seventy-three flavour molecules and work well together. A more famous example is white chocolate with caviar, which sounds bizarre. But Heston Blumenthal, who found that the two paired well, had them analysed and discovered that they had many flavour molecules in common.

We know, thanks to the work of Yong-Yeol Ahn at Harvard University, that while Western recipes are based on combining ingredients with similar (or the same) flavour molecules, East Asian cuisine is the exact opposite. In Korea and Thailand, for instance, recipes focus on combining ingredients that have few (if any) flavour molecules in common. It is the contrasting flavours that make the cuisine so distinctive.

As far as I knew, nobody had done similar work in India. But Bagler has followed roughly the same methodology as the Harvard team and has analysed Indian recipes. He has come to several interesting conclusions.

The first is that Indian recipes do not follow the Western pattern. We choose ingredients that do not share flavour molecules.

Secondly, if you were to list out the ingredients that determine flavour, there are many regional variations in India. But one thing is common across the subcontinent. The key determinants of flavour (like the four molecules that give the strawberry its essential taste) are spices. Even a tiny bit of spice will determine how a dish can taste. Take away the little dash of spice and keep all the other ingredients intact, and the dish will taste totally different.

Here at last is scientific proof of what I have long believed at an intuitive level: Indian food is about spices. The quantity of masala in a pilau may be one-fiftieth of the quantity of rice. But the dish gets its distinctive flavour from the spice.

The Harvard team led by Ahn concluded that a few foods become the key signatures of a cuisine. In North America, these include dairy (milk, butter, cream), eggs and wheat. In Korea, they are ingredients like beef, ginger, pork, onion, soya sauce and rice.

Bagler says that in India these key ingredients would just be spices. No matter which regional cuisine he studied, spice (to varying degrees) became the defining factor.

Which takes us back to the origins of pilau and kebab. When we say that the basic ingredients of the Middle Eastern kebabs and the Indian versions are broadly similar, we are right. But that, as research has now conclusively demonstrated, is not the key determinant of taste.

It is the flavour molecules that determine the taste. And the spice mixes in our kebabs and pilaus are uniquely Indian.

But I wish I knew more about the flavour molecules in Middle Eastern food. Does the cuisine—like Western food—rely on recipes that combine ingredients with the same flavour molecules? Or is it like Indian food where the opposite is true? The Middle East has its own herbs and spices. How important are those flavour compounds to the final taste? I looked at the research but found nothing about Middle Eastern food.

But, thanks to Bagler, we do have research about Indian food. And it tells us that there is no Indian food without spices.

And once our spices take over, all dishes, no matter where they originally came from, become distinctively Indian.

The Lassan Lesson

≈

Some people like the smell of garlic; others don't. And it won't necessarily make you sexier or healthier. But if you eat it for the taste alone, you'll certainly eat better.

As you have already read, there is a scale that measures the hotness of chillies. And many fans of the chilli pride themselves on the extent to which they can eat hot chillies without collapsing. My friend, the late Sabina Saigal Saikia, for instance, could consume the hottest of chillies and still smile while the rest of us would be looking for water, Coke, ice cream, anything, to put out the fires in our mouths.

But is there a similar scale for garlic? I ask because I'm pretty sure that if such a measure existed, I would be to garlic what Sabina was to chillies.

Some people complain about too much garlic. I always wonder what they mean. As far as I am concerned, there is no such thing as too much garlic. I have never encountered a dish that has been spoilt by the addition of more garlic, and while I concede that garlic has such a powerful taste that it can mask most other flavours, I have to say that, on balance, I would take garlic over all the other flavours.

In Europe, they associate garlic with the French, whom the English always describe as reeking of garlic. But any Indian who saw how much

155

garlic the French actually used would be astonished by their moderation. The French idea of flavouring with garlic is to rub a clove around a salad bowl before making the salad. Most Indians wouldn't even taste a garlic flavour that was so subtle.

In my view, the French get too much credit. The only people who really understand garlic and know how to use it are Indians.

Consider our cooking. It's hard to conceive of even the most basic Indian dish without the flavour of onions and garlic. When we make chutneys, we look for garlic: the classic chutney of Gujarati cooking, for instance, is lassan ki chutney, which is nothing more than a concentrated dose of garlic. Indians think nothing of eating garlic pickle and chomping on the whole cloves. When we go to so-called Chinese restaurants we like ordering prawns in garlic sauce or any other dish that is redolent with the flavour of garlic.

Small wonder then that India is the world's second-largest producer of garlic after China and while the Chinese export a fair amount of their crop (to India, among other places), we like to consume most of our garlic ourselves.

But we don't make a fetish of garlic. It always intrigues me how people in the West treat a love of garlic as a dangerous perversion on a par with sadomasochism or bondage. There's a restaurant in London's Soho called Garlic and Shots, which is frequented by strangely dressed people in chains and leather trousers. The food itself is rubbish, but the restaurant gets by because it goes on and on about how it puts garlic in everything. There are garlic cocktails, garlic fish, garlic meat, garlic sauce, etc. I doubt very much if anyone actually likes the food, but the idea of eating so much garlic seems to give white people a decidedly sexual thrill.

Actually, that's not so odd. Even within the Indian tradition, garlic is associated with the creation of heat and passion in the body, which I suppose is an old-fashioned way of saying that it is a bit of an aphrodisiac. Conservative Hindus will not eat garlic and all good Jains are forbidden to eat it. (As you may have guessed, I'm a very bad Jain.)

Having lived on garlic for much of my life, I can state with authority that reports of its effects on potency and desire are vastly overrated. All it does is make you smell of garlic for several hours afterwards. Some people like the smell (I certainly do) but others don't. Nevertheless, there is no way of avoiding the garlic odour, no matter what you try. Garlic is excreted by the body through the breath and the skin; so even a strong mouthwash will make only a marginal difference.

Some foods go better with garlic than others. I find that most salad vegetables and barely cooked fish improve with the addition of garlic. The French have known this for a long time and one of their most inspired inventions is aioli, a garlic mayonnaise. You may even use it as a dip for crudités, but it goes well with a simple dish of boiled prawns. You dunk the prawns in the aioli till their cool, firm flesh is soaked with the flavour of garlic and then pop them into your mouth.

Cooked vegetables also improve with garlic. Sauté mushrooms with onions, and the flavour will be nice. But add garlic and suddenly, the dish will come alive. I don't know why more people don't use garlic with potatoes: the flavours are made for each other. Similarly, asparagus improves with a garlic-flavoured olive oil.

Italians use garlic almost as much as the French do. One of the classic pasta dishes of Italian cooking is spaghetti aglio e olio, which is spaghetti simply cooked with olive oil and chopped garlic. In India, we like to add a little chilli as well (in which case the dish becomes spaghetti aglis olio e peperoncino) but most Indian taste buds are so immune to the flavour of garlic that we need to add much more garlic than Italians would regard as necessary. One of my friends, a princess, has the rare distinction of having sent back the spaghetti aglio e olio at nearly every Italian restaurant she has ever eaten at, on the grounds that there wasn't enough garlic. Now, when I order the dish for her, I tell the chef, 'Put the most excessive quantity of garlic that you can think of. And then, when you have done that once, do it all over again.'

Oriental cuisine always seems to me to rely less on garlic than our own food. The Chinese use garlic but do not accord it the almost mythic status that we do. The Thais use such a complex mixture of fresh herbs in their cooking that they are reluctant to let a single flavour such as garlic overwhelm the dish. Even so, one of the best dishes you can get on the streets of Bangkok consists of small prawns, freshly shelled and fried very quickly with lots of garlic. Like the French, the Thais know garlic and prawns are old friends and make the most of the combination.

You will often hear about the medicinal properties of garlic. In one version of the Ramayana, Kaikeyi got around Dasharath by giving him a garlic-based medicine that killed the parasites in his stomach. And in most schools of ancient medicine, garlic crops up in some form or the other.

Even modern medicine has been known to recognize that garlic can be useful in the prevention of heart disease. Recent research on the subject however is somewhat contradictory; so I would be wary of popping those garlic capsules on the grounds of good health.

But garlic is so strong that cultural traditions usually imbue it with mythical powers. For instance, it is said that vampires are put off by the smell of garlic, a useful tip to remember should you ever find yourself having dinner with Count Dracula.

My view, however, is that if you eat garlic because of medicine or myth, you are doing yourself a grave injustice. Eat it for the taste alone. It is one of the world's great flavours—better even than, say, white truffle—and it is widely available at the cheapest possible cost.

Sadly, because it is so common, we tend to take it for granted. So, the next time you step into the kitchen, look closely at that clove of garlic. Should you just be chopping it up or pulverizing it as part of some masala? Isn't that a waste of such a great taste?

Think creatively with garlic. It won't necessarily make you sexier or healthier. But you'll certainly eat better.

Vanilla Twilight

≈

Real vanilla is the product of an exotic orchid that has travelled the world, mated with bees, but has only come into its own when human beings decided that each flower needed a little loving attention. How many other spices can we say that about?

If you've been reading my work for a while, you will know that one of my favourite tastes and scents is vanilla. Most of us have grown up on a diet of synthetic vanilla—extracted from wood pulp—which is used in most Indian kitchens and ice-cream factories instead of the real thing.

Over the last decade, however, the flavour of synthetic vanilla has fallen into disrepute all over the world. And, at least in the West, there is an increasing demand for the genuine article, the fruit of a South American orchid that goes by the botanical term *Vanilla planifolia*. In India too more and more chefs will use vanilla pods in preference to the synthetic extract, and upmarket ice cream (Baskin Robbins for instance) will be made from the pod and not the wood pulp derivative.

The craze for real vanilla has many consequences. One surprising byproduct has been the rediscovery of vanilla as a fragrance. Perfumers have always used vanilla in their fragrances, but only in the 1990s did the cosmetics industry make so much money by selling products that solely smell of vanilla. Now, vanilla soap, vanilla body lotion, vanilla eau de toilette, vanilla room fragrance and even vanilla deodorant (you can just imagine the ad line: 'armpits so good you want to eat them!') dominate the shelves of any upmarket perfumery.

159

Even the taste of vanilla has found expression in new media. The old vanilla-flavoured vodkas met with limited success until Absolut launched Vanilla, its premium vodka, along with massive publicity on the TV show *Sex and the City*. Since then vanilla vodka has become an important ingredient in many cocktails. Oddly enough, few people seem to have tried to match the taste of whisky and vanilla, though I suspect they will go together well.

There is a precedent for this. Often when you taste a wine (usually a New World variety), you will sense a woody flavour. There's a reason for this. Many wine makers like their products to take on the flavour of the barrels in which they're aged. Others are more unscrupulous and simply add oak chips to the wine as it is ageing. Whatever the reason, wine tasters describe the oaky flavour as having 'vanilla notes'. At first, I thought this was mere pretension. Then I read that vanillin, the principal constituent of synthetic vanilla, comes from wood. And when wine is exposed to wood for a long time (in a barrel, say) some vanillin is produced.

If you take the line that vanilla and wine go well together, surely, it's not much of a stretch to imagine that a good wood-aged whisky would combine nicely with a dash of vanilla flavour.

All this makes the term 'plain vanilla', much favoured by writers of business books, seem utterly redundant. 'Plain vanilla' is used to refer to something that is basic and, therefore, bland and boring. The geniuses who write the business books then tell you how to make life more interesting and profitable by going beyond the 'plain vanilla' version. I imagine that the allusion is to the ice-cream parlours of their childhood where vanilla was the basic flavour. The young geniuses probably ordered butterscotch and rum-and-raisin while sneering at simple vanilla. Perhaps the sneers were justified in an era of synthetic wood-pulp vanilla. But these days good vanilla pods are so expensive and so carefully sourced that they are much harder to procure than, say, rum-and-raisins or butterscotch flavouring.

One of the tragedies of the 'plain vanilla' mindset is that we forget the adventurous origins of true vanilla. Most people don't even know that it comes from an old orchid. The plant is unusual in that it gives off none of that special vanilla aroma. You can be surrounded by thousands of vanilla plants and never think of ice cream. The flavour we call vanilla only emerges after the pod (from the fruit which follows the flower) is dried in the sun.

So how did human beings realize that this particular orchid had hidden reserves of flavour that were only available to those who treated the pods in a certain way?

We don't know.

There are few accurate historical records. As far as the Western world is concerned, the history of vanilla begins when the Spaniards arrived in South America as conquerors. The local people served them a drink made with chocolate (which Europeans had never tasted before) and vanilla. They loved both the tastes and took them back to Europe. Eventually, they discovered the secrets of cultivating both plants, but vanilla posed a special kind of problem.

In the nineteenth century, it was still regarded as absurd that plants could have any kind of sex life. The general view was that all you had to do was dig up a field, thrust in a sapling, water it and then watch it grow. The sapling would turn into a bush or a tree and fruit would be a natural consequence.

In most cases this did work but nobody realized what the reason was. The notion of pollination was largely unknown, and botanists of that era were unaware of the importance of bees and other flying insects in pollinating plants. When flowers were pollinated, fruits resulted. Without pollination, there were no fruits.

Botanists planted the vanilla orchid all over Europe in the nineteenth century but rarely did the flower turn into the fruit. And without the fruit you got no pod and thus none of the vanilla fragrance. The French, who had studied the vanilla plant in South America, decided that a certain kind of bee probably had something to do with the process of producing the fruit.

Eventually, as such scientists as Charles Darwin explained the relationship between insects and plant reproduction, the French worked out that the bee was the key.

Early attempts at vanilla cultivation in the French colonies of Réunion and Bourbon failed even though enterprising botanists tried to introduce South American bees to the plantation. Occasionally, the plants would be pollinated, but sometimes it would be by other local insects. Colonists who had planted vanilla elsewhere—the Spanish in the Philippines, the

British in India, the Dutch in Java—came to the reluctant conclusion that the odd plant would bear fruit, but commercial cultivation was an impossibility outside of Mexico.

That all of us have access to real vanilla today is entirely because of the efforts of a young slave called Edmond who worked in a plantation in Réunion. According to legend, his owner Ferréol Bellier-Beaumont was surprised one day when he found two fruits growing on a solitary vanilla vine in his plantation. He asked Edmond if he knew how this had happened.

The slave said that he had done it. He claimed that he had fertilized the orchid himself. The planter was sceptical but two days later, another vine began to show signs of bearing fruit. According to Tim Ecott in his book *Vanilla*, the planter 'demanded an explanation, and as there were other flowers on the vine, the boy proceeded to peel back the lip of the small orchid with his thumb and with the aid of a small stick lift the rostellum out of the way and press the anther and stigmatic surfaces together'.

Edmond continued to pollinate other vines on the island and soon Réunion was full of vanilla fruit. Edmond's discovery spread far and wide and to this day, this is how the vanilla flower is pollinated throughout the world. The disadvantage is that this process is labour-intensive (each vanilla pod is the result—in effect—of a sexual act between a farmer and a flower) but the advantage is that virtually anybody can do this. Consequently, vanilla cultivation picked up and the plant was soon being grown all over the world. South America lost its monopoly and the troublesome bees went out of business.

The real vanilla boom of the last decade has led to a growth in vanilla cultivation. These days if you travel through Kerala you will find that the traditional spice cultivators will, once you have smelled their cloves and tried their cardamom, persuade you to buy a few dried sticks of vanilla. They don't always find that many takers—after all, which of us uses a vanilla pod in our kitchens? And the vagaries of the international market have meant that vanilla is not a particularly reliable crop. Some years ago, many farmers went bust when vanilla prices fell on the back of international competition. Nor is Indian vanilla the best in the world. The honour probably still goes to the stuff from the French colonial tradition of planting in Réunion, Bourbon and even Tahiti.

But life is too short for vanilla snobbery. I have very little patience with chefs who tell you that the vanilla that went into their caramel custard came from Tahiti. And it's very pretentious to declare that a bottle of mid-market liquid soap is flavoured with Bourbon vanilla. As far as I can tell, the important difference is the one between synthetic and real. I'm sure there are grades within the real pod market but frankly, which of us can tell the difference?

My view is that we should enjoy the flavour and aroma of the vanilla pod without worrying about its provenance. Remember that real vanilla is the opposite of what business nerds call 'plain vanilla'. It is the product of an exotic orchid that has travelled the world, that has mated with bees but has only come into its own when human beings decided that each flower needed a little loving attention.

How many other spices can we say that about?

Staples

Bread and Better

≈

Bread making is a minefield and most of our ideas about bread are mistaken.

Sanjay Hegde, the noted lawyer and commentator on national affairs (you've probably seen him on TV), tweeted to me some months ago about bread.

Why was it, he asked, that the pav of Mumbai was always so much better than similar pav breads in the north of India?

It is a good question. And I have no real answer, just conjectures. I have written about bread and specifically, the pav. We have no ancient baking tradition in India and no history of ovens.

So bread came to India from abroad, using two different routes. The first was through Goa. The Portuguese, who conquered the region, missed their own bread. But they found no ovens, no maida and no yeast. So what were they to do?

An ingenious Portuguese baker created the Goan version of the Portuguese pao. (That, by the way, is where our name 'pav' comes from.) Instead of maida, he used atta or wholewheat flour. Instead of yeast, he added a few drops of toddy to help the fermentation process. And because proper ovens were hard to come by, he used a simple, improvised oven with a hot surface. When the dough was fermented and ready, he shaped it into a roll (or a rectangle) and put it on the surface. It usually took between five to fifteen minutes and the pao was cooked. (Ananda Solomon, who has studied the cuisine of Goa, compares it to cooking a pizza.)

As time went on, the Portuguese went beyond the basic pao and began to bake a variety of breads in normal ovens. And even today, the many breads of Goa still correspond quite closely to the Portuguese originals.

There was a second route that bread took on its journey to India. There was no maida tradition in ancient India. All the evidence suggests that refined flour (required for more elaborate breads and pastries) came to India from the Middle East as did the oven. Even today, a surprisingly large proportion of bakeries in much of India are owned by Muslims.

The Muslim bakeries of north India eventually took to making versions of the Goan pav after it spread to Mumbai and became an integral part of that city's street food. (Think of pav-keema!) And somewhere along the way, the two traditions fused. For instance, I suspect that most pavs baked in Mumbai come from Muslim-owned bakeries and the current generation of bakers has no idea of the Portuguese origins of the bread.

But do they still make it the traditional Goan way? I wonder. Bread making has changed more dramatically over the last few decades than most of us even realize. For instance if, like me, you grew up on the basic white bread that Britannia baked and sold all over India, you probably thought that this was how bread was meant to be. Later, when you noticed that some bakers were selling 'wholewheat bread', you thought that this was just a healthy variant.

And with the recent mushrooming of smaller bakeries selling dozens of varieties of bread (sourdough, baguette, rye bread, pumpernickel, etc.), you believed that these were merely exotic variants of the normal bread you grew up on.

Well, think again. Because we didn't grow up on 'normal' bread.

It's a little hard to explain because bread making is a minefield. It is an intensely complicated subject with a variety of opinions about flour, yeast, oven temperature, etc. Nor is it easy to bake good bread. Go to any of the high-priced bakeries in our metropolitan cities and you will discover that while any fool can bake a cake, rare is the man who can bake first-rate bread.

And most of our ideas about bread are mistaken anyway.

Take the baguette, that long, slim bread that symbolizes French baking in the popular imagination. The caricature Frenchman is a guy in a Breton-striped T-shirt and a beret, with a string of onions around his neck, who rides a bicycle, holding a baguette in one hand while whistling Charles Aznavour tunes.

Except that the baguette is a relatively recent innovation.

It was born in Paris in the 1920s and took several decades to penetrate the countryside—it did not become popular in some regions till as late as the 1970s. Moreover, a baguette is not the sort of bread that households keep for eating every day. A classic baguette retains its flavour for only about half a day. You can't really eat it if you wait more than twenty-four hours after it is baked.

There are as many misconceptions about white bread. In the West, nobody with any interest in gastronomy—or any foodie, for that matter—will eat the sort of industrial white bread that we were brought up on in India. And that's not because people frown on mass production. It is because packaged bread is not made the same way as real bread—or at the very least, it is not made the same way as bread has been baked through the ages.

In 1961, the British Baking Industries Research Association, based in Chorleywood, developed a new way of making bread. This method, now known as the Chorleywood Bread Process (CBP), allowed bakers to use lower-protein wheat (cheaper) and an assortment of chemicals.

In the old days, bread was made with just wheat, water, yeast and salt. (In an artisanal bakery, it still is—hence the emphasis on the skill of the baker.) This sounds simple but in reality, it is a time-consuming and expensive process.

With Chorleywood, the dough was made ready for baking quickly and the loaf that came out of the industrial oven lasted much longer than bread baked the artisanal way. It was also half the cost of the traditional method.

There was just one problem. Chorleywood produced bread with none of the complex tastes associated with real bread because these came from a long (several hours) fermentation of the dough. Worse, the texture was soft and squishy. So, if you ate a slice of bread made the CBP way, it stuck to the roof of your mouth, like plasticine.

No matter. Chorleywood rapidly spread throughout the Commonwealth and today, something like 80 per cent of all bread sold in the UK is made that way. In the US, another industrial process that led to the creation of the Wonderloaf (and the phrase 'the greatest thing since sliced bread') was already in use. And newer processes that also use chemicals to speed up the fermentation have since evolved.

Many people object to Chorleywood because of the synthetic enzymes and chemicals it uses (remember the recent fuss over potassium bromate?). But I don't really have a problem with that.

My concern is more fundamental. Now that you can easily prepare your dough with chemicals, Indian bakers no longer bother to bake real bread. Most, or nearly all, use synthetic additives with such names as bread improver or dough conditioner. I am willing to bet (though I have no proof) that the north Indian pav that Sanjay Hegde complains about is just rubbish Chorleywood-style chemically enhanced bread shaped to look like a real pav.

Because most people don't realize that industrial bread is different from real bread, the big bread companies benefit from public ignorance. Full marks then to Britannia, who, when I asked if they used a Chorleywood-type process, answered quickly, clearly and candidly. 'While Britannia does not refer to its bread-making process as "Chorleywood Bread Process", on broad terms, the process followed for making breads at Britannia is similar to CBP,' the company said.

That's why Britannia bread lasts for five days and is relatively inexpensive. Britannia is not alone. My suspicion is that 90–95 per cent of all bread sold in the organized sector in India is made using CBP-type methods. And now, a large proportion of the bread in the unorganized sector is also Chorleywood-style or made with chemicals.

Does it matter? If you don't like real bread, probably not. But, if like Sanjay Hegde, you notice that your pav tastes wrong—yes, it does.

My ire is not directed against the Britannia/Modern Bakery kind of company that does not pretend to make artisanal bread. It's the smaller bakeries that pretend to be artisanal but still make chemical bread that annoy me. So do those hotels that charge lots of money for cheaply made industrial bread at their fancy bakeries.

Make bread any way you want. But price it according to its actual cost. And tell us whether it is real bread or chemically enhanced cheap stuff.

I think we have a right to be informed of what we are actually buying.

Singing
in the Grain

≈

Rice and wheat are passé; new grains—from quinoa to the ancient cereals of our ancestors—are the talk of the town.

What do you suppose was the staple crop of our ancestors? The only cereal mentioned in the Rig Veda? The everyday grain of the people of the Indus Valley Civilization?

If you answered rice, you would be wrong. There is a long and honourable Indian tradition of rice cultivation. (South Indians may not be thrilled to know that north Indians were the first rice eaters; it spread to the south much later.)

If you answered 'wheat', you would be right—well, sort of. They have found enough evidence to suggest that wheat was a staple in Mohenjo-Daro. But excavations at later Indus Valley sites have not shown any traces of wheat cultivation. And in any case, for all its macho, north Indian associations, wheat was no favourite of the early Aryans either. It doesn't show up in the Rig Veda and turns up only in later Aryan literature.

The great staple cereal of our ancestors was, in fact, barley.

Yup, barley! That's a grain that most of us do not eat today and whose Hindi name, jau, may actually be less familiar to readers than the English word, barley.

In recent years, much has been said and written about ancient Indian grains. There has also been a move in the West to go beyond white rice and refined flour and to rediscover other grains. Frankly, I am as baffled as the next person by the sudden invasion of amaranth and quinoa, and many other grains that I had never heard of before.

So, if you share my bewilderment, here is a guide to the grains you will come across, some old, some new and some even as ancient as the hype suggests.

Amaranth

Despite what you may hear, amaranth is not an ancient Indian grain. It is not even a grain at all and the only 'Indians' who ate it were South American 'Indians'. Columbus brought the plant to Europe, colonialists planted it here and its leaves are eaten all over India. (Local names include bathua, chua, ramdhan and rajgira for the grains.)

Because it is not a real cereal, it has a high protein content and is gluten-free. That explains its current fashionability.

Barley

For all the Rig Vedic associations, barley is best known these days as a raw material for booze—in the whisky and beer industry. Pot barley is the barley version of brown rice. The germ and bran are intact. Pearl barley, like white rice, has the bran removed.

Modern chefs use barley for risottos (I have had terrific barley risottos at both ATM and AnnaMaya in Delhi) and the texture can be amazing. It is low in gluten but not gluten-free.

Buckwheat

You may have come across this in our country, where the flour is called kuttu. But it is much more popular in other cuisines. The Russians make a variety of buckwheat dishes, including blinis, the pancakes eaten with caviar. The Japanese use buckwheat for soba noodles. And in France, buckwheat is used for crepes.

Like many other fashionable so-called cereals, it is not really a grain at all and comes from a plant in the same family as rhubarb or sorrel. So it is gluten-free and probably healthier than normal wheat.

Corn

When I was a child, I used to be confused by the term 'corn'. Did it mean bhutta as I thought? Or was it something else? I was baffled because drawings in my school geography books showed a wheat-like plant. My teachers assured me that bhutta was maize and that corn was different. (Before you ask, this was at Campion School in Mumbai.)

Of course, my teachers were talking nonsense. Corn and maize are the same thing. The confusion could have arisen from the English habit of referring to any major grain crop as 'corn'. Real corn is the same as maize, which is the same as bhutta. As should be obvious, corn is not a grain but you can get flour from bhutta just as you can get cornflakes and taco chips, and God alone knows what else.

Two corn facts that may surprise you: It is the largest crop in the US not because Americans love bhutta but because it is used as animal feed (most American steaks are no more than corn that has been processed by a cow's gut), and is the basis of corn syrup, a cheap, unhealthy sweetener that the processed-food industry loves. And two, there is no ancient Indian corn tradition. So when Punjabis tell you that they have been eating makki ki roti for centuries, do point out to them that the British introduced corn (the American plants) to the region.

Indians know makki, as in the flour we make rotis with. We have some experience of cornflour (essential for Chinese food), which is a refined, finely ground version of makki, and now, polenta, a trendy Italian cornmeal is also available.

All corn products should be gluten-free unless wheat has been added at some stage, which it sometimes is, especially to make makki rotis.

Bajra

This is one of a category of grains that we call millets: it is often called pearl millet in English. India is the world's largest producer and all Indians are familiar with its uses.

Bajra is gluten-free but our cooks often mix a little wheat atta in the dough, so be careful if you want to avoid gluten.

Ragi

A currently trendy food, ragi is actually an ancient Indian grain dating back to the latter part of the Indus Valley Civilization. It is a millet (the English name is finger millet) and is gluten-free. Anecdotal evidence suggests that ragi rotis may be better for health than wheat chapattis.

Jowar

It is called sorghum in English and though it is popular throughout western India as a food, its cultivation in such countries as the US is for animal feed purposes. Jowar is gluten-free and generally recommended over wheat for rotis and the like.

Oats

Not really a part of the Indian diet except as horse feed, oats are trendy in the West because they are a good source of dietary fibre. That's why we see an explosion of oat products: breakfast oats, oat biscuits, oatmeal pancakes and the like.

Oats do not contain gluten; they contain a protein called avenin. But if you have a gluten allergy, you need to be careful because oats are often contaminated with gluten-containing grains and oat products sometime have wheat added to them.

Quinoa

The super-trendy super grain. It is a protein and not really a cereal; so, if you want to avoid carbohydrates and gluten, it is a good choice. I use it as a rice substitute but it has none of the flavour of rice; so you'll need to tart it up if you want a tasty staple.

Rye

Unless you like American whisky, the only time you will come across rye is if you eat rye bread. For example, pumpernickel, a dark, heavy

European bread is a classic rye product. But rye has very little gluten; so most commercial bakers will throw a little wheat into the dough to make sure that the bread rises.

Sago

Proper sago (called Pearl Sage) is a starch extracted from the sago plant of South-east Asia. This is used for sabudana pudding or khichri. It is popular as a fasting food because it is neither a grain nor a vegetable.

However, the term sabudana is also used for tapioca pearls, leading to some confusion.

Tapioca

The cassava is an important crop in warm countries. Tapioca, the food of the gods if you are a Malayali, is the flour made from the cassava. You can make sabudana from the milk of the cassava root.

Semolina

We call it suji (or rava) and act as if it is our own special flour. Actually, it is just a product of one stage of the processing of a hard wheat called durum. In Italy, the flour of durum wheat is used to make pasta.

Semolina usually has a high gluten content; so steer clear of that rava dosa, that upma or that suji halwa if you are avoiding gluten.

Spelt

For some reason, this is a trendy grain, much favoured by so-called nutritionists. It is just wheat, but an ancient form. The health food argument is that it may have more vitamins and minerals than normal wheat. Nutritionists sometimes forget to point out that it is also gluten-rich.

Dal Almighty

≈

Dal is the great unifier of all Indian cuisines.

When you talk to foreigners about Indian food, you run into all kinds of misconceptions about what constitutes the essence of Indian cuisine. When I was studying abroad, I was forever asked, 'Do you miss curry?' These days it is more likely to be: 'Longing for a bit of tandoori chicken, eh?'

In reality, I've never met an Indian who thinks of his own cuisine in terms of tandoori chicken, a restaurant dish we rarely eat at home. Nor do I know many Indians who stay awake at nights, when they are away from home, pining for rogan josh or chicken shahi korma or any other kind of curry.

What we do miss is something that foreigners rarely understand.

We miss dal.

I know grown men who get dal cravings when they have been away from India for long stretches. At university, I knew students who missed the taste of home-cooked dal. And even now, if you ask most Indians what it is that constitutes the heart of real Indian food (the kind that mummy makes) the answer is nearly always framed in terms of dal.

And indeed, with the possible exception of parts of the north-east, dal is the great unifier of all Indian cuisines. Nearly everywhere you go in India, you will find dal on the thali or the plate. It could be dal fry, popular at dhabas in north India. It could be the slightly sweet chholar dal that is so distinctively Bengali. It could be the many complex sambhars of the south Indian states. Or it could be the amazing sweet-sour tuvair dal that is at the heart of Gujarati cuisine.

So dal is not just an important part of Indian food. In many ways, it is Indian food.

Essential to its appeal is the fact that dal is not usually a restaurant dish. It is the sort of thing you make at home. A great home cook will make a great dal. But even a merely competent cook can turn out a perfectly reasonable dal. You can eat dal with rice. Or you can eat it with rotis. It doesn't matter too much either way. It is the sort of dish that works equally well with the two great staples of Indian cuisine.

Restaurants, on the other hand, rarely get it right. It is rare to find an Indian restaurant, no matter how fancy or famous, that makes a yellow dal that we would regard as memorable.

What restaurants do manage is a black dal. But that is a twentieth-century restaurant creation best suited to a professional kitchen.

Consequently, most foreigners, even those who like Indian food, have no idea what we are talking about when we say that for us the taste of home is the taste of dal. They've only eaten the restaurant versions and those are nothing like the real thing.

My colleague, Pramit Pal Chaudhuri, studied the economics and foreign policy implications of dal. And what he discovered intrigued me.

Pramit's information suggested that my gut feeling is accurate. India is a nation of dal eaters. But Pramit went further: we are the only dal consumers in the whole world. (In 'we', he included Bangladeshis and Pakistanis, obviously.) No other nation has a tradition of eating dal at every meal—not even the neighbouring Myanmarese, and certainly not any others in the rest of Asia.

Lentils are consumed in Europe and parts of the Middle East but consumption is relatively small and if all lentils were to suddenly disappear from the face of the earth, it would make no difference to other cuisines. Beans (rajma, etc.) are a little more popular, but they are not true dals in the Indian sense. The Chinese (and other East Asians) use soya beans (which are an important factor, as we shall see), but those are not dal lentils either.

This means that whoever grows dal grows it entirely for the Indian market. It also means that dal is the most crucial crop for any government. If the Indian sugar crop fails or if domestic demand vastly outstrips supply, the government can simply import sugar from the global market and drive prices down. The same is true for rice or wheat. But dal presents special complications.

There are only three countries, outside of India, that grow significant quantities of dal. There is Australia, which cultivates dal only for the Indian market. There is the USA. And there is Myanmar, which exports all of its dal. So, if demand for dal outstrips supply there is really nothing the government can do. There is no untapped source of supply. And it is difficult for existing suppliers to grow more dal. Pramit asked an Australian agricultural official about the prospects of greater dal cultivation and was told, 'Look mate, every acre of Australian farmland that can be devoted to dal has already been planted with dal.'

We can try to get a few global cultivators to move from other crops to dal. But even that poses problems. Dal and soya bean require the same kind of soil. The US subsidizes soya bean cultivation. So American farmers would much rather grow soya beans than dal.

On the other hand, those countries that export dal have a powerful hold on India. The Myanmarese junta would not have hesitated threatening a ban on dal exports to India in case our foreign policy appeared unfriendly to them.

When President Obama was here, a member of his team asked Pramit what the US could do to increase cooperation with India. 'Grow more dal and sell it to us,' Pramit said. The official seemed bemused and went on to talk of the things that Americans are happiest discussing: arms sales, anti-terror alliances, tariff reductions, etc.

And yet, Pramit was entirely right. Dal defines a timeless India in a way that very little else can. It is our very own staple. And we have eaten it ever since India came into being.

For instance, though the Rig Veda mentions neither wheat nor rice, it specifically mentions urad, masoor and moong dals. (As always, I am indebted to K.T. Achaya's masterly *Indian Food—A Historical Companion* for this insight.) Archaeologists have found urad and moong grains at Navdatoli (dating to 1500 BC) and urad grains at Daulatpur. Masoor has been found in excavations in Navdatoli, Ter and Chirand, dating to around 1800 BC.

The tuvair of Gujarati dal fame appears to be of south Indian origin, which would explain why it is the principal constituent of sambhar. There are references to it in Buddhist literature (around 400 BC) and it seems to have developed from a wild plant called *Atylosia*, which grows freely even today in the Western Ghats. There are two distinct varieties of tuvair. There is the south Indian version (a short plant) that yields the sambhar dal and a northern version (a tall shrub) that is called arhar in some north Indian languages.

There are many other things that make dal a symbol of India. Here's one: almost every cuisine that has come into contact with Indian cooking has found some way of introducing dal into its food. When the Parsis first came to India, in the seventh and eighth centuries, they encountered dal, which was not a staple in their native Iran. They had landed in vegetarian Gujarat, but they invented their own dal, with chunks of meat, made with four different lentils: the famous dhansaak.

The Mughals came later and quickly incorporated dal—largely unknown in Samarkand—into their cuisine. But they also made another discovery. In the sixteenth and seventeenth centuries, the staple food of Indian peasants was khichri, made with dal and rice (or sometimes, millets). The Mughals, who were used to the pilaus of Central Asia, were unfamiliar with the idea of cooking rice with dal. They fell in love with khichri and in the fifteen years that Humayun spent in exile, his Indian cooks made khichri for his guests, including the Shah of Iran. Jehangir was so fond of Gujarati khichri that he ate it regularly in his palace.

But here's my question: Indian food has given so much to the rest of the world in terms of dishes and ingredients. Why is it that dal, so vital to Indians and so eagerly embraced by visitors, has never successfully travelled beyond our shores? Why does it remain the one basic Indian dish that only Indians understand?

I have no answers. Perhaps, even in this age of globalization, there are some dishes we like to treat as our very own.

Maharajma

≈

You can count on the rajma bean to make a delicious dish.

North Indians always look surprised when I tell them this, but it is true. Until I went to boarding school in Rajasthan, I had no idea what rajma was.

And even today, when Indian food is much more pan-national, I'm sure there are millions of Gujaratis (like myself), Maharashtrians, Bengalis and south Indians who have never eaten rajma in their lives.

Every time you explain to people north of the Vindhyas that rajma is not really an ancient Indian staple, they act as though you are mad. But surely, we have all heard of the glorious rajma tradition of Kashmir, they say. And what about the simple rajma dishes that are regularly cooked in every Punjabi home? Surely, rajma is just another kind of dal? And we all know that Indians were eating dal in Vedic times, don't we?

Well, yes and no. Yes, because dal is one of the original Indian foods, pre-dating even the Vedic period. Masoor, moong and urad have all been found in Indus Valley sites. No, because rajma is not what ancient Indians would call dal. In fact, as the great food historian K.T. Achaya wrote, we find no mention of rajma in any Indian text, ancient or medieval, till about a century ago. It simply did not exist in our part of the world.

The evidence suggests that it was the French colonialists who brought the rajma bean to India and later, the British who turned it into a commercial crop in the north. Wherever there was a tradition of black dal (in much of India, dal is a yellowish colour and rarely black), households took to rajma and it soon became a kitchen staple. But despite the speed with which it became part of the north Indian diet, rajma did not travel well, which is why you are unlikely to be served rajma at homes outside of the north.

Which is sad, because a well-made rajma can be delicious. It is one of those Indian dishes that restaurant chefs can never improve on. To enjoy good rajma-chawal, you must either eat at a north Indian home or at a highway dhaba, where truck drivers depend on rajma for protein and sustenance. Even great chefs have come up with no good rajma recipes. In his book, *My Great India Cookbook*, Vikas Khanna does not even attempt to give his own spin on rajma but reproduces a recipe from a home cook called Bishambhar. It is a fine recipe and I've reproduced it here, with due acknowledgement to Bishambhar and Vikas.

But Punjabis are not the only people to claim a misplaced ownership of rajma. The French are far worse. One of the classic dishes of French cuisine is the cassoulet. Frenchmen get into fist fights with each other about the perfect cassoulet recipe. What we can agree on is that the dish takes its name from the earthenware pot it is cooked in. There is also a broad consensus that 30 per cent of the constituents of the dish should be pork (ham, salt pork, bacon, pork shoulder, sausage, etc.). The rest can consist of duck, goose or lamb and, of course, beans.

Ah yes, beans. According to legend, the dish was created in 1355 during the siege of Castelnaudary. Besieged by the English, the plucky townspeople put a large pot on a fire in the town square and threw in all the pigs, lambs and birds they could find along with white haricot beans. Ever since then, the dish has been the symbol of rural France, especially of the Languedoc region.

It is a good story, which illustrates that famous French maxim: When in trouble, cook.

The trouble is that the story is a load of cobblers. The good people of Castelnaudary could not have made a haricot bean stew in 1355 because there were no haricot beans in France in that era. The bean was brought back from the New World by Christopher Columbus in 1493 and took another century to reach the French countryside. The earliest reference to the haricot in France dates to 1565 (over two centuries after the siege of Castelnaudary) and the dish was probably invented in the seventeenth century. (Two centuries or so later, the French took the bean to India.)

Which brings us to the other interesting thing about the haricot bean (*Phaseolus vulgaris*). We know that cassoulet is made with white beans while rajma is a dark red bean. And indeed, we use different terms for each large bean: kidney, pinto, cannellini, borlotti, black, etc. But the truth is that they are all the same bean. The changes in size and colour have only to do with climate, market requirements, cultivation, etc. Whether it is the plump white bean of the cassoulet or the dark, homely rajma bean, they are all offshoots of *Phaseolus vulgaris*. And all of them come from South America. Which means that none of them can have an ancient history in Europe or India because they are relatively recent visitors.

Chefs will tell you that a good cassoulet cannot be made in a restaurant, that the dish takes several hours to cook and up to four days to prepare, because the ingredients are so complicated. They are right. To look at a recipe for authentic cassoulet is to want to slit your own throat: you know that you will never have the patience or the ingredients required to make the real thing. Life is too short to make a genuine cassoulet unless—like the residents of Castelnaudary in the legend—your town is under siege and you have nothing else to do.

But what exactly is the real thing? In France, there are about a thousand cassoulet recipes all based on a bean they only had access to relatively recently. So, just as there is no one authentic rajma recipe, you can make your own kind of cassoulet, depending on the ingredients you have available. I make my own and though they will probably cancel my Schengen visa when they see how inauthentic it is, I'm reproducing the recipe here anyway.

It is a measure of the versatility of the rajma bean that French peasants and Punjabi housewives all regard it as something of their own. And no matter what the cuisine is—French or Kashmiri—you can count on the rajma bean to make a delicious dish.

Cassoulet à la South Extension (Deuxième Partie)

Ingredients

1 confit duck leg (available at gourmet stores or on order at any Oberoi hotel deli)

300 grams fresh pork, cut into pieces
1 packet streaky bacon (pancetta is better but harder to find)
1 packet chorizo sausages (the Oberoi kind will do but many foreign brands are available)
1 sachet bouquet garni (a herb potli available at upmarket groceries)
1 packet good-quality European sausages
2 cubes chicken stock (real stock or the stock they sell in tetra packs is better)
2 cans haricot beans (widely available, though you can soak and boil dried beans)
Onions, garlic to taste.

Method

Chop the onion and garlic. With a pair of kitchen scissors, cut the bacon into small pieces. Shred the duck confit into little bits. Slice the chorizo thinly.

Fry the onions, garlic, bacon and chorizo in olive oil in a large pan over medium heat till the bacon is rendering its fat and the onions are sweating. In another pan, lightly fry the whole European sausages and reserve.

When the bacon fat seems to have coated the onion-garlic-chorizo mixture, add the pork pieces and brown quickly. When done, add the shredded duck confit and the whole cooked sausages. Add enough stock to reach the top of the pan. Throw in the bouquet garni.

Bring to the boil and then cover and simmer at medium to low heat for at least an hour. If the pan seems too dry you can keep adding more hot stock. You will know you are nearing the end when the pork seems tender and ready to fall apart. Now add the canned (or pre-boiled) beans. Simmer on low heat for twenty minutes or more.

Watch the pan. The dish is ready when the bacon and duck confit have almost disappeared and the pork is tender enough to eat with a spoon. Once you've got there, check the seasoning. You should not need more salt because commercial stock is quite salty. But you can add pretty much anything you like at this stage—garlic purée, a dash of Tabasco, some herbs, etc.—to whoosh up the flavour.

In restaurants, they would now sprinkle breadcrumbs on top of the stew and brown it under the grill or finish it in the oven, but you don't need to do that at home. (But if you are entertaining, a cassoulet with a breadcrumb crust looks more impressive.)

If you like the dish, you can improvise on the recipe the next time. Sometimes I've added fresh duck legs, mushrooms, button onions, spicier sausages and some lamb.

Whatever you do, remember that this is as authentically French as Banta Singh is. So, don't bother about the real recipe; the French only got the beans from South America relatively recently anyway.

Bishambhar's Rajma Recipe

Ingredients

1 cup red kidney beans (rajma)
1 tsp salt or to taste
3 tsp ginger-garlic paste
1 tbsp oil
Half a cup onions, finely chopped
Half a cup tomato puree
7–8 pods black cardamom
2″ stick cinnamon
One-and-a-half tsp fennel powder
2 tsp dried ginger powder
A pinch of asafoetida powder
Half a tsp red chilli powder

Method

Wash beans and soak in water overnight. Drain and rinse thoroughly. In a pressure cooker, combine beans with three cups of water, salt and half the ginger-garlic paste. Pressure-cook for 7–9 minutes over low heat after the cooker reaches full pressure. Remove from heat and allow the pressure to settle. Meanwhile, put oil in a frying pan over medium heat. When hot, add remaining ginger-garlic paste and sauté for a few seconds. Add onions and sauté till translucent. Mix in tomato purée and cook for 2–3 minutes. Spoon contents of pan into the pressure cooker containing the beans. Mix in the remaining ingredients and pressure-cook over low heat for 10–12 minutes. When the pressure settles, open cooker and serve the beans hot.

Fire and Rice

≈

Let's celebrate the diversity of India's rich rice culture.

It is a funny business, all these prejudices about rice. North Indians think of themselves as wheat eaters; it is the south Indians who are rice eaters, they say.

In the Middle East, they act as if they discovered rice, claiming pilaus and biryanis for themselves. In Europe, Italians will lecture you about the virtues of Arborio versus Carnaroli, as though rice is their very own thing.

So it is with rice varieties. All over north India basmati is the only breed that counts; everything else is regarded as inferior. In the south, they are less respectful of basmati and far more knowledgeable about rice varieties. In such states as Kerala, they grow so many interesting kinds of rice that they earmark each variety for a particular kind of dish: a small-grained rice for payasam, a large-grained red variety for sambhar-rice, broken rice for upma or porridge (kanji) and yet another variety for the delicious biryanis of the Moplahs.

In fact, all Indians should take special pride in rice. Yes, it is true that archaeologists have found evidence of rice cultivation in China, dating back to 6000 BC. But this does not mean that rice originated in China. All the evidence suggests that rice is Indian, the one food that we gave to the rest of the world. The wild grasses that turned into rice have been around pretty much since the beginnings of time. But rice was first cultivated—from those wild grasses—in the foothills of the Himalayas, long before it turned up in the Yangtze Valley. Archaeologists have found terraced fields in Kashmir, suggestive of rice cultivation, that have been dated to 10,000 BC or 4000 years before the Chinese first thought of any kind of fried rice. So yes, rice is ours. We found the wild grass. We cultivated it. And we gave rice to the rest of humanity.

So, despite all this nonsense about fair, wheat-eating Aryans and north Indians, the reality is that rice was really the staple food of north India. It did not actually reach south India till 1000 BC or many, many centuries after north Indians had been cultivating it. In contrast, wheat, which north Indians are so proud of, came to India from the Middle East and is not our own grain at all.

There is some evidence to suggest that the people of the Indus Valley Civilization cultivated wheat. But the Aryans, from whom north Indians like to claim they are descended, had no interest in wheat at all. There are virtually no references to wheat in Vedic literature (the Aryans ate rice—though perhaps, not with sambhar) and we have to wait till the Buddhist period for mentions of wheat in texts. Somehow, the notion of brave Aryan warriors fighting and banishing the Dravidians (largely mythical but widely subscribed to in north India) seems less compelling when you realize that after these fair-skinned horsemen had finished with battle they probably sat down to a meal of curd rice (or perhaps payasam to give them some energy).

If north Indians are reluctant to see themselves as descendants of curd-rice-wallahs, what of all the other people who act as though rice is their own invention? If I hear another Pakistani telling me that Arabs brought biryani to the subcontinent, I will throw up.

The reality is that rice took centuries to reach the Middle East. It did not even get to Japan till after the birth of Christ (about 10,000 years after we were cultivating it). The Middle East became familiar with rice after Persian traders took it to their part of the world around AD 500. It only reached Egypt in the seventh century. And it became popular among Arabs because the Prophet was said to have liked rice and ghee. The Prophet's dates are: born AD 570, died AD 632. So that makes the Islamic connection with rice a seventh-century phenomenon. As for pilau, which the Arab/Turks claim to have invented, yeah, well . . . in fact, the earliest pilau recipes date back to the thirteenth century AD, by which stage every Indian knew how to make hundreds of rice dishes. As for khichri, it may well be the oldest rice dish that is still regularly eaten by millions. The Egyptians got it from us and made it a part of their cuisine long before the Turks started bragging about their pilaus.

I'm a little more patient with Europeans when they brag about the red rice of the Camargue (in France) or the fat rice of Italian cookery because the poor sods don't know any better. When Alexander and his European army arrived in north India in 326 BC, they had never heard of rice. Contemporary accounts from Macedonian writers treat our staple grain as though it was some magic food. Perhaps some Europeans took rice back from India with them (though I doubt it—there is not one mention of rice in the Bible). But rice really only reached Spain (where they are proud of their paella) when Arab/Moorish soldiers introduced it to the Spaniards. And as for Italians, the earliest recipes for risotto date only to the nineteenth century.

So rice is our thing. It is the great Indian food. There are over 8000 varieties of rice and my guess is that we can probably grow several thousand of them in our subcontinent. And indeed I can think of hundreds that we do grow.

But here's my complaint: we make too little of rice. If you hear restaurateurs talk, they will brag about a roti/paratha/naan chef and will praise the touch of his fingers. But no rice cook ever gets any respect: he is just the mundu who boils the grains. Worse still, despite being the land of rice, most Indians have no clue about the many different varieties that are available in our country.

For this, I lay the blame entirely on north Indians. First of all, they subscribe to all this Aryan wheat eater rubbish that has no historical basis. And when the Muslim kings and emperors arrived, north Indians quickly abandoned their own rice tradition and became slaves to the rice dishes of people from Central Asia and the Middle East who knew nothing about rice. Too much fuss was made over biryani and pilau. (Even now if you ask for rice at a restaurant in north India, they will try to put peas in it on the mistaken assumption that ordinary rice is too humble and that some kind of pilau is called for.)

But the worst thing north Indians have done is to elevate basmati to the status of the king of rice. It is considered cheap to serve any rice other than basmati to guests and all that Mughal court nonsense about rice (dreamt up by people who were essentially illiterates ou rice) prevails:

it must have long grains, each grain must remain separate after cooking, the rice should smell of butter, etc.

It is only once you leave north India, its restaurants and its ignorant chefs that you get some sense of the richness of India's rice tradition. You cannot enjoy a Goan meal unless you eat it with the fat, partly polished rice of the region. You cannot possibly serve basmati with many Malayali dishes—you must use one of the magnificent varieties of rice of Kerala. You can't make appams unless you have the right rice for the flour. And you cannot make payasam with the rice you use for kheer.

But north Indians are prisoners of their prejudices, willing and credulous followers of traditions established by ignorant Central Asian dynasties who knew nothing about rice. I've been to fancy south Indian restaurants in Delhi where they serve basmati. I've even got into arguments with moronic executive chefs at hotels who insist that Chinese fried rice should be made with basmati. Of the big hotel chains, only the Oberois care about rice, always offering a brown rice option at buffets. ('It won't work,' a chef at a rival chain told me. 'Indians want rice that is very white'.' What utter nonsense!)

So let's abandon these prejudices. Let's celebrate the diversity of India's rich rice culture. Without our ancestors, there would be no rice and therefore no sushi, no risotto, no rice pudding, no pilau, no paella and no nasi goreng. As inheritors of that proud legacy, let us not bury it under a mound of basmati (served with peas, no doubt).

They See
Me Rolling

≈

The kathi roll is so popular that you will find it (or its variations) in much of India. Yet, we know little about it.

Ask most people to give an example of an Indian sandwich and they will point you in the direction of the chicken-tikka sandwich so beloved of English sandwich shops. But a sandwich made with bread isn't really Indian, no matter what the filling is.

In fact, an authentically Indian sandwich does exist, is widely available all over the country, and deserves its popularity. The only problem is that we don't think of it as a sandwich.

I refer, of course, to the kathi roll.

If you define a sandwich as being a bit of meat (or cheese or vegetables, etc.) encased in bread, the kathi roll conforms to the definition. At its most basic, it consists of a kebab of some description (the meat) wrapped inside a roti of some sort (the bread).

The roll is so popular that you will find it—or variations thereof—in much of India. In Delhi, Khan Market sophisticates swear by Khan Chacha. In Mumbai, they prefer the Frankie, which is essentially a kathi roll, after a weekend in Dubai. And in Kolkata, they worship the Nizam's roll. I'm not as familiar with the south but I'm sure you can find kathis in Hyderabad and Bengaluru.

And yet, we know little about the roll. While researching this piece I spoke to a variety of chefs and food historians. Not one could tell me, with any degree of certainty, which part of India the original kathi came from or how it became so popular all over the country.

So, what follows is largely guesswork based on my conversations with people and my own memories of rolls that I have eaten all over the country—after all, the very first *Rude Food* centuries ago (all right, a few years ago) was about the Nizam's roll.

As far as I can tell, what we call the kathi kebab roll is actually not one roll at all—it is at least two. The first roll seems to have originated at Nizam's in Kolkata.

I have many memories of eating at the original Nizam's. A large tawa, which I was assured was 100 years old (the next time I went, they said sixty years old, so let's just agree it was very old), was put on an open fire. The cook had already rolled a maida paratha on the tawa. Then, he broke an egg on the paratha and cooked it on both sides so that the result was part paratha and part omelette. Then he shiftily took a few pieces of pre-cooked 'mutton' kebab, looked nervously at a sign that said 'No beef is served here' (but we thought we knew better) and put them in the centre of the paratha. He added raw onions and chutney, rolled the paratha and put the finished roll inside a wrap of shiny paper.

You could have the roll without the egg but I always thought this was a waste of time. You could have it with chicken (rubbish). And no doubt there was a vegetarian version, which the chefs made while they held their sides and laughed.

When I moved to Kolkata, Nizam's was one of a whole bunch of Muslim restaurants (with such names as Aminia, Sabir and Shiraz), which specialized in curries, chops and biryanis. But only Nizam's had the roll and they guarded its ownership zealously with signs that read 'We have no branches'.

This may or may not have been true but the roll was found everywhere in Kolkata, often at restaurants with such names as New Nizam's. Unlike most imitations, the average quality of the rolls at these other restaurants was nearly always high. And so while many people preferred the Nizam's originals (or not—Arvind Saraswat came to Kolkata to open the Taj Bengal's restaurants, went to Nizam's kitchen and swore never to eat there) there were lots of options in every area of Kolkata.

Ask most people now about the kathi kebab roll, and you will be told that it was invented by Nizam's and travelled eastwards from Kolkata. There are two problems with this view. The first is the name. Nizam's never called its roll a kathi roll. It was simply a mutton roll or a chicken roll or, in moments of hubris, a Nizam's roll. Nor did anybody else in Kolkata (at least in that era) use the term 'kathi kebab'. It was just called a roll.

Secondly, the rolls that people in Delhi enjoy, have nothing to do with the Nizam's roll. For instance, I went to Khan Chacha in Khan Market last week. The street stall was legendary, and when the chefs fought with their landlord (who, they say, stole their name and offered it to franchisees) in court, the story made all the newspapers with half the population of Delhi rooting for the chefs against the landlord. (The other half of the population is vegetarian.)

Now the Khan Chacha chefs have new partners, the Kalras, the owners of Dayal Opticals. This seems a happier arrangement because the Kalras have set them up in a restaurant of sorts (you buy a coupon and queue up for your food, but you get a table), which does a roaring business. Apparently, M.S. Dhoni and various other celebrities are regulars.

The Khan Chacha roll has damn all to do with the Nizam's version. For a start, most Delhi operations use tandoori kebabs, while Nizam's kebabs are never tandoor-cooked. The Khan Chacha roll is based on the roomali and on thin rotis. The Nizam's roll depends on the richness of a crisp, egg-covered paratha.

The Khan Chacha formula is to make three kebabs: a chicken tikka, a thin seekh of the kind we used to buy from street vendors when we went out drinking in our youth, and a so-called Kakori, which is probably not a Kakori at all but is more like a real seekh kebab than the thing they call a seekh.

You can order the three kebabs separately. Or they will wrap them up in rotis and serve them to you. In that sense, the Khan Chacha roll (in any of its three avatars) is a true Indian sandwich. (I can't be sure but there must be a vegetarian roll somewhere on the menu too.)

Any fool can see that a tandoori chicken tikka wrapped in a roomali roti is entirely different from the Nizam's roll. But somehow, we tend to lump them together as examples of kathi kebab rolls.

I asked Monish Gujral, whose grandfather Kundan Lal Gujral popularized tandoori cooking in India at his Moti Mahal in the 1950s, whether he recognized the Khan Chacha roll. Monish says that this roll does not have its origins in the Nizam's tradition at all.

According to him, it was his grandfather who invented the chicken tikka roll and the seekh kebab wrap. When these dishes became popular at Moti Mahal, Kundan Lal looked for takeaway versions. He began by putting his kebabs into kulchas and rolling them with onion and chutney. Later, Moti Mahal shifted to using lighter rotis. In the Moti Mahal version, the roll was only a means of transporting the kebab. In the Nizam's version, the roll was the point of the exercise.

The Khan Chacha rolls seem to me to be extensions of the Moti Mahal wraps. They are essentially wrappings for kebabs rather than great rolls in themselves. This is not to deny that they're very good: millions of Punjabis cannot be wrong. But I doubt if they've descended from the Nizam's roll.

I asked Manjit Gill, ITC's corporate chef and one of the most knowledgeable people I know, which version of the roll ITC serves at all its properties.

Manjit says that they discussed the roti options when they were standardizing the recipe. Eventually, ITC took the line that it was creating a roll, not providing a wrap for its kebabs.

So, the ITC version uses a Mughlai paratha, and the chefs pay special attention to the filling. Often ITC uses chopped or ground meat, and one version requires lots of fresh vegetables. Manjit's view is the same as mine. A roll is a dish in itself. It is not an excuse to eat a seekh kebab on the run. In this health-conscious era, however, most ITC hotels will offer lighter versions made with thinner rotis should guests be frightened of the Mughlai paratha, but the standard recipe uses the paratha.

I don't want to play any favourites between the two avatars of the roll. Some time ago, at the Four Seasons in Mumbai, I got the chef at Café Prato to make me a roll with atta (their standard version uses maida), so I understand that people often want to eat healthily. When I lived in Anand Lok in Delhi, I was a regular at the local Al Kauser where they would wrap a Kakori in a roomali roti for me and very nice it was too. Equally, whenever I stay at an ITC hotel I usually order some version of the kathi roll because ITC chefs have been astonishingly creative in tinkering with the filling. So yes, there is room for all kinds of rolls.

After all, the damn thing is a sandwich and the whole point of a sandwich is that you can play around with the bread and the filling.

But if you strap me to a lie detector and hold a gun to my head and ask me to choose just one roll, the truth is that I will go for the Nizam's roll. I'll take the so-called mutton (nudge nudge, wink wink) version made with an egg paratha, stuffed with crunchy onion and that tangy Nizam's sauce, and rolled tightly in shiny grease-proof paper.

It is not that this is necessarily the best roll in the world. It is just that I can never forget those days in 1986 when I would eat a Nizam's roll for lunch every day. I had just come from Mumbai (then Bombay), had no experience of rolls (a Frankie does not count, I'm afraid, despite the resemblance) and was blown away by the excellence of the Nizam's version.

Since then, I have tried various establishments that use the Nizam's name in other cities but none of the rolls has been up to the standard of those I ate in Kolkata (then Calcutta). Perhaps the real thing was genuinely better.

Or perhaps everything tastes better when you are young.

Biryani
as Birthright

≈

My worry is that the regional biryanis will slowly die out.

Every Indian knows that dal is not a single dish.

Yes, it is always made from lentils but that is about all the various dals of India have in common. A person with no experience of Indian cuisine would—if he was simultaneously served the black dal of the Punjab, the sambhar of Udupi and the chholar dal of Bengal—not immediately realize that all three were lentil preparations of the same general category.

But, even though we accept that dal is the name we give to a family of dishes, rather than a single dish, we have difficulty in arriving at the same conclusion when it comes to biryani. In our minds, we still think of biryani as being a single dish.

Few Indian menus would ever describe a dish as 'dal'. We would usually feel the need to add a descriptor of some sort: 'mah ki dal' or 'Chholar dal' or of course, sambhar, because we know that these are entirely different dishes. (And rajma would not even be described as a dal.) Even when two dals are made from the same lentil—say sambhar and the classic Gujarati dal, both of which use tuvair—we recognize that they are different dishes and describe them as such.

In the case of biryani, however, no such distinctions are made. The most you'll get is a description of the meat used for the dish (chicken biryani or mutton biryani, etc.) and just perhaps, some meaningless descriptor (nawabi biryani).

And yet, as most of us intuitively recognize, biryani is as much a family of dishes as dal. Yes, all biryani should have rice (just as dals use lentils), but once you get beyond that basic criterion, the situation becomes immensely complicated. Even in north India, the biryani of Delhi is totally different from the biryani of Bhopal, which is different from the biryani of UP (assuming that there is such a thing—the biryanis of Lucknow and Rampur are of different styles).

Outside of north India, the divergences increase. Of the famous restaurant biryanis, the Hyderabad one (especially the Kacha biryani) is the south Indian version that usually makes it to menus in the rest of India. But even within Hyderabad, you will find an Andhra-style biryani, which is a spicy, more robust, food-of-the-common-people dish than the courtly and elegant Hyderabadi biryani.

There are many other classic south Indian biryanis, some made with local varieties of rice, not the long-grained basmati-style rice of court biryanis. The delicious biryani of Calicut (Kozhikode) has as much in common with a Lucknawi biryani as an appam has with a butter naan. In eastern India, the biryani of Kolkata (often made with potatoes to save on adding more meat) is justly famous at local restaurants but largely unknown outside that city. The pilaus of Assam have an entirely different character.

The general rule of thumb is that wherever in the subcontinent you find a Muslim community, you will find a local biryani. And just as the Muslims of Kerala have little (except religion) in common with the Muslims of Kashmir, so too are their cuisines entirely distinct.

I have tried to find the history of biryani (something of a personal obsession, as regular readers of *Rude Food* and viewers of my TLC show will know) but, as I have often said, there is no authentic or convincing explanation of how the pilaus of Central Asia were transformed into the subcontinent's biryanis. Nor has anyone been able to explain exactly how to distinguish a biryani from a pilau (I don't think there is always a dividing line). And it is still not clear to me how every Muslim community in every corner of India makes its own biryani. (Could this be because of religious feasting? Possibly, but I have yet to find somebody who is certain.)

My worry, these days, is that the regional biryanis will slowly die out. Already, the vast majority of restaurants are graduating to a bland biryani of no specific origin. The upmarket restaurant version, here and at Indian restaurants abroad, complete with dough-purdah and lots of wisdom about dum-cooking, is essentially a rip-off of a recipe perfected by ITC in the 1980s. And while the ITC Dum Pukht biryani is still better than its many imitations are, it is an entirely modern creation, invented in the kitchens of the Maurya by combining some of the techniques of Lucknow biryani with some of the flavours of Hyderabad. As an example of modern Indian cooking, the ITC biryani deserves our respect. But as an example of regional cuisine, it is not very convincing.

I was reminded of all this some time back, ironically at an ITC hotel. When the chain opened its Grand Central hotel in Mumbai's Parel area some years ago, it packed the menus with Mumbai dishes. Many of these have been subsequently dropped but I was impressed to see that, on its room-service menu, it did not just offer the famous Dum Pukht biryani but served a Bohra biryani too. Out of curiosity, more than anything else, I ordered it. To my surprise, it was absolutely outstanding. The next time I was in Mumbais, at another hotel, I made the Grand Central pack a takeaway for me to carry it to Delhi. And a week later, the excellence of the biryani was a key factor in making me choose to stay at the Grand Central again.

For those of you—most of you, I would imagine—who do not know what a Bohra biryani is, it is an example of one of the finest Gujarati biryanis. Though we do not always realize this, some of Gujarat's most accomplished trading communities are Muslims. The Bohras are one such community as are the Memons. The most famous—outside of India, certainly—are the Khojas, partly because of the global prominence of the Aga Khan, their spiritual leader.

It is hard to find—even in Mumbai—restaurants that serve the authentic food of these communities these days. To enjoy the cuisine you need to be invited to a private home. But you can see traces—vulgarized, bastardized and mutated, admittedly—of the Gujarati biryani in most popular Mumbai biryani restaurants (Delhi Darbar, Jafferbhai, etc.), even though the Gujarati connection is rarely trumpeted.

I pick the Gujarati biryani because I grew up in Mumbai. But every state has its own biryanis and often, in south India, the biryani recipe varies from district to district just as much as the sambhar recipe varies. The south Indian biryani that gets served most often at restaurants in north India as a so-called 'regional biryani' is the Moplah biryani of Kerala, which is just one of the many excellent biryanis of the region, though it has become a staple of restaurant and hotel 'south Indian festivals'.

So it is with eastern India. When I lived in Kolkata I would frequent the local restaurants (Shiraz, Sabir, etc.) for biryani, but I always waited for Muslim festivals because that was when friends would send over their home-made biryanis—which were delicious and based on local recipes handed down over generations. (I am not sure about this but my guess is that home-style biryani always differs from chef-type biryani because while wedding caterers and restaurant chefs tend to be men who make robust, meaty biryanis, the ghar-ki-biryani is made by mothers and has a more delicate, feminine touch.)

I respect the biryani of Lucknow (or pilau as they call it in Lucknow, where the term biryani is not usually applied to the dish) and I admire the Kacha biryani of Hyderabad (though you rarely get a great biryani at restaurants in that city these days). And of course, nobody can deny the influence and quality of the Dum Pukht modern biryani.

But let us not restrict ourselves to these old standbys. Let's explore the enormous regional variety of biryani and recognize that this is the one dish that unifies India because it is found nearly everywhere in the country. Nobody denies its Muslim origins but like modern India, biryani is about more than just religion or region. It is a symbol of a country that takes differences and divergences and then merges them into one India.

The Length and Bread of It

≈

Why doesn't the Indian bread tradition get the respect it deserves?

In the West, bread is a really big deal. When the French food revolution took off in the 1770s and '80s, one of its greatest heroes was a baker called Lionel Poilâne who introduced a loaf with a note of acid running through it.

Poilâne bread became so famous that even today, it is a global benchmark for quality.

So it is with other kinds of bread. Food critics will often judge a restaurant by the quality of its bread. Bakery chefs are in great demand and they fight battles over the starter cultures that are required to make good fermented loaves.

I can understand this. The West is a bread-based culture. No matter where you go, you will find a local bread. The French have their baguettes and their croissants (which may or may not be of Turkish origin); the Italians have focaccia; the Germans have a dark bread; and the English, well, the English have nasty sliced industrial white bread that sticks to the roof of your mouth.

In contrast, Asia is a rice-based culture. And so, most Asian cuisines will make much of the quality of their rice. For instance, the Japanese will complain about Thailand's fragrant jasmine rice, arguing that the taste is too strong and will ask for their own blander variety of rice. Rice dishes—from nasi goreng to fried rice to the pellets they use for nigiri sushi—will be the subject of endless discussions and debate.

Which brings us to India, a relatively unusual society in the sense that we are both rice and wheat eaters. The caricature has it that the north eats wheat but the subcontinent's most famous rice dishes—biryani and kheer, for instance—actually have north Indian roots. And of course, the south is a rice-eating society.

But here's my problem: While we are prepared to make much of our rice dishes ('the best biryani is in Lucknow', etc.) we are strangely reluctant to brag about our breads. And God knows India has a huge variety of breads. Forget about wheat. Indians can make great breads (rotis) from virtually any kind of grain or pulse—from bajra to jowar to chickpeas (besan) to many varieties of dal.

But restaurant guests do not pay enough attention to our bread-making skills. I know people who will choose a restaurant on the basis of the quality of the biryani or the pilau, but hardly anybody comes back from a restaurant raving about the quality of the naan or the rotis. Even when dishes revolve around bread, it hardly gets a mention. People may praise the pav-bhaji at a stall, but it will be the bhaji they focus on; the pav will be taken for granted.

When we do talk about bread, we focus on the extras. I have heard people say, 'The keema naan is delicious at this restaurant,' but rarely will they talk about a plain naan. Even when parathas are discussed, it is usually the stuffing that is talked about, not the paratha itself.

Contrast this with the West. A man who makes a terrific chocolate croissant or puts great toppings on his focaccia will not be taken seriously unless the croissant itself (without the chocolate filling) or the basic focaccia are perfect.

Why should this be so? Why don't we take our naan/paratha/roti/puri/thepla tradition as seriously as the West takes its bread? Why is a man who makes a great biryani hailed as a genius while a guy who makes great naans or parathas languishes at the back of the kitchen?

Some of this, I suspect, has to do with our traditional inferiority complex about refined flour or maida. Though obviously there are as many views on this subject as there are food historians, the broad consensus seems to be that Indians specialized in wholegrain flours (atta, bajra, etc.) till Muslim traders brought in maida from the Middle East. West Asia had a strong baking tradition (in India we tended to make our breads on tawas or fried them), which used refined flour and when this eventually became the preferred style of the royal court, chefs all over India began adopting it.

Even today, there is a bogus snobbery associated with maida, which is seen as superior to plain old atta. When I lived in Kolkata, I was forever being told by uppity Bongs that they did not allow atta into their kitchens. Their parathas and luchis (puris) were made from maida. So it is with cooks at most north Indian restaurants. Tell them that a tandoori roti (which is of Hindu Punjabi origin and has nothing to do with Samarkand, Peshawar or Bukhara) should be made with atta and they will act as though you have insulted them. Unless you push them, they will always prefer maida.

In many ways this is bizarre because, the world over, the trend is to give up on maida and to return to wholewheat. But in India, the prejudice endures.

The fancy, imported image of maida (and of the refined-flour breads that came relatively late in our culinary history) also has a colonial link. When the Portuguese landed in Goa, they rejected the local breads and tried to make their own. Without the starter culture that they were used to back home, they started using a little alcohol (even feni) to begin the process of fermentation in the dough that was crucial to their kind of bread.

That tradition endures today in the humble pav (or pao) that is in direct descent from the bread that the Portuguese introduced to Goa. (There are three theories about the name. One is that the dough was mixed by people walking on it—hence 'pav' for foot. More plausible is the version that each pao was made in a batch of four, so an individual piece was a quarter of the total—or a 'pao'. Or it's just a variation on the Portuguese word for bread.)

By the time the British got to India, our native bread-making tradition was held in contempt. They did not understand how bread could be made on tawas, favoured the Muslim maida-baking approach and in any case, gave us their own tasteless white bread.

Though things have changed a little since those days, I am still surprised by how complete the imported maida domination of our local roti tradition is. Think about it. Most of us eat phulkas or some variation thereof at home. But how many restaurants in India bother with phulkas or chapattis of any kind? You'll be encouraged to order naan or tandoori rotis. Chapattis will rarely be on the menu.

And even where restaurants do make an effort, how often do you see the traditional Indian breads made from such grains as bajra on the menu? Even though, in terms of health, such grains as bajra and jowar are much, much better for you than maida, they are usually banished from the menu.

Some dishes survive—especially in this day and age—because chefs and restaurants persist with them. With Indian breads, the opposite is true. The only reason the chapatti is so ubiquitous is that we cook it at home. Leave it to restaurants and it will die. So it is with the puri. Except for halwais, most chefs do not bother very much with it. Only the home cooks keep the tradition alive. When chefs do approach the paratha, they either overload it with fancy stuffings or (claiming inspiration from Parathewali Gali) deep-fry it so that one paratha is enough to knock you out and two put you in queue for a heart attack.

My other theory about why we don't take our breads seriously enough (apart from our fascination with maida) is that Indians take rotis for granted. In the West, they eat bread on its own (or with a little butter or olive oil). In India, we treat a roti as no more than the wrapping for a subzi or piece of meat or whatever. So naturally, we focus less on the wrapping and more on the stuff that it is wrapped around. So, if a meat curry is great, we'll rave about that and ignore the roti we eat it with.

In doing so, we shortchange ourselves. No matter how great a mutton curry is, a bad roti will always destroy the experience. A delicately spiced subzi needs a soft phulka for its full flavour to emerge. A plate of chana is worth nothing without a fluffy bhatura. A garlicky yellow dal improves 200 per cent when you dunk a nice, crisp tandoori roti into it. A simple plate of sookha aloo can be transformed into a superlative meal if the puri is any good. A bowl of dahi, coloured with a little achar, becomes a gourmet meal if you eat it with a spicy thepla, full of the goodness of methi.

In short, unless you eat rice at every meal, there is no way you can really enjoy Indian food if you don't get the bread right. You can eat a Western meal—say a steak or a piece of fish—without any bread and not really miss it. But can you imagine eating a subzi by itself? You have to depend on the roti to transform most Indian dishes into great meals.

Which brings us back to where we started. Why don't we have our own Poilâne? If bakers are so prized in the West, why do we take our own roti chefs for granted? Why doesn't the Indian bread tradition get the respect it deserves?

I don't know. But unless things change, I think Indian cuisine will pay the price for our neglect.

Dreaming
of Dosas

≈

**As quick snacks go, they are quite delicious—and now they can
be healthy too.**

I have a deep admiration for dosa, which I consider the ultimate Indian
fast food.

It's not that difficult to make (after all, it is served in nearly every
office canteen in India), does not cost a lot and provides a high-quality
filling meal.

Unlike American fast food, however, the dosa is a proper dish,
made to order from a batter that has to be freshly prepared each day
and does not depend on pre-packaged, frozen or processed ingredients.
The vegetables for the masala (if you order a masala dosa) must be fresh;
the chutneys do not really work unless they are ground only a few hours
before being served and a good sambhar can be a gourmet dish by itself.

Innumerable books have been written about the techniques that
go into creating a McDonald's or Pizza Hut operation and while there
is much to admire in the US fast-food model, my own view is that a
restaurant like Sagar in Defence Colony, Delhi, or MTR in Bengaluru is
far more impressive in its ambition and execution. It is not easy to serve
hundreds of dosas each day, ensuring that the batter ferments perfectly
each time and that, even though each dosa is made from scratch, there is
no variation in quality.

My only concern with the dosa has been one of health. In this era when people worry about their consumption of complex carbohydrates, how healthy can it be to eat dosas that are fried and where ghee or butter is used almost as a matter of course?

The first indication that somebody was trying to protect the dosa from the health lobby came when I went to the ITC Mughal hotel in Agra in 2008. The then general manager, Anil Chadha, made me try a multigrain dosa, which, he assured me, was a healthier version of the traditional dish. I loved it. And so, I guess, did many others because you can now get multigrain dosas at most ITC Luxury Collection hotels. (Chadha took the dosa with him to Bengaluru's ITC Windsor.)

I thought of the multigrain dosa as being an ITC preserve till I was served one for breakfast at Mumbai's Taj Lands End. It was clearly not a traditional dosa but it tasted terrific and I asked chef Anirudhya Roy, who runs the Lands End kitchens, where he had got the idea from. Roy, a modest man, refused to accept any of the credit. The dosa had been created by chef 'Nat' Natarajan, one of the Taj's most respected chefs (he opened Southern Spice in Chennai in the 1990s) and Roy had merely reproduced Nat's recipes.

The two competing multigrain dosas got me thinking. Were Indian chefs now coming around to the view that something needed to be done to make the dosa healthier? Perhaps the ITC experiment was not an isolated one. I got Roy to send me a copy of Nat's recipe and Chadha sent me the original ITC multigrain recipe.

I've reproduced both recipes here so that you can judge for yourselves, but my sense is that the two dosas are quite different even if they work on the same basic premise.

Natarajan's multigrain dosa takes its name seriously. Of the 400 gm of rice that go into the dosa, 300 gm consist of raw rice and there is another 100 gm of boiled rice.

Traditionally, dosas are made of rice and urad dal in a 2:1 ratio, and in a sense, Natarajan keeps to this formula with 200 gm of dal to 400 gm of rice. But he uses two dals—100 gm urad and 100 gm moong. Then, in addition, he adds a full 300 gm of other grains: 100 gm of broken wheat, 100 gm of oats, 50 gm of ragi and another 50 gm of barley.

So while you get the traditional components of a dosa, you also get a lot of other grains as well.

The ITC version takes a different track. It has two distinct processes. First, it uses a dosa batter that is different from the 2:1 rice-to-dal formula. It requires 900 gm of basmati rice and only 100 gm of urad dal, thereby significantly cutting down the dal content. The second process consists of making a grain mix from flax, rye, cornmeal, wheat bran, barley, etc., and grinding it. Then, you add the dosa batter to the grain mix in the ratio of 5:3. This is significantly different, not just from the Taj dosa but also from the traditional dosa.

I've known Nat for years, from the days when he was a sous-chef in the old Rendezvous in Mumbai through his adventures in the south. For my money, he is the single most underrated chef in the country, largely because of his own retiring nature and partly because he is based in Chennai, and not in the media hot spots of Delhi and Mumbai.

I phoned him to ask about his dosas. It turned out that as corporate chef for the Gateway Hotels (one of the Taj's four brands along with Taj Luxury, Vivanta and Ginger), he set out to create lighter dishes for all his menus. He was guided by such nutritional principles as the glycaemic index. (Simply put, this posits that foods with a high glycaemic index stimulate the release of insulin, which converts food to fat, so we should eat foods with a low glycaemic index to stay thin.) His aim was to invent a menu that cut out the foods high on the glycaemic scale.

He found this easy enough to do with lunch and dinner, but for breakfast, he decided to eschew the usual chef's trick of simply making his breads with wholewheat (lower on the glycaemic index than maida) and to do something truly imaginative. Not only did he come up with this dosa but he also tinkered with the masala that goes into a masala dosa, reducing the potatoes, adding lots of peppers and using olive oil.

Nat says you can get his multigrain dosa at most Gateway Hotels, though it does not seem to have caught on at the fancier Taj properties. The reason I got to try it at the Lands End was because chef Roy visited a Gateway Hotel, tried the dosa, liked it and asked Nat for the recipe. As yet, the Taj has no plans to serve healthy dosas to guests who pay high room rates.

The ITC story is almost the opposite. While the Taj's dosa was created by one of the group's senior-most and experienced chefs, the multigrain dosa at the Mughal was invented by Pratish Nair, a young and enthusiastic chef in the hotel's kitchen. I tracked down Pratish and discovered that his motives were almost the same as Nat's.

When ITC opened its award-winning Kaya Kalp spa in Agra, Pratish was handed the job of trying to evolve a spa cuisine. Frankly, this is not as difficult as it sounds. There are thousands of spas all over the world serving rubbish food in the name of good health; so all he had to do was to steal a few recipes.

But Pratish wanted to do Indian breakfasts that were healthy. All over ITC, chefs live by Nakul Anand's axiom—now regarded as gospel by the hotel industry—that the one meal guests always eat in the hotel is breakfast and most Indians want idlis or dosas for breakfast; so, unless a hotel gets its south Indian breakfasts right, it will never be regarded as a food and beverage (F&B) success.

Pratish's experience had taught him that guests like their dosas crisp, almost like paper dosas. But how can you make a healthy dosa, full of grains and seeds and still achieve crispness unless you use lots of cooking fat (butter, ghee, etc.) that rather defeats the point of the exercise?

He began experimenting and created about forty-five different recipes before junking them all. But eventually, he cracked it. If he made the dosas with basmati rice, he discovered, they got crisp quite easily. Moreover, if he put flax seeds into the batter, the seeds released enough oil for him not to have to worry about adding any extra fat to the tawa.

So, when Pratish makes his multigrain dosas now, he uses a special tawa meant only for this dish and—here's the best part—he cooks them without any oil, ghee or butter at all! Still, he gets crisp, perfect dosas each time!

I've eaten both versions of the multigrain dosa, though admittedly my experience of the Taj dosa is limited to chef Roy's interpretation rather than Nat's original. A few things seem clear.

One, you can't compare them. They are quite different. Two, both are terrific. Three, you must eat them fresh from the tawa. They do not survive the inefficiency of the average room-service waiter. And four, they represent an interesting new way forward for Indian food. I doubt if they will ever catch on in home cooking (too many ingredients) but they prove that there are chefs all over India, who strive to make the familiar seem more interesting—and healthier!

Chef Pratish Nair's Multigrain Dosa

Portion: 4

Ingredients

For the grain mix:

90 gm flax seed
40 gm wheat flour
20 gm wheat bran
25 gm linseed
50 gm soy flour
30 gm barley
15 gm sunflower seeds
50 gm cornmeal
20 gm wholemeal oat flour
5 gm sesame seeds
30 gm rye flour
5 gm cumin seeds
Salt to taste

For the dosa batter:

900 gm basmati rice
100 gm urad dal

Accompaniments

1 portion coconut chutney
1 portion tomato chutney
1 portion garlic chutney
1 portion sambhar

Method (dosa batter)

Soak rice and urad dal together for five hours. Grind to a fine paste and ferment overnight. Soak all the seeds in warm water for ten minutes.

Grind to a coarse paste and mix with fermented dosa batter (60 gm grain mix to 100 gm dosa batter). Rest the batter for thirty minutes at room temperature after mixing in the coarsely ground seeds. Pour the batter on to a hot plate and cook without adding oil.

Chef Natarajan's Multigrain Dosa

Portions: 21

Ingredients

For the grain mix:

300 gm raw rice
100 gm boiled rice
100 gm urad dal
50 gm barley
100 gm broken wheat
100 gm green moong dal
100 gm oats
50 gm ragi flour
Salt to taste

Vegetable mixture:

100 ml olive oil
2 tsp mustard seeds
50 gm garlic, chopped
500 gm onion, sliced
12 green chillies, chopped
500 gm tomatoes, chopped
400 gm green capsicums, diced
400 gm red capsicums, diced
1 kg large potatoes, diced
20 gm basil leaves, shredded

Red chutney:

30 gm garlic cloves

50 gm small onion
750 gm tomatoes, chopped
100 gm dry red chilli
50 gm tamarind pulp
Salt to taste

Green chutney:

½ cup grated coconut
3 cups coriander leaves
15 green chillies, chopped
50 gm tamarind pulp
Salt to taste

Method

Stuffing: Heat the oil in a skillet and add mustard. Add garlic, onion and green chillies and sauté. Add vegetables and toss in a slow fire until they are cooked well and become soft. Add basil, salt and check the seasoning.

Dosa: Soak all the ingredients, apart from the ragi and oats, in water for two hours. Grind to a fine paste in a grinder, as you do with regular dosa batter. Now mix oats and ragi flour into the batter. Add salt and leave to rise overnight. When fermented well, make thick dosas out of the batter on a hot plate.

Presentation: Apply green chutney and red chutney on rough side of the dosa and place vegetable filling. Top with second dosa. Garnish with cherry tomato, olive and basil. Serve with hot sambhar and the chutneys.

Noodle Me This

≈

Will noodles become an Indian staple?

Some foods are more or less universal: meat, fish, vegetables, wheat, rice, fruit, etc.

No matter where in the world you go, you will find that they play some role in the local cuisine. Some cooked foods are as ubiquitous. In nearly all of the world, they cook rice in much the same sort of way (boiling in water). Fish tends to be fried, in one way or the other, all over the world.

After that, however, it gets more complicated. Is bread a universal food? You find it in the West, in the Middle East and in Indian cuisine. But it is largely absent from the cuisines of the Far East. The Chinese steamed bun is a Western import. The Japanese have no real bread tradition. Nor do the Thais.

And what of noodles?

There is a tendency among Western food writers to regard noodles as a global food, as the one dish that unites both the East and the West. The Italians have pasta. The Chinese have noodles and everybody else has some variation of those two dishes.

In fact, a persistent legend has it that the Italians got their pasta from China. According to this version, Marco Polo arrived in China, ate a bowl of chow mein, was so thrilled that he rushed back to Florence and Italian pasta was born.

Like most culinary legends, this is rubbish. First of all, there is some dispute over whether Marco Polo actually made it to China at all.

(Did he just make it all up?) Secondly, Italians were eating pasta long before Marco sat down to his chow mein or chop suey or whatever. Thirdly, the Italians were actually ahead of the Chinese in the noodle–pasta game. The Chinese only knew how to make fresh noodles, which had to be consumed soon after they were made. The Italians, on the other hand, had started making pasta with durum wheat (what we call suji in India), which allowed them to keep the pasta for a long time before they cooked it (through the winter, for instance).

Nevertheless, 'the world eats noodles' is a superficially attractive thesis. Of how many foods can you find so many global varieties? You can eat pasta with pesto in Italy, macaroni cheese in America, chow mein in any Chinese restaurant in the world, noodle soup in Thailand and soba noodles in Japan.

The problem with the global noodles hypothesis is that one of the world's greatest cuisines has no real room for noodles.

And that is Indian cuisine.

Think about it. Rice may well be the food that links South Asia and the Far East. But surely that's not true of noodles? Can you come up with any great noodle dish from an Indian cuisine?

I've been racking my brains and the best I can conjure up is the idi-appam of Kerala, which becomes a sort of noodle-like tangle when it is cooked. But even there, the Malayalis do not see it as a noodle dish. They see it as a broken-up variation of the appam, which is essentially, a pancake.

Some Indian desserts do use vermicelli (seviyan), especially in Muslim cuisines. But these are not staples (they are cooked usually on festive occasions) and the use of vermicelli is not Indian in origin. These desserts come from the Middle East where there has been trading contact with Europe for centuries and where vermicelli probably was first imported from Italy.

Other than that: zilch.

It is not as though we do not like playing around with our staples. We make hundreds of dishes with wheat. Rice turns up in everything from khichri to the idli. But somehow, the noodle has never entered our consciousness.

So, here's my next question: even though noodles are not part of our culinary tradition, could we be on the verge of introducing them into our cuisine?

This is not as strange as it sounds. Dishes often find fame and popularity far from their original homes. The noodle is now a Thai staple—go to any street in Bangkok and you will find vendors selling bowls of a flavourful soup containing noodles, herbs and (probably) fish balls. And yet, all the evidence suggests that noodles came to Thailand from China and are not indigenous to that country.

It is the same with Italian food. Pizza may have originated in Naples, but it is America that is the real home of pizza today. Spaghetti Bolognaise was created in England and became such a global phenomenon that restaurants in Bologna are now forced to put it on their menus. The American home staple of macaroni cheese has an Italian origin, but most people think of it as being as American as apple pie. (And anyway, apple pie originated in Europe . . .)

So, are we going to get Indian pasta or noodles?

For a long time I would have said no. Despite the best efforts of restaurateurs, pasta never caught on in India as anything other than an Italian dish. There was a stage when I thought that a masala-keema version of spaghetti Bolognaise might work, but the truth is that if Indians want to eat keema they will eat it with naan, roti, rice or even white bread. Spaghetti just does not go with Indian flavours. That is why the Indianization of the pizza (at the upper end, the chicken tikka pizza and at a mass level, the so-called Jain pizza) has never been extended to pasta.

But now I am more optimistic about noodles than I ever was about pasta. It is not the number of noodle houses that are opening all over our cities (with such names as Tasty Tangles) that make me reassess my position. These are successful and popular restaurants, but their menus are determinedly non-Indian and distinctively Far Eastern in character.

My optimism is based on the home and the street. Though they never get the credit that is their due, there is no doubt that instant noodles (whether loaded with trans fats or not) have had a significant influence on the quick home-cooked Indian meal.

If people want a relatively cheap snack between meals (or even a light meal), they often use noodles cooked vaguely Indian-style with garlic, onions, masala, etc. It is a filling option and it involves a minimum of effort. Some noodle manufacturers now offer ready-made Indian flavours to feed into this trend.

Those of us who take the instant-noodle option know that we are not cooking an Indian dish even if the flavours seem Indian. But do our children know this? This new generation lacks the kind of grounding in Indian food that older people have. It is entirely possible that when these kids grow up they will associate noodles with home cooking and not see them as a foreign food in the way that we do.

The second factor is the street. Despite all the romanticization of the dabbawallah tradition and the caricature of the devoted wife who wakes up early to cook her husband's lunch before he goes to office, the reality is that fewer and fewer people are getting lunch from home. Instead, they buy something to eat near office.

If you examine office areas in Mumbai and Kolkata (I'm not so sure about Delhi—but it will happen), you will find that roadside stalls, small restaurants and canteens are turning increasingly to instant noodles (and in some cases, proper noodles). There was a time when these dishes were dressed up as 'Chinese food' (to the horror of the Chinese). But now there is less and less pressure to do so. Indians are quite happy to eat masala noodles without pretending that they are experimenting with Chinese food.

So, will noodles become an Indian staple? Will we finally join the rest of Asia? I'm not sure. But I think that there is a chance that it could happen in this century.

Momos, Tandoori Chicken and Refugee Food

≈

Political demonstrations are an everyday affair in India. A significant part of the whole ritual of political protest is the burning of an effigy. Over the years, every leader of consequence (from Donald Trump to Mao Zedong to Indira Gandhi) has been burned in effigy while demonstrators cheer. But how about burning an effigy of a momo to protest against China.

In the troubled Indian border state of Jammu and Kashmir, demonstrations are even more common than in the rest of India. Even so there was something unusual about the protests organized by Ramesh Arora, a legislator from the Bharatiya Janata Party (BJP). Arora and his followers were not demonstrating against any political party or leader. The target of their ire was the 'momo', a dim sum–like dumpling that is popular all over India.

The momo, Arora declared, is 'more dangerous than alcohol or psychotropic drugs'. Worse still, he added, teenagers were getting 'addicted to momos as they do with drugs.' So, the 'Chinese momo', as he called it, had to be banned for its 'negative impact on Indian food culture'.

216 · VIR SANGHVI

Then, as his supporters carried placards with such slogans as 'Momos—Silent Killer' and 'Momos—Slow Death', Arora drew the media's attention to the effigy that was the centrepiece of his demonstration. This time it was not a political leader but it was, instead, an effigy of the momo, the 'Silent Killer' from Arora's rhetoric.

Even by the not-very-exacting standards of Indian political protests, there was something surreal about this demonstration. It is the first time in Indian history that a humble dumpling had been granted its own effigy. And though Arora got his fifty seconds of airtime on TV bulletins that evening, the general response was one of incredulity, if not outright hilarity.

Things did not get better when Arora declared that he wanted a ban on Chinese cuisine in general because it causes cancer of the intestine. (It is a miracle that there are any healthy Chinese people left in the world!)

Arora tried to find a pseudoscientific justification for his views, referring to the alleged ill effects of monosodium glutamate, an old Indian obsession that led the government of India to halt the sale of Maggi noodles some years ago. But obviously, nobody had told him that many Indian restaurants and locally made packaged foods also use monosodium glutamate. And perhaps it would not have mattered because the real target of his protest was China and its cuisine.

One problem with Arora's anti-Chinese protest is that not only is the momo not really Chinese, but most Chinese people, I suspect, have never even heard of it. So it seems like an odd choice of target for an anti-Chinese demonstration. (Even the second target of the protest, Ajinomoto, a popular brand of monosodium glutamate flavour-enhancers, is not Chinese. It is a Japanese company.)

But the story of the momo and its journey to near ubiquity in India (now including political protests!) tells us something about how the country's cuisine has developed. So many of the dishes that the world regards as Indian are either recent inventions or are adaptations of dishes from elsewhere.

Sometimes the dishes came from abroad with traders. The sambusak of the Middle East, originally a baked turnover, became the deep-fried Indian samosa that is popular the world over. The pilaus of Turkey were Indianized by court cooks and evolved into the biryani. Even the chilli, regarded internationally as the building block of Indian cuisine, was introduced to India (from the New World) by the Portuguese. It was so adroitly incorporated into Indian dishes by local chefs that most Indians now regard it as an ancient Indian vegetable/condiment.

But some of the greatest dishes came from refugees, from those forced to flee their homes because of some upheaval. The best example is modern tandoori cooking (tandoori chicken, butter chicken, and all tandoori kebabs, including the chicken tikka). It was only popularized as late as the second half of the twentieth century by refugees.

In 1947, when the British announced that they would leave their former colony of India, they also declared that they would hand over power to two nations. There would be India, of course. But they would create a new country called Pakistan as a homeland for the subcontinent's Muslims.

Initially, people on both sides of the border believed (and were assured) that Hindus and Muslims would continue to live happily in either country. But as the British rushed through the partition of India, Hindu–Muslim riots broke out and millions of people, on both sides of the border, feared for their lives. Muslims left India for Pakistan and terrified Hindus fled to find new homes in India.

Hindus and Muslims had lived in peace, side by side, for centuries in such Punjabi cities as Lahore. But Partition divided Punjab between India and Pakistan and once the riots began, many Hindus left the Pakistani part of Punjab and headed first to Indian Punjab and then, to Delhi, a larger city with more opportunities.

The refugees fled with not much more than the clothes on their backs. When they arrived in Delhi, the government set up refugee camps for them and they struggled to find work. Some drifted into the food business.

Among them was a man called Kundan Lal Gujral who had worked at a restaurant in Peshawar (now in Pakistan). Gujral had learned how to make innovative use of the tandoor, a clay oven that has traditionally been used in Punjab to bake breads (of which the naan is the most famous).

In Peshawar, Gujral had seen cooks at his restaurant put whole chickens on skewers into the tandoor. He was determined to replicate the idea in India. Not only was the chicken delicious, it was a cost-effective way of cooking. You could put three whole chickens on to a single skewer and cook them simultaneously in the tandoor.

Gujral opened a restaurant called Moti Mahal in Delhi and built a large tandoor. He cooked naans and chickens in their dozens at the same time in his massive tandoor. And his business flourished because it required no elaborate menus, few cooking vessels and virtually no cutlery. As Moti Mahal's fame spread, the menu expanded. Pieces of cut chicken went into the tandoor and were called chicken tikka, lamb chops cooked the same way became burrah kebabs and so on.

Then, Gujral hit on his second good idea. He needed a way to use up the leftover tandoori chicken and chicken tikka. So, he created a tomato-and-butter sauce and began to rehydrate the dried-out leftover chicken in the gravy. That dish became butter chicken. Later he added the same gravy to home-style Punjabi dal and created the buttery black dal that most Indian restaurants now serve.

This was Indian-cuisine-in-a-hurry, based on one tandoor and one sauce, a far cry from the haute cuisine of Delhi or north India's food capital of Lucknow. So, the great chefs sneered at it. But the public lapped it up.

Hundreds of Punjabi refugees decided to follow Gujral's example and set up tandoori restaurants. To help them along, the government allotted them land near New Delhi's central Pandara Road to open stalls. (That market still exists as a tandoori-lovers' paradise, though the stalls have now become full-fledged restaurants.)

As the refugees spread out all over India, they took their tandoors with them. By the late 1950s tandoori chicken had arrived in what were then Calcutta and Bombay. By the 1960s, it was a menu staple all over India. By the 1970s, virtually every Indian restaurant in the world had its own tandoor. And today, tandoori chicken is the world's most famous Indian dish.

Not bad going for a dish created by hard-working refugees in their desperation to make a fresh start!

Something similar happened to the momo, long before it was turned into an effigy and became the subject of dim-witted political protests.

The original momo is a Tibetan dish. Given that Tibet has been in China's sphere of influence for centuries, it seems reasonable to assume that like the gyoza of Japan, it had its roots in the Chinese tradition of dim sum.

But, unlike the fancier dim sums of Cantonese cuisine, this was a peasant dish. It was made of the cheapest, most easily available flour and filled with minced yak meat and flavoured with local spices.

In 1959, the tense relationship between Tibet's spiritual leader, the Dalai Lama, and Beijing (which had taken effective control of Tibet in 1951) finally collapsed. The young Dalai Lama fled to India, eventually making the northern Indian town of Dharamshala his home.

Some Tibetans arrived with the Dalai Lama, and throughout the early 1960s, Tibetan refugees kept streaming into India. The government, which had some experience of dealing with refugee arrivals after the Partition, provided them with housing. Then, recognizing their entrepreneurial skill, it gave them stalls along Janpath, one of New Delhi's main roads, to sell artefacts, antiques and the like.

But the Tibetans chose to wander. Many went to India's north-east, to Nepal and to the Indian protectorate of Sikkim (now fully integrated into India) where they looked for business opportunities.

Like the Punjabis before them, they decided that food offered the quickest route to making some kind of living. Momos were easy to make. Flour was readily available and steamers were not difficult to procure. There were no yaks so they made their momos from minced goat (the dominant meat in Delhi) or minced chicken. As they moved east, first to Kolkata and then to the hills of the north-east, they also began using pork, which made for a tastier momo.

By the early 1970s, the Tibetan momo had taken over the east. Nearly everywhere the Tibetans went, the momo followed. As canny business people, the Tibetans refined the recipe for the filling depending on the market they were catering to. In Kathmandu, Nepal, you get momos with a dark filling that are packed with spice. In many north-eastern towns, they incorporated the local flavours of pork and chilli. And so on.

Around 1980 or so, the Tibetans had done so well as business people that they found the returns from making momos too small to bother with. So others entered the fray, and as Bengalis, Khasis, Nepalis and others began making their own kinds of momos, the dish's Tibetan origins were largely forgotten.

It wasn't till the beginning of the twenty-first century, however, that momos went truly national. A fast-food chain (Momobelle) dedicated to momos was launched, the fancy new Four Seasons hotel in Mumbai put momos on the menu, and in every Delhi market, you could find two or three momo sellers.

Inevitably, the business became secretly corporatized. In Delhi, there are central kitchens where momos are made in their thousands. Local hawkers buy the dumplings each morning and then take them to their markets. They are steamed at the stalls and naturally, the hawkers claim their mothers or sisters made them at home.

Nothing in India remains purely regional. So now, momo stalls are mushrooming all over Jammu and Kashmir—hence the demonstrations and effigies! And two great culinary traditions have merged. All over Punjab, restaurants and stalls that would once have sold only chicken tikka or butter chicken now sell tandoori momos.

Tandoori momos?

Well, think about it. What is a momo? It is a steamed dim sum. What's a tandoor? It is an oven. So haven't you ever heard of dim sum baked in an oven?

Put that way, it doesn't sound that absurd, though Indian foodies regard the dish with derision.

So, is the momo still refugee food? Clearly not. What's more, it's not even regarded as a Tibetan dish in most of India. As the BJP's Jammu leader Arora (the man who called momos the 'Silent Killer') put it: 'This is a Chinese dish.'

Chinese?

Well, at least Beijing would approve, even if the Dalai Lama would not. With a single effigy, a slow-witted Indian politician has settled the issue of whether Tibet should be considered a part of China or not!

But his foolishness should not detract from the real story: Every refugee who has sought shelter in India has enriched its culture and, especially, its cuisine.

There is tandoori chicken. There is the momo. And now, there are even tandoori momos!

Tasty Triangles

≈

All we need is for the great Indian cooks to rediscover the samosa and treat it with the respect it deserves.

The samosa is the archetypal Indian snack. You can have hot samosas with your tea or you can have them cold, several hours after they have been made. You can have your samosas filled with spicy keema or you can have totally vegetarian versions filled with potatoes, paneer or even peas and French beans. You can enjoy the hefty Punjabi version or you can have the thinner, more delicate Bohra version from Mumbai. You can eat your samosa on the railway platform in Ambala or you can buy it from a bakery in Alappuzha.

What's more it is now one of the most internationally renowned Indian snacks. Once I had dinner at a French restaurant in Montreal. Part of the first course was a samosa with a cheese filling. The French usually describe filled pastries with terms derived from their own extensive gastronomic lexicon or call them pastillas or whatever. But this was called a samosa on the menu. As Montreal is a bit of a hick town, I wondered if this would confuse other diners with less experience of Asia. Not at all: they all seemed to know what a samosa was, even though there was no explanation on the menu.

Somewhat less surprisingly, the samosa has also been welcomed into the British mainstream. It frequently turns up in upmarket picnic hampers sold by such shops as Harrods and Fortnum & Mason. I've seen it on display at many tea and sandwich places. And British supermarkets usually sell some version of the samosa: fresh, frozen, ready to cook, etc.

All this should make people from the Middle East very angry.

Because the samosa is not really an Indian dish at all.

Push Indian food writers and they will eventually concede that the earliest mentions of the samosa in Indian literature can only be found after the Muslims established their kingdoms in India. Samosas turn up again and again on Mughal menus, usually as savouries stuffed with various kinds of keema. At the risk of alienating the Rashtriya Swayamsevak Sangh (RSS), I have to state that I was unable to find a single Hindu source for this dish. Even the great K.T. Achaya, who usually managed to assert that every famous Indian dish originated long before the Muslims arrived, perhaps even during the Indus Valley Civilization (he speculates that as early tandoors have been excavated there, maybe even tandoori cooking started in Mohenjo-Daro), seemed unable to locate an ancient Tamil kingdom where the samosa was the court dish.

The problem with trying to pretend that we invented the samosa is that it makes extensive appearances in Middle Eastern literature of the medieval era. Even today, a version of the samosa, called a sambusak, is eaten all over the Middle East.

According to Alan Davidson's *Penguin Companion to Food*, the very name samosa comes from the Persian word *sambosag*. By the tenth century, Arab cookbooks were already giving the recipe and called it a sambusak.

The samosa/sambusak spread all over the Middle East as conquerors and traders travelled and it took various forms and various shapes in every country. The original sambusak was probably a half-moon but as it moved, it acquired its current triangular shape. In some countries (Turkey and Afghanistan, for instance) both triangular and semicircular shapes continue to coexist.

So what was India's contribution? How did we turn the sambusak into the samosa?

I can think of several Indian innovations. It is almost certain that Indians were not into baking (the Indus Valley Civilization notwithstanding) until the Muslims got here. Nor were we very familiar with refined flour or maida. We used atta, which, while healthier, is somewhat more limited when it comes to the possibilities for pastry.

The original sambusak was probably made from maida. It might well have also been baked. In that sense it was related to the pastilla of Morocco and Spain and the pastele of the Sephardic Jews. Other European pastry dishes such as the puff and the pasty are probably derived from the same source.

But an army cannot bake. Nor can a wandering trader. Somewhere along the way, the people of the Middle East began frying their sambusaks. It is easy to see why they would do this: You can fill a dekchi with oil and build a fire pretty much anywhere you go. An oven is much more difficult to construct.

So, by the time traders and conquerors had made the journey to India from Europe and Central Asia, they had given up on the baked version. The sambusak they brought to India was probably fried.

Then, the genius of Indian cooking took over. India has a long tradition of taking ordinary Middle Eastern foods (the pilau or the kebab, for instance) and turning them into delicacies. At the Mughal court, the sambusaks or samosas were not filled with pumpkin and walnuts as they had been in the Middle East. Instead, Indian cooks devised delicate and more innovative fillings.

It used to be said that Mughal chefs loved keema because it was the perfect medium for transferring any kind of flavour. So, court chefs took the boring sambusak and turned it into a haute cuisine dish. I'm not sure—and records are unclear on this—how the court chefs abolished the baked version of the dish, but my guess is that they preferred the delicate crispiness of a well-fried samosa to the stodginess of a baked sambusak.

When did the samosa make the transition from the courts to the kitchens of ordinary people? And why have today's great Mughlai chefs given up on it, treating is as the sort of thing best left to halwais?

I don't know. And try as I might, I have been unable to find an answer in literature.

What is clear is that, even in the Middle East, there is a tradition of vegetarian sambusaks. In Central Asia, those made with puff pastry (and baked) are non-vegetarian. Those made with dough (leavened or unleavened) are often vegetarian.

My conjecture—and it is only a conjecture—is that Indian cooks (or to be less politically correct: non-court cooks and Hindu halwais) took the sambusak/samosa and married it to another Indian tradition: the deep-fried snack such as the pakora, vada, bonda or kachori.

Indians have always liked the idea of taking a filling and encasing it in some kind of dough (atta, besan, etc.) before deep-frying it. When the samosa moved out of the court kitchens, it was quickly turned into that kind of a halwai snack.

More significantly, it ceased to be the sort of haute cuisine dish that had to be eaten as soon as it was made. The distinguishing feature of the samosa these days is that it is often served several hours after it has been cooked.

As deep-fried foods do not stay very well, cooks have had to make compromises. Vegetarian fillings are not just cheaper but they are also less likely to go off. A thin and delicate batter will get soggy quickly, so fat Punjabi-style shells have been used to encase the filling. And because even these do not stay crisp for very long, halwais have invented samosa chaat in which the samosa is broken up and then doused with chutney (and sometimes, dahi) so that the texture of the casing does not matter much.

I have nothing against halwai samosas or their regional variations (such as the spicier, smaller shingara of Kolkata) but the best samosas are still the small, crisp ones with a thin casing that are served soon after they are made.

The Gujarati samosa falls into this category. The non-vegetarian version is associated with Gujarati Muslim communities (the Bohras, the Khojas, the Memons, etc.) and there is a delicate vegetarian version (with such fillings as French beans and peas) that most traditional maharajs will make.

In the old days, it was easy enough to get the small Gujarati samosa in Mumbai. The old MG Café on Queen's Road was famous for it and many restaurants (including the now defunct Bombelli's) would buy ready-made uncooked samosas from central suppliers and fry them just before serving.

You can still get them but it is getting more and more difficult. The fat Punjabi samosa has taken over just as the Punjabi chef has at most hotels and restaurants.

Now, all we need is for the great Indian cooks—the Imtiazs and the Raeeses, etc.—to rediscover the samosa and to treat it with the respect it deserves.

There is a lost tradition waiting to be revived here.

Culture Curry

≈

Thanks to our ownership of the term 'curry' we can claim that our cuisine has conquered the world—all the way from Thailand to Trinidad.

If I had continued to make more episodes of *A Matter of Taste*, the food show I did for the Discovery Travel and Living channel, here's one that I would certainly have done: Curry Around The World.

We think of curry as being one of the defining dishes of Indian cuisine. And certainly, foreigners often use curry as a synonym for Indianness. For instance, when *Sholay* went to European film festivals it was described as 'shootout at the OK curry' (after the famous Western *Gunfight at the O.K. Corral*) or simply as a Curry Western. Americans claim that Indian homes smell of curry. And the traditional term for a cheap Indian restaurant in the UK is a 'curry house'.

But, as Indian food writers never tire of reminding the rest of the world, curry is more or less unknown to us. Of course, we'll make gravy dishes and we'll make such specialities as rogan josh or vindaloo, but we'll never think of them as curries.

Ask a great Indian chef about the strength of his cooking and the chances are that he'll brag about his gravies. Most Lucknow cooks will be noted for the secret mixture of spices that goes into their gravies. And in that sense, gravies are to Indian cuisine what sauces are to French. But rarely if ever will you find an Indian chef saying that he makes a great mutton curry or a killer chicken curry.

So why has the term 'curry' taken off all over the world? The traditional explanation is that it is a corruption of 'kari' from the 'kari patta' that the Brits took to their mother country from their stints in the colonies. There is some controversy over this theory but nobody can deny that few countries are as curry-fixated as Britain. 'Going out for a curry' is a fairly common way of referring to an Indian meal and many British Indian restaurants list innumerable curries on their menus. Indians may find it slightly confusing to be confronted with such curries as a patia, which bears no relation to the Parsee dish of the same name, or a vindaloo that has nothing to do with the vinegar-flavoured Goan dish but is merely the restaurant's basic curry with extra chillies.

And yet, however sniffy we are about curries, it's hard to deny that they do represent one of the unifying factors of Indian cuisine. In his introduction to *Curry*, a famous cookbook featuring recipes from global chefs, Vivek Singh (most famous as the chef at London's Cinnamon Club) argues that any fish, meat or vegetables cooked with spices and in a liquid is a curry. If you use that definition, you find curries all over India—the nalli gosht of Lucknow is as Indian as the fish curry of Goa.

What's more difficult to explain is why we find curries in other parts of the world. Often it is because of migrants or because foreigners have taken a fancy to Indian curries. The British are the most famous example, but let's not forget the Japanese. Bizarrely, curry (directly descended from the Indian version but almost unrecognizable to us) is one of the most popular dishes of Japanese cuisine. According to Yasuko Fukuoka (who's done the Japanese chapter in *Curry*), the British took curry to Japan in the nineteenth century because their Indian cooks kept making curry dishes and the Japanese couldn't get enough of them. Intriguingly, while the Japanese are rice eaters, many prefer to eat their curries with noodles, a combination that most Indians find odd.

Similarly, curry in Africa and the Caribbean is also a consequence of migration. The curries of Trinidad owe their origins to the indentured Bihari labourers who went off to the West Indies to work on the sugarcane plantations. And African curries are largely a consequence of the migration of Gujaratis and Punjabis to East Africa.

However, try as I might, I have been unable to link the curries of South-east Asia to Indian cuisine. It is traditional for Indians to be patronizing about South-east Asian cuisines and to say things like

'Thai food is really a cross between Chinese and Indian' but the truth is that many East Asian cuisines—Thai in particular—are remarkably sophisticated and complex and have grown entirely on their own.

It's hard to see how Indians can claim that a Thai green curry or red curry travelled from our shores before being colonized by the Thais. Apart from the completely different nature of the spicing, there's also the dependence on coconut milk, which is not typically Indian (though, of course, you find coconut-milk-based curries in Indian coastal cuisine).

The Thais claim that they developed their own curries and this may well be true. Thai cuisine itself has a complicated history. The Thais were fish-eating vegetarians till the Chinese arrived and introduced them to meat and chicken. It's easy to trace the Chinese influences in Thai cuisine (all Thai dishes are seasoned with nam pla or fish sauce, but the ones that have a Chinese origin usually require some soya) but more difficult to find an Indian connection.

The exception perhaps is the masaman curry, which has its origins in Thailand's Muslim community (largely concentrated in the south), and the word masaman is probably a corruption of Mussalman. You could argue that Arab or Indian traders taught coastal Thai Muslims to make a curry that has more in common with our food than with the herby cuisine of central Thailand.

But that's about it. I haven't found any other evidence of Indian influence in Thai curries. On the other hand, there is a reason to believe that a reverse migration also took place. Bengalis claim chingri malai curry as one of the star dishes in their cuisine. But the style of cooking (in coconut milk) is so different from most other dishes that one view is that the curry was brought back by Bengalis after they had worked in the rubber plantations of Malaya. The malai in chingri malai curry refers not to coconut cream, as Bengalis like to believe, but to Malay, after the country where that particular curry originated.

If I had shot an episode of *A Matter of Taste* on curry (and one was planned, though we never got around to shooting it) I would have travelled around Thailand, Malaysia and Laos trying to see if I could find some link, however tenuous, to the curries of India.

My suspicion, however, is that it is the English name 'curry' (not one that the people of those countries use themselves) that gives us a false sense that all Asian curries are somehow related. In fact, the practice of cooking meat or vegetables in a gravy is not restricted to Asia or even to the countries of South-east Asia. You could argue that an Irish stew is a curry of some description. And you could also make a case for claiming that boeuf bourguignon is a Burgundy curry. To say that these cannot be curries because they have no spices is to miss the point. History suggests that medieval European cooking used many spices (that's why the traders first came to India) before herbs came into vogue. And in any case, the curries of South-east Asia also depend on herbs rather than spices.

So perhaps we should define curry more narrowly. A catch-all description makes it difficult to exclude those dishes that are clearly not curries. On the other hand, it also gives India a sense of great importance because thanks to our ownership of the term 'curry' we can claim that our cuisine has conquered the world—all the way from Thailand to Trinidad.

Sweet

Kheer
for Dessert

≈

Kheer is the greatest rice pudding in the world. It is an international dessert combining three cooking traditions—Indian, the Middle Eastern and the Western.

Can you think of a dessert that is truly international? One contender would be bread pudding, which turns up in various guises (shahi tukra, bread-and-butter pudding, etc.) all over the world but suffers—at least in my view—because wheat is not regarded as a staple in many parts of the world.

That leaves us with rice. Nearly everywhere you go, you'll find some kind of rice dessert, even if it is as simple as, say, mango with sticky rice, the sort of dish you come across all over the Far East where sweet sticky rice is an important constituent of desserts.

My own vote, however, goes to kheer.

Yes, I know it sounds odd to think of kheer as an international dessert, and certainly it is not known by that name outside of India. But kheer unites three different cooking traditions—Indian, the Middle Eastern and the Western. We may use different names for the dessert, but it is, essentially, the same dish.

If you take the defining characteristic of kheer—it is a mixture of sweetened (often reduced and thickened) milk with whole rice—you'll find that it is not very different from the rice pudding of Western cuisine. And of course, in the Middle East, there is a glorious rice-and-milk dessert tradition.

Kheer differs from many Indian desserts because it has two quite distinct origins. The first is the ancient Indian tradition of payas, which survives to this day in south India as payasam and in Bengal, also as payas. And the second is the Middle Eastern sheer brought to India by Arabs in the medieval age.

According to the great K.T. Achaya, still our most reliable source on the food of ancient India, we find mentions of payas in Buddhist-era literature. At that stage it was a mixture of rice, milk and sugar—a formula that has endured for over 2000 years.

When Hinduism returned to India and drove Buddhism out to the Far East, the payas became a staple temple food. In particular, it was associated with Lord Shiva and served as prasad to his devotees.

But even while this tradition endured, another was on its way.

In the Middle East, rice puddings have been around for a very long time. In Persia, their version of kheer, the sheer biring, was, according to legend, made by angels on the seventh floor of Heaven when the Prophet ascended there to meet Allah.

But there are many other kinds of Middle Eastern rice pudding. Shola (or sholleh) is the name given to several rice dishes, most of them savoury, but which allow for sweet variations.

Then there is the muhallabia, also essentially a kheer but one where the rice is ground. And, of course, we know one variation of muhallabia, the Mughal phirni, which also uses ground rice, rather than whole, as the thickener for sweetened milk.

The name kheer suggests that the dish came to India from the Middle East sheer, which means milk in Farsi. Also, the fact that many Muslim communities in India make it with seviyan (certainly a Middle Eastern import) suggests a West Asian or Arab origin.

So is the kheer related to the sheer biring or the payas? It is an interesting question that admits of no easy answer because Hindu and Muslim cuisines have always flourished side by side.

My guess would be that, as with so many other foods, the dishes merged at some stage. For instance, many Muslim chefs will use kewra as an aromatic flavouring for kheer. But kewra is not from West Asia. It is part of the genus *Pandanus*, which we see all over East Asia and India.

(It turns up in Thai cooking again and again and is much prized in Bali for its vanilla-esque flavour.) As the Arabs rarely used *Pandanus*, it is safe to say that the tradition of using such flavourings came about because of Hindu influences on Muslim kitchens.

But kheer is just one kind of rice pudding. The dish turns up in Western cuisine in various forms. It is often prescribed as a dish for sick people or children (which is understandable given its comforting texture and reassuring sweetness) but also (less understandably) as an aphrodisiac!

The 'aphrodisiac property' may have reflected a great truism of all cuisine—whenever a dish is based on expensive or hard-to-find ingredients, mystical erotic properties are instantly ascribed to it.

In medieval Europe, rice was an expensive import and consumed only on special occasions. Sugar was also expensive and the spices required for flavouring (cinnamon and nutmeg were frequently used in rice puddings) also came from the East and often were regarded on a par with gold—sometimes they cost as much as gold, ounce for ounce.

Consequently, Western cuisines combined rice with cheaper meat products (this was common in those days and many desserts included meat, a tradition that only survives today in the jellies made from animal bones) to create rice puddings that sound too disgusting for modern tastes.

According to Alan Davidson's *Penguin Companion to Food*, one seventeenth-century recipe included sugar, breadcrumbs, eggs, rosewater, nutmeg and bone marrow! A traditional Cumberland rice pudding included suet, marrow and other animal products.

Fortunately, as time went on, and rice, sugar and spices became readily available, the rice pudding also became largely vegetarian.

Today's Western rice pudding differs from our kheer in only one basic respect—it usually includes egg, which would hardly be appropriate in India where the dish is often used as prasad.

But otherwise, chefs all over the world are the same. Ask an Indian chef to make kheer and he will do his best to tart up the dish by adding new flavours (fruit kheers are a cliché these days), reducing the milk so much that the dish loses much of the liquid that is so essential to its enjoyment or putting it in the oven before serving so that it looks like a Western pudding.

Western chefs use the same tricks. They muck around with flavours (real vanilla, liqueurs, etc.), use milk that is reduced or condensed, and try fancy presentation tricks. Some chefs even make their rice puddings risotto-style claiming that this is a traditional Italian recipe (which it may well be). The usual trick, however, is to 'soufflé' the pudding, which is to say that the chef adds eggs, puts it in the oven and waits for it to rise. This looks fancy but misses—at least from my perspective—the point of a rice pudding.

And what is the point?

Well, according to me, several things are obvious. The first is that the English and the French do not know how to cook rice. (I'll grant the Italians, the Spaniards and other truly Mediterranean people—though not the Greeks—their rice dishes.) Their rice puddings are, at origin, rather dull. And these days, they are overdone and needlessly fancy.

Secondly, the Middle Eastern rice pudding tradition, though worthy, has none of the richness of our mix-of-religions traditions. Indians make the best rice puddings in the world, which given that we grow so much rice (unlike the Middle East) is only fair enough.

I respect the Chinese/Far Eastern way with rice but according to me, to simply mix glutinous rice with fruit (which is what all of their rice puddings consist of) is not a very creative way of making a dessert.

Far better therefore to stick with the Indian tradition where rice is slow-cooked with milk and spices. My view is that a good kheer should learn from the delicacy of the south Indian payasam. It should not be made with condensed milk, your tongue should not be coated with milk fat, and it should not spend time in the oven.

Rather, the point of a great rice pudding—and especially a kheer— is the contrast between milk that is sweetened and delicately flavoured with spices and the texture of rice. You can add extra textures of course— raisins, coconut (a nod to the south) or nuts. But the point must be the rice.

But, of course, chefs don't bother with kheer these days. They have contempt for it, treat it as a dish any housewife or temple pandit can cook and refuse to put in on their menus. South Indian chefs have more respect for their traditions—which is why it is easier to get a good payasam at a restaurant than it is to get a good kheer.

Which is a shame because (a) the kheer is the greatest rice pudding in the world and (b) it is a truly secular dish, marrying Muslim and Hindu traditions.

If we can't even protect, nourish and restore the kheer to its former glory, there is something wrong with the way in which we treat our cooking traditions.

Cream
of the Crop

≈

**What made crème caramel such a hit with Indians is its
sweetness and simplicity.**

It is a dessert that is unquestionably Western in origin. And yet, you will
find it served at restaurants all over India, including small towns—places
where nothing else on the menu is remotely Western.

It is a dish you will find at top restaurants and one which grand
pastry chefs will make. But it is also that one Western dessert that many
Indian housewives will have no problem in cooking at home.

What's more, you will sometimes be hard-pressed to tell the difference
between the version served up by your aunt in her small suburban kitchen
and the version made by some fancy chef in a tall white hat. Many of us
grew up eating crème caramel even if we didn't always call it that. We may
have known it as caramel custard or as caramel pudding. But whatever
you call it, the dish is the same. I asked Rohit Sangwan, executive sous-
chef at Mumbai's Taj Lands End and, for my money, India's best pastry
chef, what made the dessert such a hit with Indians.

Rohit reckons that it is the sweetness. In his experience, the Indian
attitude to desserts is shaped by the Indian mithai. And because our
mithai is so much sweeter than Western desserts, we like our puddings
to be as sweet as possible. I have another theory. I think it has to do with
texture. We may enjoy cakes and pastries, but we are not that keen on the

texture of baked maida. Our own sweets use no pastry at all. So we like desserts that are not based on maida.

Moreover, our sweets tend to be made from milk, whether it is shrikhand or sandesh or even the rasgulla. Essentially, Indians think of pudding as something made with milk and sugar. And a crème caramel is really no more than milk and sugar with some eggs thrown in. When you bite into it, you get a nice clean feeling without the crumbly pastry nature of most pies and cakes.

Then, of course, there is the simplicity factor. Any fool can make a crème caramel. All you need to do is make a custard with milk, eggs and sugar (and a drop of vanilla essence) and then cook it in a water bath or a double boiler. You don't need skill. You don't need to understand baking. You don't even need an oven—and, until recently, most Indian kitchens did not come equipped with ovens of any kind.

What makes for a good crème caramel? In my experience, the basic difference between a successful crème caramel and a failed one is the consistency. A great crème caramel is firm, but it quivers slightly when your spoon first goes in. It always slices easily without collapsing. A bad crème caramel is thin, has a slight curdled-milk quality, does not retain its shape and falls apart when you try to eat it.

Rohit says that the difference between good and bad is not really one of technique. The trick lies in the ingredients. If your milk is the thin, watered-down stuff that some doodhwallahs provide, it is almost impossible to make a good crème caramel. Buy milk from a reputed dairy, and your dessert will succeed. Plus, he adds, it has to do with the eggs. Sometimes people cheat and add too few eggs with consequences that are fatal for the consistency of the crème caramel.

When fancy chefs get in on the act, there is not much they can do with the basic structure of the dessert. There are only two parts of the recipe that provide room for manoeuvre. The first is the caramel. In a classic crème caramel, a caramel sauce (i.e., a sugar sauce) will go into the dish before the custard is poured in to give the dessert its brown top. Top chefs muck around with the caramel sauce, adding ingredients here and there to make it seem fancier. (It is not uncommon to try to add an orange flavour, though frankly, I think it is a waste of time.) The other option is to add flavour to the custard. Professional chefs should not use vanilla essence, which is usually synthetic in origin, and should invest in real vanilla. But they can also add nutmeg and other spices in an effort to make the dish seem grander. As you may have guessed, I am not a fan of fancy crème caramels. Give me a simple caramel custard with a nice, rich texture and I will often prefer it to nearly everything else on the dessert menu. It is a foolproof dish that is almost always satisfying no matter whether you pay hundreds of rupees for it or whether you make it yourself at home for a fraction of the cost.

There was a time in the 1970s when chefs built on the popularity of crème caramel to introduce diners to a fancier version—crème brûlée. By the '80s, crème brûlée was ubiquitous on restaurant menus all over the world. In the '90s, its popularity began to recede and though you still find it on many menus today, chefs try to avoid straightforward crème brûlées because they've become so common.

So, when it does turn up on menus these days, it is usually in some tarted-up form with fruit or dry fruit flavouring (apricots, for instance) or reeling under the influence of some kind of alcohol (a whisky crème brûlée, for example).

Unlike a crème caramel, a crème brûlée is not a dish for the home cook. For a start, it uses cream over milk (in Rohit Sangwan's version, an astonishing amount of cream!), which is only fair because the name itself means 'burnt cream' in French. Secondly, the dish's signature is a hard crust of sugar, which, in theory, you can get by placing the dessert under the grill once you've sprinkled it with sugar. In reality, however, you only get a proper crust if you put a blowtorch to the sugar. And most kitchens, even in the West, do not come equipped with blowtorches.

Like all caramel desserts, there is a controversy over the origins of the crème brûlée. The English claim that they invented it. (But then, so do the Spanish.) The French laugh away this claim and point to the name, which is distinctively French.

What is clear is that Trinity College, a college in the English university town of Cambridge, served a variation of the crème brûlée over a century ago. Chefs would bake a custard, sprinkle sugar on it, and would then brand it with the Trinity crest. But did Trinity's chefs actually invent it? Or were they adapting an existing dessert?

Trinity College itself makes no claims for the invention of the crème brûlée. It says that the dessert already existed by the time the college's variation was introduced.

These days, crème brûlées tend to be made in the bakery sections of most hotels. They are then refrigerated for several days until somebody orders one. At that stage, the restaurant in question takes it out of the fridge and either puts it under the salamander or blowtorches it. The result is usually a crème brûlée that may be warm at the top but is cold at the centre and is therefore not terribly appetizing.

Nearly a decade ago, I got into an argument with a chef at a Delhi hotel about the right temperature for a crème brûlée. It was meant to be a warm dessert, I said. It was completely wrong to serve it ice cold with a warm crust on top. No, said the chef, the recipe required the dessert to be refrigerated overnight.

I checked with Rohit about the Lands End crème brûlées. He says that he does not like refrigerating his brûlées for exactly the reasons I mentioned. He makes his crème brûlées fresh and then leaves them to set at room temperature for five to six hours. The blowtorching happens right at the end. As a chef, he has a technical objection to refrigeration. According to him, a refrigerated crème brûlée will have lots of moisture and so, no matter how much blowtorching you do, the crust will never get hard enough to make a satisfying crunch when you push your spoon into it.

Rohit also makes another point that had not occurred to me. In his experience, vegetarians prefer crème brûlées to crème caramels because of the egg factor. Both desserts are made with eggs, of course—you can't make a real custard without them. But a crème caramel tends to smell and taste slightly of egg white, which makes many vegetarians a little uncomfortable. On the other hand, because a crème brûlée depends on egg yolks, it has no real egg smell.

There was a phase when I loved crème brûlées. But as I get older I find that they are too rich for me. Oh yes, those golden crusts are a delight but once you break through, the sheer richness of the cream can be a little overwhelming.

So give me a nice crème caramel any time! Rohit says that Indian chefs tend to put too much sugar in their custards, forgetting that the caramel sauce will also add lots of sweetness. He reckons that a crème caramel properly made with less sugar, lots of eggs and good-quality milk is hard to beat.

I know I agree. And so, I think, do millions of Indians.

Crème Caramel

Ingredients

1 litre milk
2 vanilla pods
11 whole eggs
200 gm sugar
150 gm sugar for making caramel

Method

Caramel: Pour the sugar in a pan and cook on a slow flame. Once the sugar turns golden brown, remove from flame and very carefully pour into moulds.

For the custard: Preheat the oven to 150°C; boil milk with slit vanilla pods. Meanwhile, mix the egg and sugar together lightly, just enough to combine them. Pour the boiled milk over the egg and sugar and strain.

Baking: Pour custard over caramel and place the moulds in baking tray half-filled with water. Bake for about twenty minutes, until the custard is set. To test, gently shake the ramekins; the custard should not wobble.

If you are not sure, you can insert a knife to see if the custard is cooked in the centre of the dish.

Demould and serve chilled upside down.

Crème Brûlée

Ingredients

800 ml double cream
200 ml milk
3 vanilla pods
10 egg yolks
100 gm caster sugar
150 gm caster sugar for glazing

Method

Preheat the oven to 150°C. Heat the cream and milk in a saucepan. Slit vanilla pods open lengthways. Using the back of a knife, scrape the seeds from inside the pod into the cream. Mix the egg yolks and sugar (100 gm) together, pour the boiled cream over the mixture and keep mixing.

Strain and fill the dish with the custard. Fill a baking tray with cold water to two-thirds of the way up the sides of the ramekins and place in the oven; bake for fifteen to twenty minutes. Place the baked ramekins on a small tray. Cool. Using a teaspoon, spread sugar (150 gm) over the top of the custard. With a blowtorch or an oven, toaster and griller (OTG) (with only the top filament put on), burn the sugar until it melts to create a thin sheet of golden caramel.

The Cookie Crumbles

≈

Above all, biscuits must be simple and tasty.

Not only has it been a long time since Britannia ruled the waves, it has also been many years since Britannia ruled the Indian biscuit shelves. In my youth, Britannia and biscuits were synonymous. You had the Parle Gluco biscuit, of course (apparently the largest-selling biscuit in India in that era), but the ones that ordinary middle-class families like ours chose to buy were Britannia's versions of such British favourites as Bourbon, Marie, Thin Arrowroot and Nice (pronounced, we were told, like the city in France—not that it mattered as long as we got to eat the layer of sugar on the outside).

I discovered later that this had to do with Britannia's original corporate parentage (British companies with such reassuringly dated names as Huntley-Palmer) and the colonial desire to export great British brands to each corner of the empire.

Then, the Brits were taken over by Americans. Such giant conglomerates as RJR Nabisco (maker of the mighty Oreo, which is to the US biscuit—sorry, cookie!—market what Coca-Cola is to its soft drink sector) were placed firmly in control and the sweet old colonial brands started vanishing. Eventually, it all got very complicated with Nabisco being taken over by Wall Street bankers, Indian Britannia being sold, its new owners fighting with its new French partners, etc. In any case, I am assured now that this avatar of Britannia, part of Nusli Wadia's empire, has its own Indian identity and is so successful that foreigners try to steal its brands (Tiger biscuits, for instance). Fair enough.

But two points are worth making. One: it is not the Britannia I grew up with. (But then, this is not the India I grew up in either; so I guess that's only to be expected.) And two: that the relaxation of food imports means that the shelves at my local grocer's groan under the weight of so many imported biscuits and cookies from all over the world that the biscuits of my childhood (the great Britannia varieties) end up being relegated to the back of the shop while fancy expensive ones with French and German packaging occupy pride of place.

I am a bit of a reactionary when it comes to biscuits. They are not—at least as far as I am concerned—some fancy gourmet food for great chefs and corporate focus groups to experiment with. They must be tasty. They must be simple. And above all, they must give you the reassuring feeling of sitting at home with a nice cup of tea (or coffee) into which you can (if your manners are as bad as mine) dunk your favourite biscuit. As for the great German and French brands that now clog our supermarket shelves, I have only one thing to say: If you can't pronounce the name, don't bother eating the biscuit.

I have already lamented much over the long-time absence of a great British biscuit from our shores. This was the digestive, the biscuit that, in my prejudiced view, made Britain great. We never got it in India because Britannia couldn't be bothered or because it was too closely associated with another British biscuit company, McVitie's.

Nowadays, however, you can buy digestives from every conceivable foreign manufacturer in Indian shops, though, to my mind, the McVitie's version is still clearly superior to all others. My belief that the digestive is truly the king of the biscuit world (gosh, I feel like a traitor to Bourbon when I say things like that!) is based on several factors.

First of all, there's size. (No jokes about how it doesn't matter, please.) A digestive is a clunking great thing, a large-diameter biscuit that leaves you satisfied rather than hungering for more. Then, there's the texture. They sell you digestives these days by focusing on the wholewheat element. A digestive biscuit, some manufacturers suggest, is made with wholegrain, not maida. This is not entirely true—there's an awful lot of maida in each digestive. Even the health claims originally made for the biscuit (the reason why it is called a digestive) have now been exploded. In the old days, they said that because digestives used lots of sodium bicarbonate, this released carbon dioxide during the baking process, making the biscuit an aid to digestion (to wind, more likely). McVitie's does not bother to make this claim any longer, which is just as well.

But even if all the health stuff is rubbish, what is true is that a digestive has a wonderful, slightly crumbly texture unlike the one-dimensional hard wheatiness of, say, Thin Arrowroot or Marie. This gives it a completely different mouth-feel from most other biscuits and contributes to its distinctive taste.

As brilliant as the digestive is, however, it is its cousin that is probably better known. This is the chocolate digestive (either in milk or in dark-chocolate avatars), so popular in England that it is often simply referred to as a chocolate biscuit, its distinctiveness making it a generic biscuit. (Remember Hugh Grant, the prime minister in *Love, Actually*, asking at Number Ten, 'Who does one have to sleep with to get a chocolate biscuit here?' And at that stage the heroine appears with a plate of chocolate digestives?)

I like the dark-chocolate version, though apparently the original was created many years before its cousin. A young Scottish baker called Alexander Grant invented the original digestive at the end of the nineteenth century. Around 1925, the McVitie's bakery in Edinburgh came up with the milk-chocolate version, which is exactly the same biscuit with a thin layer of milk chocolate on top. Eventually, the dark-chocolate version was created and so, the world's best biscuit was born.

You don't get chocolate digestives easily in India. I suspect that this is because the chocolate melts easily in our climate, causing the biscuits to fuse together when the chocolate solidifies again. But you do get a huge variety of European chocolate biscuits.

I've tried the German Choco Leibniz, which is essentially a Petit-Beurre biscuit (though I doubt if they call it that in Germany) with a lump of good-quality chocolate. (You know the Petit Beurre, of course? It's the buttery biscuit that they now make in India as well.)

The same idea gets a French twist with the Petit Écolier biscuit. This is also a version of the Petit Beurre with a thick slab of chocolate stuck on to it. It is expensively packaged (there is a detailed drawing of a little schoolboy on each biscuit) and looks suitably upmarket, but it doesn't work for me because it lacks the crumbly intensity of the digestive.

When I can't get chocolate digestives (which, frankly, happens a lot of the time), I fall back on the good, old-fashioned Bourbon of my childhood. Contrary to what we grew up thinking, Bourbon is not a Britannia brand. In England, for instance, the version I have most often come across is made by a company called Crawford's.

Bourbon seems to be a generic term for a particular kind of sandwich biscuit. Within the biscuit industry, sandwich biscuits are regarded as a bit gimmicky. They consist of two separate biscuits with a sticky filling in the middle. My own opinion is that most sandwich biscuits are let down by their fillings: the so-called 'custard' in custard creams is uniformly disgusting; ditto for alleged jam fillings. And as for the stuff they put inside an Oreo, you have to be an American to love it (which, of course, they do).

The reason the Bourbon works is that (a) even though the chocolate filling would not win any gourmet prizes, it is entirely acceptable and (b) because the biscuit itself is so good. Take a cup of strong black coffee (the kind of thing they serve at Café Coffee Day or Barista or somewhere like that) and dip your Bourbon into it. Now, eat the Bourbon. The flavours of coffee, sugar, wheat and chocolate will have merged so perfectly that you will be conscious of enjoying a superior gastronomic experience.

There are problems with the Bourbon though. Unlike the digestive, it is less filling. So you'll find it hard to stop eating them till you finish the packet. And, if you are at one of those office meetings where they place a plate of mixed biscuits in front of everyone, you'll have to move quickly because the Bourbons will always be the first to go. (Why do they bother with mixed biscuits when people eat the Bourbons only?)

So here's my ranking. If you are feeling chocolatey, hold out for a dark-chocolate digestive. If that's not available, take the Bourbon. Never waste money on the fancy European stuff with unpronounceable names. And if you want something satisfying, you can't do better than a plain digestive. It'll fill your stomach and, more importantly, it'll make you feel good.

Choc-a-bloc

≈

Real chocolate is like fine wine.

The first thing you need to remember about chocolate is that there are two quite distinct categories of products that go by that name.

The first includes the mass-market, industrial chocolates we grew up on—the Cadbury's, the Snickers, the Mars bars, the Kit-Kats, etc. And the second is the high-end chocolate crafted by skilled chocolatiers, derived from high-end beans and usually made by a different process than the industrial stuff.

What both categories have in common is the cocoa bean. As you probably know, the bean has been cultivated in South America for thousands of years, though originally it was used to make a savoury drink. When the Spanish invader Hernando Cortéz landed in the Americas, the Aztec king Montezuma made one of those errors that transformed history. He mistook Cortéz for a reincarnated deity and welcomed him with a pot of chocolate.

Cortéz and his men slaughtered the Aztecs, colonized their country and took chocolate back to Europe where inventive chefs created a sweet version. Later, chemists were able to figure out how to harden chocolate, leading to the creation of the chocolate bar, and then eventually, to 'filled' (with nuts, nougat, wafers, etc.) chocolates like, say, Snickers or Kit-Kat.

Though chocolate has been around for millennia, milk chocolate, oddly enough, is of relatively recent origin. All chocolate is based on fat (80 per cent is cocoa butter) while milk is based on water (89 per cent).

The two are natural enemies, and it wasn't till 1875 when Henri Nestlé, who had invented condensed milk (still a big seller for Nestlé), joined hands with a chocolate chemist called Daniel Peter to add cocoa powder and sugar to the condensed milk, that milk chocolate was born and with it, the craze for commercial chocolate bars.

But milk chocolate is not the same all over the world. There are now different industrial processes and each yields a distinctive flavour. Hershey, the American chocolate giant, uses milk powder and its chocolate has a distinctive taste (like sour or spoilt milk). In Switzerland, Nestlé's successors add condensed milk to unsweetened chocolate for a creamier flavour.

In India we have grown up on Cadbury's, which gave us a taste for its English-style caramelized milk chocolate loaded with sugar. One theory about Cadbury's early success in India is that the oversweet, caramelized milk taste reminded Indians of our own milk-based sweets. (Another is that Cadbury's were the first and created the chocolate palate in India.)

All this conditioning has made us resistant to other kinds of chocolate. But it hardly matters these days. Because cocoa is expensive, most commercial chocolate brands don't use much chocolate. The point of a Kit-Kat or a Snickers or even a Mars bar is not the chocolate covering—it is the non-chocolate stuff inside.

I have a lot of respect for the industrial chocolate sector and for some of its creations (the Snickers bar is magic!), but I don't think it has much to do with real chocolate. Instead, this sector, with its emphasis on packaging, marketing, innovation, etc., reminds me more of Coke and Pepsi.

Real chocolate, on the other hand, is like fine wine, which is why it falls in a completely different category. And in fact, the parallels with wine are striking. The cocoa bean is an agricultural product. Its quality varies from season to season, different regions produce beans that taste significantly different. Ghana produces reasonable-quality chocolate while Congo does not. Chocolate from Chuao in Venezuela is better than chocolate from anywhere else in that country. And so on.

Unlike wine, chocolate is not a First World product—no cocoa grows in Europe. The general rule of thumb is that a First World product is always spoken of in terms of terroir (Burgundy for wine, Parma for ham, and now Kobe for beef). But with Third World products, the raw materials are rarely spoken about while the attention is paid to the First World guys who work with them.

So, the centres of the chocolate world are places like Belgium, Switzerland and France. And the heroes are so-called artisanal brands, most of which are really fully industrial or are subsidiaries of conglomerates. Valrhona is owned by the giant Bongrain. Godiva is now owned by the Turkish Yildiz Holdings. Suchard is owned by Mondelez, the multinational that owns Kraft, Cadbury's and Kool-Aid.

Even so-called hip brands like Max Brenner, famous in America and Australia, are divisions of global giants. Max Brenner is a subsidiary of the Strauss group, the Israeli food giant. Royce, with over forty stores abroad and many more in its native Japan, is a large company that sells drinking water, coffee, crafts and even insurance.

None of this is to say that the 'luxury' chocolate brands make bad chocolate but only to point out that these days, they are as much into marketing and packaging as Mars or Hershey. And image alone is no guarantee of quality.

So what should you look for in a luxury chocolate? Well, speaking for myself, I look for two things. Like good wine, the chocolate should interpret the flavour of the bean. And if you are tasting chocolates made by famous chocolatiers such as Michel Chaudun or the pastry chef Pierre Hermé (who buy their chocolate from big manufacturers), you look for creativity in fillings, delicacy of construction and, of course, the dark taste of good chocolate.

You need to remember that the overwhelming taste of commercial chocolate is that of sugar and milk. Real chocolate should (ideally) have no milk and much less sugar. You judge the cocoa content (anything below 40 per cent is a waste of time), the colour (and the gloss) and the fragrance—good chocolate should contain fruity aromas. It really is a lot like judging wine!

Making high quality chocolate involves a process so complex that were I to describe it in detail, you would probably turn the page. But one key element is the conching, a process invented in the nineteenth century that creates texture and shifts the flavour compounds between the particles of chocolate so that each flavour emerges in your mouth at intervals creating the multilayered taste that good chocolate and good wine share.

Conching is an expensive process, so commercial chocolate is quickly conched, but quality chocolate needs to be conched for several hours. The same is true of tempering (carefully heating, cooling, heating again, etc.), which gives the fat in the chocolate a stable crystalline structure (I told you the process was tedious!) leading to a sheen on the surface of the bars, a cleaner snap when you break off a piece, and resistance to 'bloom' (when the outside of the chocolate turns white).

In 2007, Yogi Deveshwar, ITC's long-time chairman, decided that he wanted the company to make world-class chocolates. ITC's consumer products and foods are wildly successful but they have no great reputation for luxury. So Deveshwar made this a challenge for ITC Foods. It took ten years of experimentation and research, and the expertise of some of the world's best consulting chocolatiers but they came up with a line of chocolates called Fabelle.

This is top-of-line chocolate, sourced from several different countries, conched for at least twelve hours and then handcrafted. As we have seen, if you buy high-quality beans and treat them with respect, it doesn't matter whether you make the chocolate in Japan (Royce) or Switzerland (Suchard). One factor that does matter is how soon you eat the chocolate. All bars and all chocolates—even if they are well packed—begin to lose flavour over time (think olive oil, not wine). And yet most foreign brands can take months to reach consumers. ITC pushes its chocolates into the shops within twenty-four hours of manufacture. And if a packet does not sell within the stipulated time, they will discard it only because the taste will not be at its peak.

I have to say, in all honesty, that I was very sceptical when I tried my first Fabelle chocolate. To my surprise, the quality of the chocolate itself was outstanding. Fabelle will market bars marked by single origin (Madagascar, Equador, etc.) but their moulded chocolates are masterful, with delicate construction and unusual fillings (Fleur de Sel, Nacho chili, acacia nectar, etc.).

I first tried Fabelle at the chocolate boutique at the ITC Gardenia hotel in Bengaluru. (Because of the obvious synergy, the Foods division is teaming up with the Hotels division to run the boutiques at ITC luxury hotels.) I was so struck by the effort and expense that had gone into creating the chocolates that I wondered how ITC would ever make money on such a niche product, no matter how excellent it was.

I am told by the head of ITC Foods that they have opened new boutiques at other hotels and the response has been phenomenal. Apparently, Indians love eating and gifting high-end chocolates.

Which is encouraging. Because it is nice to see how Deveshwar's passion to make something I never thought was possible in India—a truly world-class chocolate—is translating into commercial success.

Clearly, the rest of us have been underestimating the Indian consumer!

Afterword

≈

This Afterword is an afterthought. My wife, Seema Goswami, who is the world's best (unpaid!) editor, went through two sets of galley proofs for this book before declaring that it ended too abruptly. Yes, some of the chapters were interesting, she conceded (she is not generous with praise), but they were written over a period of several years and needed to be bookended with an intro (which I had written) and something at the end.

She is right, of course. And a book of this nature can't end without a look ahead at what is to come.

I am, in equal parts, optimistic and pessimistic about the future.

My optimism stems from two factors. Now that food is such a big deal for all levels of the middle class, we are becoming more quality conscious and more adventurous. Shows like *MasterChef Australia* and the vast world of the Internet have brought us closer to global standards. We no longer feel like yokels when we go to fancy restaurants abroad and, thanks to Instagram, we are more connected to the global food scene.

At a not-so-elevated level, even people who don't care who Gary Mehigan is, are much more interested in food. I have had intense arguments with guys who work in semi-clerical jobs in offices about the perfect samosa. Should the filling contain saunf? How thick should the pastry be? Should it be good enough to eat on its own? Or does a samosa always need chutney?

There are no right or wrong answers, so these debates continue all over the country.

251

At no time, since I became a journalist, have Indians been so passionate about food.

So that is why I am optimistic.

But I am pessimistic too. Fewer and fewer people cook. You could be cynical and say that our mothers never really cooked as much as we like to believe they did. But Indian regional cuisines were kept alive, not just by mothers but also by cooks. Often this was a hereditary job. And often a domestic cook who learned great dishes in one household would take those recipes to other houses he worked, where they would also quickly become favourites.

It was those cooks who kept the diversity of Indian cuisine alive. In a city like Delhi, for instance, the term 'mutton curry' referred not to one dish but to a whole family of dishes.

The Punjabi Hindu mutton curry was a relatively simple dish. The Kayasth curry was more complicated. And the Muslim curries, whether from Delhi or from Lucknow, were too numerous to even enumerate.

And depending on whose house you went to, you would get a completely different curry.

All that may soon come to an end. There are fewer and fewer cooks out there. Prosperity and social mobility have meant that the children of cooks have opportunities in other fields that were never available to their parents. And when people do become cooks, it is in restaurant kitchens where they are rarely encouraged to make the authentic specialities of their regions.

In terms of progress, we must applaud the new opportunities available to young people who don't want to follow in the footsteps of their parents. But we must also accept that despite all the media hype about a boom in regional cuisines, the reality is that regional cuisines are slowly disappearing from our homes. Instead, a bland, bastardized Pan-Indian cuisine has developed in homes across our big cities.

Another measure of (largely welcome) changes in Indian society is that a) more and more women work and b) their husbands no longer expect them to come home and cook full meals for the family every evening. (Though, on a separate note, I am still astonished by the number of men who are unwilling to change, who expect their wives to wake up early, pack lunch for the kids, work a full day and then rush home to cook dinner. It is changing but it is not changing fast enough.)

A consequence of these changes is that people prefer to eat packaged food (instant noodles, etc.) at home or, if they can afford it, to order dinner from one of the many delivery services.

In the beginning the delivery services picked up food from restaurants. But because few people could pay restaurant prices more than once or twice a week, a new takeaway sector has developed. This consists of places geared only to take-out such as Domino's Pizza, which has spread rapidly all over India. A newer development is cloud kitchens. These tend to be low-cost operations, not attached to any restaurant, that exist only to create takeaway food at lower-than-restaurant prices.

I applaud these innovations for the convenience factor they bring to food but the sad truth is that while the variety of cuisines on offer is large, rarely is the food remotely authentic or even very good.

What will happen, I suspect, is that over the next decade or so, Indians will be able to eat a multiplicity of cuisines at restaurants and at their own homes. The price we will pay for this will be the slow subsumption of distinctive regional cuisines into please-all blandness.

I make no value judgements about this. You can't fight progress and demographic changes are irreversible.

But Penguin had the right idea when they called this book *The Indian Pantry*.

Because soon, there won't be many regional pantries, just one big Indian pantry.

And that, let's be honest, is sad.